starting out:
classical Sicilian

ALEXANDER RAETSKY
MAXIM CHETVERIK

EVERYMAN CHESS

Gloucester Publishers plc   www.everymanchess.com

First published in 2007 by Gloucester Publishers plc (formerly Everyman Publishers plc), Northburgh House, 10 Northburgh Street, London EC1V 0AT

British Library Cataloguing-in-Publication Data
A catalogue record for this book is available from the British Library.

ISBN: 9781 85744 537 4

Distributed in North America by The Globe Pequot Press, P.O Box 480, 246 Goose Lane, Guilford, CT 06437-0480.

All other sales enquiries should be directed to Everyman Chess, Northburgh House, 10 Northburgh Street, London EC1V 0AT
tel: 020 7253 7887; fax: 020 7490 3708
email: info@everymanchess.com: website: www.everymanchess.com

EVERYMAN CHESS SERIES (formerly Cadogan Chess)
Chief Advisor: Byron Jacobs
Commissioning editor: John Emms
Assistant editor: Richard Palliser

Typeset and edited by First Rank Publishing, Brighton.
Cover design by Horatio Monteverde.
Printed and bound in Great Britain by Clays, Bungay, Suffolk.

Contents

Bibliography   4

Introduction   5

1   Rare 6th Moves   7

2   The Boleslavsky: 6 Be2 e5   23

3   The Sharp 6 Bc4   37

4   The Sozin Attack   68

5   The Velimirovic Attack   88

6   6 Bg5: The Richter-Rauzer   108

7   The Traditional 6...e6 7 Qd2 Be7   119

8   The Modern 7...a6   144

Index of Variations   170

Index of Complete Games   175

Bibliography

Books

Chess Explained: The Classical Sicilian, Alex Yermolinsky (Gambit 2006)

Dangerous Weapons: The Sicilian, John Emms & Richard Palliser (Everyman 2006)

Easy Guide to the Classical Sicilian, Jouni Yrjola (Everyman 2000)

Experts vs. the Sicilian, eds. Jacob Aagaard & John Shaw (Quality Chess 2004)

Sicilianskaya Zaschita: Scheveningen, Garry Kasparov & Alexander Nikitin (Fizkulture i sport 1984)

Starting Out: The Sicilian, John Emms (Everyman 2002)

Periodicals

Chess Informant 1-98

New In Chess Yearbook 1-83

Software

ChessBase 9.0

Chess Assistant 9.1

Rybka 2.1

Introduction

During the past hundred years the Classical Sicilian has been one of the most popular variations of the Sicilian Defence. Unlike systems like the Najdorf and the Dragon, Black even has a choice of ways to reach the Classical depending on personal taste: both 1 e4 c5 2 Nf3 Nc6 3 d4 cxd4 4 Nxd4 Nf6 5 Nc3 d6 **(Diagram 1)**, which we've adopted as our standard move order, and 1 e4 c5 2 Nf3 d6 3 d4 cxd4 4 Nxd4 Nf6 5 Nc3 Nc6 occur roughly the same number of times in our database.

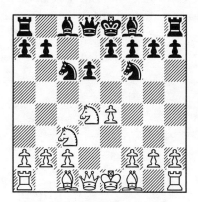

Diagram 1 (W)

The Classical Sicilian

The Classical Sicilian was brought into use in the second half of the Nineteenth Century by Louis Paulsen; a highly original player who was even happy to meet 6 Be2 with the modern and anti-positional 6...e5. By the 1920s the future World Champion Max Euwe could be found at the forefront of developments in the Classical: the Dutchman might have usually met 6 Be2 with 6...e6, transposing to the Scheveningen, but he introduced many important ideas against the aggressive 6 Bc4.

Nowadays a number of very strong players make good use of the Classical Sicilian, especially our compatriots Alexei Dreev and Vladimir Malakhov, the American Alex Yermolinsky and the Greek Vasilios Kotronias, as well as the creative British grandmasters Jonathan Rowson and Peter Wells. However, for reasons of fashion the Classical isn't quite as popular in 2007 as it was in the mid-nineties, when it was regularly seen in the repertoire of no less a player than Vladimir Kramnik, but we are confident that the opening will shortly regain its previous popularity.

From the point of view of the clubplayer the attraction of the Classical Sicilian is clear: Black develops quickly and has good chances to develop early counterplay, while white players are often less well prepared than they are for the Najdorf and Sveshnikov. Our coverage begins with White's less common 6th move options (at grandmaster level at least), before examining Black's many options against both 6 Bc4 and the popular 6 Bg5, the critical Richter-Rauzer Attack. Thus we hope that black players will be able to construct a repertoire to suit them and this work should also be of interest to those who strive as White to create problems whenever Black selects the Classical Sicilian.

We hope that you will enjoy our voyage into the fascinating world of the Classical Sicilian. Before that begins we must offer our special thanks both to those who helped with the translation and to Richard Palliser at Everyman Chess.

Alexander Raetsky & Maxim Chetverik

Voronezh

July 2007

Chapter One

Rare Sixth Moves

- **The English Attack**
- **White Fianchettoes**
- **6 f4 and Others**

The English Attack

1 e4 c5 2 Nf3 Nc6 3 d4 cxd4 4 Nxd4 Nf6 5 Nc3 d6 6 f3 (Diagram 1)

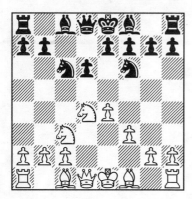
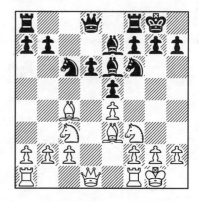

Diagram 1 (B)	**Diagram 2 (W)**
White prepares Be3	Exchanging the active bishop

The English Attack (characterized by the moves Be3, f3, Qd2 and 0-0-0 followed by a kingside pawn advance) is a very popular system against the Classical's sister variation, the Najdorf.

 NOTE: There is an important difference between the Classical Sicilian and the Najdorf: ...Nc6 is much more of a developing move than ...a6 and that allows Black to quickly counter in the centre should White try an English Attack-like set-up.

The text does not develop a piece, but does prepare Be3 without allowing ...Ng4 in response. White can also begin with 6 Be3 when apart from the Scheveningen approach (6...e6), Black has two main options:

a) 6...e5 7 Nb3 Be7 8 Be3 transposes to our coverage of 6 f3. White can also play more positionally with 7 Nf3 when we recommend 7...Be7 8 Bc4 0-0 9 0-0 (according to Adams 9 Bg5 Be6 10 Bxf6 Bxc4 11 Bxe7 Nxe7 equalizes) 9...Be6! **(Diagram 2)**.

 TIP: Black should not fear the resulting doubled pawns in this type of position. On the contrary any exchange on e6 strengthens Black's centre and gives him useful control of the d5- and f5-squares.

O.Eismont-R.Scherbakov, Cappelle la Grande 1996, continued 10 Bb3 Na5 11 Qe2 Qc8 (with the idea of supporting a knight on c4; a good alternative is to exchange on b3) 12 Bg5 Nc4 13 Rab1 Rb8 14 Bxf6 Bxf6 15 Qd3 b5 16 Nd5 Bd8 with counterplay.

b) 6...Ng4!? **(Diagram 3)** disturbs White's bishop and prevents his English Attack scheme. White must now choose between:

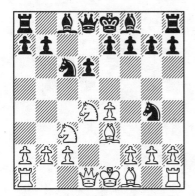

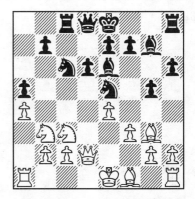

Diagram 3 (W)

Disrupting White's development

Diagram 4 (W)

Black enjoys dynamic counterplay

a) 7 Bb5!? allows White's structure to be smashed in the name of rapid development and we will return to this aggressive move in Game 1.

b) Rather rare is 7 Qd2, but perhaps this isn't so bad if White continues very actively as he did in Y.Shabanov-A.Obukhov, Krasnodar 1991: 7...Nxe3 8 Qxe3 g6 (emphasizing White's lack of a dark-squared bishop) 9 Bb5 Bd7 10 Bxc6 bxc6 11 e5!? dxe5 12 Qxe5 f6 13 Qe4 Qb6 14 0-0 e5 with quite a complex situation.

c) 7 Bg5 h6 8 Bh4 g5 9 Bg3 Bg7 (this is very similar to a popular variation of the Najdorf, except that there's no need for Black to resort to ...a6) 10 Nb3 (Black seizes the initiative after 10 Nxc6 bxc6 11 h3 Qa5!? 12 Qd2 Qb4! 13 Rb1 Rb8! and 10 Nf5 Bxf5 11 exf5 Qa5 12 Qf3 Rc8 also promises him good counterplay) 10...Be6 (rather tempting too is 10...Bxc3+!? 11 bxc3 Be6; for example, 12 Be2 Nge5 13 0-0 Qc7 14 Nd4 Bc4 15 Bd3 0-0-0 16 Qe2 Na5 17 a4 Kb8 18 Rfc1 Rc8 19 f3 Rhg8 favoured Black in R.Tischbierek-S.Krivoshey, German League 2004) 11 Qd2 a5 12 a4 Rc8 13 f3 Nge5 **(Diagram 4)** 14 Nd5 Nb4 15 c3 Nxd5 16 Bb5+ was H.Nakamura-R.Ramesh, Isle of Man 2004, and now the simple 16...Bd7 17 Bxd7+ Qxd7 18 Bxe5 Bxe5 19 Qxd5 b6 would have been fine for Black.

Returning to 6 f3:

6...e5

Dislodging White's knight from d4, but a reasonable alternative is the modified Dragon with 6...Nxd4!? 7 Qxd4 g6 and after 8 Bg5 Bg7 9 0-0-0 0-0 neither 10 e5 nor 10 Qb4 promise White any advantage.

7 Nb3

White has also been known to retreat with 7 Nde2, but Black is fine after 7...Be6 whether White allows ...d5 or plays 8 Nd5, leading to an exchange of bishop for knight on that square (compare with our next note).

7...Be7 (Diagram 5)

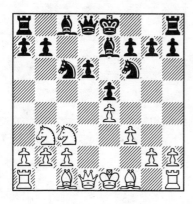

Diagram 5 (W)	**Diagram 6 (W)**
Black develops quickly	Black hopes for ...d5

8 Be3 0-0

A decent alternative is 8...Be6; for example, 9 Nd5 (otherwise Black can break with ...d5) 9...Bxd5 10 exd5 Nb4 11 c4 a5 12 Qd2 b6 13 Be2 0-0 14 0-0 Na6 15 Nc1 Nc5 was satisfactory for Black in S.Movsesian-S.Atalik, Sarajevo 2001.

9 Qd2

 NOTE: White has two main plans in the English Attack: he will either continue aggressively on the kingside or hope to gain a positional advantage by occupying the d5-square.

9...a5!?

A standard and strong way of gaining counterplay: Black wants to push his pawn all the way to a3, breaking up White's queenside and undermining both his knights. Instead 9...Be6 looks quite logical, but after Motylev's 10 Nd5! Bxd5 11 exd5 Nb8 12 Na5!? Black has a few problems on the queenside.

10 Bb5

White is loath to weaken the b4-square with a4 as he still hopes to go long, and so aims to halt Black's a-pawn with his pieces. He can also play very ambitiously with 10 Na4, hoping to exploit the hole on b6: 10...Be6 11 Nb6 (consistent; instead 11 Bb6!? Qb8 12 Bb5 Nd7!? 13 0-0 Nxb6 14 Nxb6 Ra7 creates the unobvious threat of 15...a4! 16 Nxa4 Rxa4 17 Bxa4 Qa7+ winning two pieces for the rook) 11...a4! (a strong exchange sacrifice to seize the initiative) 12 Nxa8 Qxa8 13 Nc1 a3!? 14 b3 (probably stronger was 14 bxa3) 14...d5 15 Bg5 dxe4 16 Bxf6 Bxf6 17 fxe4 Nd4 18 Nd3?! Bh4+ 19 Nf2 and here in A.Rodriguez-G.Milos, Sao Paulo 2005, Black missed the decisive 19...Bg5! with the point that after 20 Qxg5 Nxc2+ 21 Ke2 Nxa1, 22 Qc1 is impossible because of 22...Nxb3! 23 axb3 a2 24 Qa1 Qa3.

 TIP: It's well worth studying Milos's play here: Black thematically broke up the white queenside with his a-pawn and then achieved the ideal Sicilian ...d5-break after which White came under some pressure.

10...Be6 (Diagram 6)

We will return to this crucial position for the assessment of 6 f3 in Game 2.

Theoretical Conclusion

In recent years theory has developed quite quickly after 6 f3, but Black gains sufficient counterplay after 6...e5 by aiming for the liberating ...d5-break and with a timely advance of the a-pawn. White can also begin with 6 Be3 when 6...Ng4 leads to some fairly dynamic and sharp positions which are fully satisfactory for Black.

Illustrative Games

Game 1
□ **A.Rodriguez** ■ **G.Hernandez**
Ayamonte 2004

1 e4 c5 2 Nc3 Nc6 3 Nge2

A slightly unusual move order, but it's not at all easy to move order a Classical Sicilian player.

3...d6 4 d4 cxd4 5 Nxd4 Nf6 6 Be3 Ng4 7 Bb5!? (Diagram 7) 7...Nxe3

Correctly taking up the challenge. Instead 7...Bd7 8 Nxc6 Nxe3 (or 8...bxc6 9 Bxc6 Nxe3 10 Bxd7+ Qxd7 11 fxe3 when White is better) 9 Nxd8 Nxd1 10 Bxd7+ Kxd8 11 Rxd1 Kxd7 fails to equalize on account of 12 e5!.

8 fxe3

White doesn't have to allow his structure to be wrecked, but 8 Nxc6 Nxd1 9 Nxd8+ Kxd8 10 Rxd1 e6 11 0-0 Kc7 12 Rd2 Be7 is very comfortable for Black: his bishop pair and especially the unopposed dark-squared bishop should come into their own as the game progresses.

8...Bd7 9 0-0 e6!

Prudent. Instead 9...Ne5?! 10 Nf3! Bxb5 11 Nxb5 Qb6 12 Nxe5 dxe5 13 Qd5 is quite awkward and 9...g6 10 Bxc6 bxc6 11 Qf3 f6 12 e5! dxe5 13 Nxc6 is also worth avoiding.

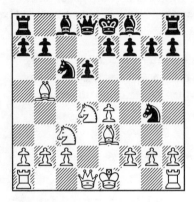

Diagram 7 (B)

Very uncompromising play

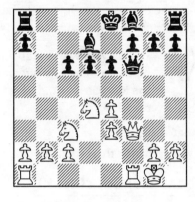

Diagram 8 (W)

A strong pawn sacrifice

10 Bxc6 bxc6 11 e5!

White has also tried 11 Qf3, but this has been neutralized by Polugaevsky's 11...Qf6! **(Diagram 8)**: for example, 12 Qxf6 (or 12 Qe2 Qg5 13 Rf3 Be7 14 Rg3 Qe5 15 Nf3 Qa5 16 Rxg7 Bf6 17 Rg3 Qb4 with excellent dark-square compensation) 12...gxf6 13 Rxf6 Bg7 14 Rf3 Rb8 15 b3 c5 16 Nde2 Bc6 17 Raf1 Rb7 and Black's powerful bishops at least made up for the sacrificed pawn in T.L.Petrosian-A.Motylev, Tiayuan 2005.

11...Be7

It might appear a little strange to allow Black's centre to be broken up, but practice has shown this to be the most accurate. Instead both 11...d5 12 Qf3 Qe7 13 b4! and 11...dxe5 12 Qh5 Qe7 13 Qxe5 slightly favour White.

12 exd6 Bxd6 13 Qh5 0-0 14 Ne4 Be7 (Diagram 9) 15 Rad1 Qb6

A safer and probably better choice is 15...Qc7. White must then act before Black puts his bishops to good use, but 16 Ng5 Bxg5 17 Qxg5 e5 18 Nf5 Bxf5 19 Qxf5 Rad8 gives Black easy equality.

16 Rf3 Be8 17 Rh3 h6 18 Rg3 Kh7 19 Rf1 f5?

Under some pressure Hernandez slips up. Instead 19...Qxb2 was called for, although after 20 Nf6+! Bxf6 21 Rxf6 Qc1+ 22 Kf2 Qd2+ 23 Ne2 g6 (and not 23...gxf6?? 24 Qg4 followed by mate on g7) 24 Qc5 White retains strong compensation for the pawn.

20 Rxg7+! Kxg7 21 Nxe6+ (Diagram 10) 21...Kh7

Now some accurate manoeuvring is enough to finish Black off, but neither would 21...Kg8 have saved him on account of the decisive 22 Qxh6 Qxb2 23 Nxf8 Bxf8 24 Qe6+ Kg7 25 Rxf5 Bg6 26 Rg5.

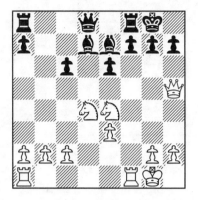

Diagram 9 (W)

Black is very solid

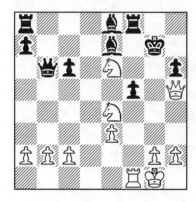

Diagram 10 (B)

White's attack is lethal

22 Nxf8+ Bxf8 23 Qxf5+ Bg6 24 Nf6+ Kg7 25 Qe6 Bf7 26 Qg4+ Kh8 27 Qe4 Bg8 28 Nd7 Qb4 29 Qxc6 1-0

Game 2
□ **V.Tseshkovsky** ■ **R.Scherbakov**
Ekaterinburg 2002

---

1 e4 c5 2 Nf3 Nc6 3 d4 cxd4 4 Nxd4 Nf6 5 Nc3 d6 6 f3 e5 7 Nb3 Be7 8 Be3 0-0 9 Qd2 a5 10 Bb5 Be6 11 Rd1

Preventing ...d5, but giving up on the idea of castling long. Let's see why that might be: 11 0-0-0 Nb4!? 12 a3 d5! **(Diagram 11)** 13 axb4 d4 14 Nxd4 (or 14 Bxd4 exd4 15 Qxd4 Qc7 16 Nd5 Nxd5 17 exd5 Bf5 18 Bd3 Bxd3 19 Rxd3 Bxb4 and Black has dangerous compensation) 14...exd4 15 Qxd4 Qxd4 16 Rxd4 axb4 17 Nb1 Rfc8 gave Black excellent play for the pawn in A.Fedorov-V.Ivanchuk, Moscow 2005.

White also has two positional alternatives:

a) 11 Nd5 a4!? 12 Bb6 (Black seizes the advantage after 12 Nc1 Bxd5 13 exd5 Nd4 14 Bxd4 exd4 in view of 15 Qxd4?? Qa5+ and 16...Qxb5) 12...Qb8 13 Bxc6 (or 13 Bc7 Qa7 14 Bb6 Qb8 with an early and unusual repetition) 13...bxc6 14 Bc7 cxd5!? (a very creative queen sacrifice) 15 Bxb8 axb3 **(Diagram 12)** 16 exd5 Nxd5 17 c4 Nb6 18 Bxd6 Nxc4 19 Bxe7 Nxd2 20 Bxf8 Nc4 saw White return the queen, but Black retained good play for the exchange in O.Brendel-R.Tischbierek, Deizisau 2000.

b) 11 0-0 provokes ...d5:

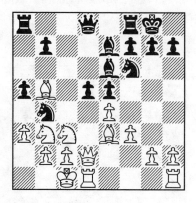

Diagram 11 (W)

Blowing open the position

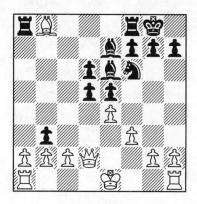

Diagram 12 (W)

A promising queen sacrifice

 WARNING: Here 11...d5 is not a simple equalizer because 12 exd5 Nxd5 13 Nxd5 Qxd5 14 Qxd5 Bxd5 leaves Black's queenside vulnerable and the awkward resource Bb6 will win White the d-file.

Instead the correct 11...Na7! 12 Be2 Nc8 13 Nd5 Bxd5 14 exd5 Nb6 15 c4 Nbd7 (the knight completes its tour and now prevents White's key c5-advance) 16 Rab1 Ne8 17 Rfd1 b6 kept White at bay on the queenside and was about equal in O.Salmensuu-A.Lugovoi, Jyvaskyla 1999.

11...Na7! (Diagram 13)

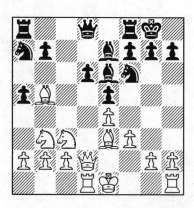

Diagram 13 (W)

The knight heads for b6

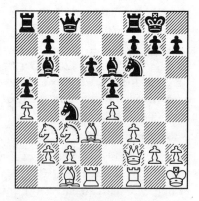

Diagram 14 (W)

Black has good activity

Again we see this manoeuvre, driving the bishop back and bringing the knight to the more active b6-square.

12 Bd3 Nc8 13 a4

White doesn't have to hold up ...a4, but after 13 Qf2 a4 14 Nc1 Qa5 15 0-0 a3 16 Nb3 Qb4 it is clear that Black has plenty of counterplay.

13...Nb6 14 Qf2 Nc4 15 Bc1

White can win a pawn with 15 Bxc4 Bxc4 16 Bb6 Qc8 17 Nxa5, but this is rather risky as it forfeits castling rights and after 17...Ba6 18 Qd2 Qe6 19 Be3 Rfc8 (Scherbakov) one has to like Black's compensation.

15...Qc8 16 0-0 Bd8

Scherbakov continues to manoeuvre well.

 TIP: It's rarely a bad idea to improve your worst-placed piece.

17 Kh1 Bb6 (Diagram 14) 18 Qe1 h6 19 Na1!

White was in danger of drifting into a worse position, but suddenly he highlights the fact that the c4-knight is short of a square to move to.

19...Qc5 20 Nb5 Rad8 21 c3 d5!

The ideal break, although here it does entail a piece sacrifice.

22 b3 dxe4

No doubt when deciding on his active 19th Scherbakov had already realized that the text was the way to go, rather than 22...Ne3? when 23 b4! would have been strong.

23 Bxc4 Bxc4 24 Ba3 Qc6 25 bxc4 exf3 26 gxf3 e4! (Diagram 15)

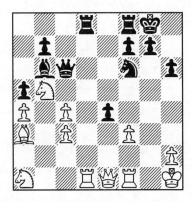

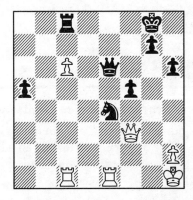

Diagram 15 (W)
Opening up the white king

Diagram 16 (W)
A superbly placed knight

27 Nd4

Black was right to offer further material because 27 Bxf8 exf3 28 Qg3 Nh5 29 Qg4 f5! 30 Qxf5 f2+ 31 Rd5 Qxc4 (Scherbakov) leaves Black with very dangerous compensation and indeed White is probably best advised to repeat with 32 Qe6+ Kh7 33 Qf5+.

27...Bxd4 28 cxd4!?

Tseshkovsky has ambitious hopes of putting his extra material use to some use. Instead 28 Bxf8 exf3 29 Qg3 Ne4 would have led to perpetual with 30 Qxf3 Nf2+ 31 Kg2 Qg6+ 32 Qg3 Qe4+ 33 Qf3 Qg6+.

28...Rfe8 29 Qe2 Qxa4 30 Bc5 exf3 31 Qxf3

Wisely removing the dangerous f-pawn. Instead 31 Qd3 f2 32 d5 b5! would have seen Black retain excellent counterplay.

31...Qxc4 32 Nb3 Re2 33 Nc1 Re6?!

A slip in the time scramble. Instead 33...Rc2 would have maintained the dynamic equilibrium in view of 34 Qxb7 Ng4 35 Rde1 Nf2+ 36 Kg1 Nh3+ and again it's perpetual.

34 Nd3

Missing his chance with 34 Qxb7 when Black would have had to defend an exchange-down ending after 34...Qd5+ 35 Qxd5 Nxd5 36 Rde1.

34...b6 35 Nf4 bxc5 36 Rc1 Qa6 37 Nxe6 Qxe6 38 dxc5 Ne4 39 Rfe1 f5 40 c6 Rc8 (Diagram 16)

Time control reached and Black's strong knight and two pawns fully compensate for the exchange.

41 c7 Qe5 42 Qb3+ Kh7 43 Qb7 Qf4!

Wisely opting to force a draw, whereas the tempting 43...a4? 44 Qxc8 Qd5 would have failed to 45 Qg8+! Kxg8 46 c8Q+ Kh7 47 Qc6.

44 Rf1 Qd2 45 Qxc8 Nf2+ ½-½

White Fianchettoes

1 e4 c5 2 Nf3 Nc6 3 d4 cxd4 4 Nxd4 Nf6 5 Nc3 d6 6 g3 (Diagram 17)

This quiet approach is seen in most variations of the Sicilian Defence. As a rough rule White doesn't hope to gain an edge from the opening, preferring to fight for the advantage in the middlegame.

6...e5

A consistent response for the Classical Sicilian player, but we should note that Black can also take play into a Scheveningen (with 6...e6) or a Dragon (after 6...Nxd4 7 Qxd4 g6); both of which are good alternatives.

Another option is the fairly rare 6...Bg4!? with the idea that after 7 f3 Bd7 White might well prefer not to have inserted f3. That's certainly true if White continues 8 Bg2, but an experienced Sicilian player might well prefer the aggressive 8 Be3 after which play takes on the contours of sharp English Attack or Dragon lines depending on whether Black prefers 8...e6 or 8...g6. We should note too that Black has also tried meeting 7 f3 with 7...Nxd4, but after 8 Qxd4!? Bxf3?! (8...Bd7 is somewhat safer) 9 Bb5+ Nd7 10 Rf1 White has a strong initiative for the pawn.

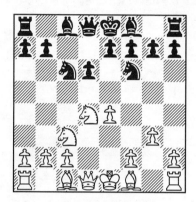

| **Diagram 17 (B)** | **Diagram 18 (B)** |
| A positional line | Black must counter on the queenside |

7 Nde2

The knight has more prospects here than on b3. The plan is now to seize space on the kingside with h3, g4 and Ng3.

7...Be7

It looks tempting to attack with 7...Bg4!? 8 Bg2 Nd4, but after 9 0-0 Rc8 10 f3 Nxe2+ 11 Qxe2 Be6 12 Qb5+ Qd7 13 Qxd7+ Nxd7 12 Be3 White is slightly better.

8 Bg2 0-0 9 0-0 (Diagram 18)

Here Black usually chooses between 9...Be6 (the subject of Game 3) and the Najdorfesque 9...a6. We prefer the former because after any queenside fianchetto the c6-knight can turn out to be misplaced.

Theoretical Conclusion

As in other lines of the Classical, meeting 6 g3 with 6...e5 is a reliable method for Black. White will usually counter by bringing a knight to d5 and after an exchange of pieces there, an unbalanced but roughly equal position-type is reached.

Illustrative Games

Game 3
□ **R.Kholmov** ■ **E.Kovalevskaya**
Pardubice 1997

1 e4 c5 2 Nf3 d6 3 d4 cxd4 4 Nxd4 Nf6 5 Nc3 Nc6 6 g3 e5 7 Nde2 Be7 8 Bg2 0-0 9 0-0 Be6 10 h3 Rc8 11 Be3

White can also occupy d5 immediately and after 11 Nd5 Bxd5 12 exd5 Nb8 Black should look to the kingside for counterplay; for example, 13 g4!? Ne8 14 Ng3 Bg5! (exchanging off the bad bishop) 15 Bxg5 Qxg5 16 Qc1 Qxc1 17 Rfxc1 g6 **(Diagram 19)** 18 g5 f5 was quite comfortable for one of your authors in R.Edouard-A.Raetsky, Sautron 2005.

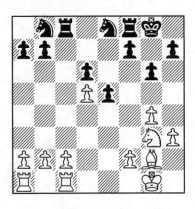

Diagram 19 (W)

...f5 is the plan

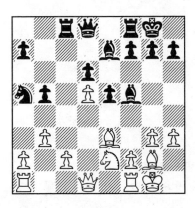

Diagram 20 (W)

White can't advance his c-pawn

11...b5!? 12 Nd5

Continuing the plan, rather than allow Black easy counterplay with 12 Nxb5 Qd7 13 Kh2 Rb8 14 a4 a6 15 Nbc3 Rxb2.

12...Na5 13 b3

White might also play on the queenside with 13 a4 and after 13...bxa4 14 Nxe7+ Qxe7 15 b3 Nb7 16 Rxa4 Nc5 the position is roughly balanced.

13...Nxd5 14 exd5 Bf5 (Diagram 20) 15 Rc1 Nb7!

Recycling the knight from the rim and thereby making it difficult for White to expand on the queenside.

16 g4 Bd7 17 Qd2

A more ambitious option was 17 f4, but after 17...f5 18 gxf5 Qa5 Black has sufficient counterplay.

17...f5 18 gxf5 Bxf5 19 Ng3 Bg6 20 Ne4

Thematic play from White. However, Black is actually doing quite well here since she can challenge White's control of e4 and we should not forget too that White's kingside structure has been split.

20...Qd7 21 Kh2 Nc5 (Diagram 21)

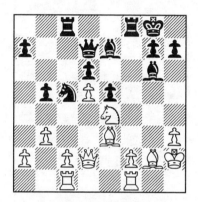

Diagram 21 (W)

Challenging for control of e4

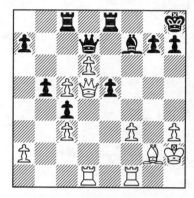

Diagram 22 (W)

Simplification beckons

22 f3 Bd8

A provocative choice, but probably better was 22...a5!? and after 23 Nxc5 dxc5 24 c4 b4 Black is slightly for preference: d6 is well blockaded and there are options on both flanks.

 WARNING: A protected passed pawn can be a very useful asset, but beware having one when it is both well blockaded and the opponent is the side with the superior activity.

23 Bxc5 dxc5 24 d6 Kh8 25 Rcd1 c4 26 b4

The veteran might have tried 26 f4!? when 26...Qe6 27 fxe5 Qxe5+ 28 Kh1 Bb6 29 Rxf8+ Rxf8 remains rather murky.

26...Bb6 27 Qd5 Rfe8 28 c3 Be3 29 Nc5 Bxc5 30 bxc5 Bf7 (Diagram 22)

Now c5 appears a little weak, but Kholmov has realised that he is in time to trade that pawn.

31 c6! Rxc6 32 Qxb5 a6 33 Qb4 Rd8

Winning the d6-pawn in return for the e-pawn as a draw begins to look likely.

34 f4 e4 35 Bxe4 Rxd6 36 Rxd6 Qxd6 37 Qxd6 Rxd6 38 Rb1 g6 39 Rb7 Bd5 ½-½

6 f4 & Others

1 e4 c5 2 Nf3 Nc6 3 d4 cxd4 4 Nxd4 Nf6 5 Nc3 d6 6 f4 (Diagram 23)

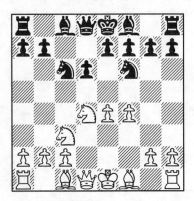

Diagram 23 (B)

Black has several options

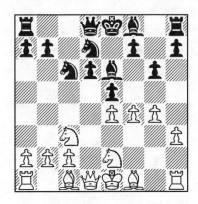

Diagram 24 (W)

Original play from White

The advance f2-f4 is applied quite often against different variations of the Sicilian Defence, but against the Classical it is not very popular largely because Black has a number of decent replies. Even rarer options are:

a) The primitive pin 6 Bb5 is unpopular because any exchange on c6 simply strengthens Black's pawn structure, while if White doesn't exchange he must lose time retreating his bishop after an eventual ...a6.

b) The prophylactic 6 h3 makes more sense as this can be followed up with an early g4. As well as the Dragon option (6...g6), Black can select one of:

a) 6...e5 was seen in S.Movsesian-V.Baklan, Groningen 1998, which continued 7 Nde2 Be6 8 f4 (in the case of 8 g4 Black can break in the centre: 8...d5 9 exd5 Nxd5 10 Bg2 Bb4 with a good game) 8...g6 9 g4 Nd7 **(Diagram 24)** 10 Be3 Be7 11 Bf2 exf4 12 Nxf4 Nde5 13 Bg2 Bg5 14 Ncd5 h5! and in this complex position Black enjoyed good counterplay.

b) 6...e6 7 Be3 Be7 8 g4 takes play into a line of the Scheveningen, but here h3 can turn out to be a waste of time. One possible way of handling the black position is 8...h6!? 9 Qd2 d5 (our favourite Sicilian break; admittedly White can now inflict an IQP, but he will struggle to take advantage of it having weakened himself with g4) 10 Bb5 Bd7 11 exd5 Nxd5 12 Nxd5 exd5 13 Nf5 Bxf5 14 gxf5 a6 15 Bxc6+ bxc6 16 0-0-0 Qd6 was dynamically balanced in A.Grischuk-A.Sokolov, French League 2002.

6...e5 (Diagram 25)

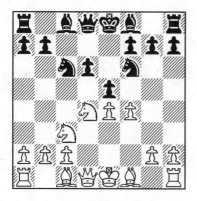

Diagram 25 (W)

Contesting the centre

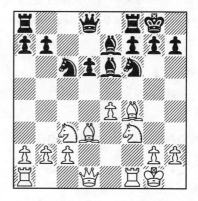

Diagram 26 (W)

...Qb6+ is one option; ...d5 another

Thematic and also the most ambitious counter. Once again 6...e6 and 6...g6 are decent alternatives, but probably not 6...Bg4 since 7 Nxc6 bxc6 8 Be2 Bxe2 9 Qxe2 e6 10 Be3 is a little better for White.

7 Nf3

Instead 7 fxe5 dxe5 8 Nxc6 Qxd1+ 9 Nxd1 bxc6 10 Bd3 Be6 is very comfortable for Black, but White might try to prevent Black from castling with 7 Nxc6 bxc6 8 fxe5. However, against this there is the strong reply 8...Ng4! when accepting the sacrifice with 9 exd6?! creates problems only for White after 9...Bxd6 10 Bg5 Qc7. Instead 9 Be2 Nxe5 10 Be3 Be7 11 0-0 0-0 12 Qd2 Be6 13 Rad1 Qc7 14 Bd4 Rfe8 was approximately level in C.Astengo-A.Lugovoi, Gausdal 2003.

 NOTE: White can also retreat with 7 Nb3 and after 7...Be7 8 Be2 0-0 9 0-0 we've transposed to the Boleslavsky variation; see the move order 6 Be2 e5 7 Nb3 Be7 8 0-0 0-0 9 f4 in our next chapter.

7...Be7 8 Bd3

More active appears 8 Bc4, but after 8...Qa5!? Black generates some threats and 9 Qe2 (or 9 Bd2 exf4 10 Nd5 Qc5! 11 Qe2 Nxd5 12 exd5 Ne5 13 Bb5+ Kf8 and Black should be fairly happy with this unclear situation) 9...Be6 10 Bxe6 fxe6 11 0-0 0-0 saw him developing quite comfortably in Y.Yakovich-E.Alekseev, Krasnoyarsk 2003.

8...0-0

A decent alternative is the sharper 8...Qb6!?; for example, 9 f5 (taking up the challenge; instead 9 Qe2 0-0 10 Rb1 Be6 11 Be3 Qa5 12 0-0 exf4 13 Bxf4 Rae8 is about equal) 9...0-0 10 Qe2 Re8 11 Qf2 Nd4! which gave Black good, active counterplay in M.Petrov-B.Avrukh, Nikea 2003.

9 0-0 exf4 10 Bxf4 Be6 (Diagram 26)

Completing Black's development after which the central strike ...d5 will secure him a reasonable game; for example, 11 Kh1 d5! 12 e5 (12 exd5 Nxd5 13 Nxd5 Qxd5 14 c4 Qh5 is fine too for Black) 12...Nd7 13 Qe1 Nc5 14 Qg3 Re8 15 Bh6 Bf8 was very solid for Black and about equal in B.Maryasin-L.Yudasin, Ramat Aviv 1998.

Theoretical Conclusion

With 6 f4 White tries to escape from theory, but objectively the direct counter 6...e5 gives Black good counterchances.

Chapter Two

The Boleslavsky: 6 Be2 e5

- **Introduction**
- **White Retreats to b3**
- **White Retreats to f3**

Introduction

1 e4 c5 2 Nf3 Nc6 3 d4 cxd4 4 Nxd4 Nf6 5 Nc3 d6 6 Be2 (Diagram 1)

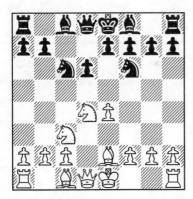

Diagram 1 (B)

Classical play from White

Diagram 2 (W)

The Boleslavsky Variation

Nowadays at grandmaster level this classical approach is rarely seen with 6 Bg5 and 6 Bc4 being much more common. At lower levels, however, 6 Be2 retains some adherents and Black should most certainly be ready for it, whether he wants to counter with 6...e6 (transposing to the Scheveningen), 6...g6 (reaching a Dragon) or 6...e5, the independent Classical Sicilian approach which we will consider here.

6...e5 (Diagram 2)

At first sight a rather radical move, but by no means a bad one. As its great pioneer, Isaac Boleslavsky, wrote as early as 1943, 'the positional merit of 6...e5 is that it deprives White of free play in the centre and on the kingside... and White cannot effectively exploit the hole on d5'. Nowadays we see ...e5 played in all manner of Sicilian positions and Boleslavsky's discovery has most certainly stood the test of time.

 TIP: In the Boleslavsky Black should arrange to meet Nd5 by exchanging that knight, after which exd5 transforms the structure, leaving Black set to play on the kingside and White on the queenside.

After 6...e5 White usually retreats with either 7 Nb3 or 7 Nf3 since 7 Nxc6?! bxc6 only strengthens Black's centre; for example, 8 Qd3 Be7 9 0-0 0-0 10 Rd1 Nd7 11 Be3 Nb6 12 a4 a5 13 b3 f5! was already slightly better for Black in R.Ortega-V.Smyslov, Havana 1964.

White Retreats to b3

1 e4 c5 2 Nf3 Nc6 3 d4 cxd4 4 Nxd4 Nf6 5 Nc3 d6 6 Be2 e5 7 Nb3 (Diagram 3)

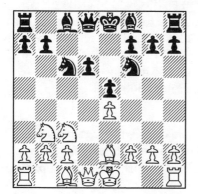

Diagram 3 (B)	**Diagram 4 (W)**
White keeps his f-pawn free	White has a choice of plans

This might be less popular than 7 Nf3, but it does lead to more of a dynamic game.

7...Be7

Wisely developing the kingside first. Instead 7...Be6 (hoping to free Black's game with ...d5) 8 f4! exf4 9 Bxf4 Be7 10 Qd2 0-0 11 0-0-0 in Yermolinsky's view favours White due to his pressure against d6.

8 0-0

By far White's main move. We should note that before Boleslavsky was even born, Gunsberg tried 8 Be3 0-0 9 g4 Be6 10 g5 against Paulsen (Frankfurt, 1887), but this aggressive plan is no longer considered dangerous: 10...Nd7 11 Qd2 a5 12 a4 Bxb3 13 cxb3 Nd4!? (a decent alternative is 13...Nc5!? 14 Bc4 Ne6 15 h4 Ned4) 14 Bxd4 exd4 15 Qxd4 Nc5 16 Bc4 Bxg5 gave Black good counterplay in O.Hilbig-S.Agdestein, German League 2002.

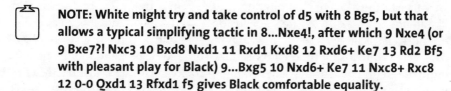

> **NOTE: White might try and take control of d5 with 8 Bg5, but that allows a typical simplifying tactic in 8...Nxe4!, after which 9 Nxe4 (or 9 Bxe7?! Nxc3 10 Bxd8 Nxd1 11 Rxd1 Kxd8 12 Rxd6+ Ke7 13 Rd2 Bf5 with pleasant play for Black) 9...Bxg5 10 Nxd6+ Ke7 11 Nxc8+ Rxc8 12 0-0 Qxd1 13 Rfxd1 f5 gives Black comfortable equality.**

8...0-0 (Diagram 4) 9 Be3

Continuing to develop, but White has a couple of important alternatives:

a) 9 Kh1 Be6 10 f4 exf4 11 Bxf4 transposes to the note to White's 11th move in variation 'b', below. Black can also play more dynamically with 9...a5!? as we'll see in Game 4.

b) 9 f4 is more direct: 9...exf4 10 Bxf4 Be6 11 Bd3 (Black equalizes more straight-forwardly after 11 Kh1: 11...d5! 12 exd5 Nxd5 13 Nxd5 Qxd5 14 Qxd5 Bxd5 15 Rad1 Be6 16 c3 Rad8 is obviously pretty comfortable for him, and 12 e5 can be met by either 12...Ne4!? or the more solid 12...Nd7 13 Nxd5 Ndxe5) 11...Ne5 (worthy of attention too is 11...d5!? 12 exd5 Nxd5 13 Nxd5 Qxd5 14 c4 Qd7) 12 Kh1 Qb6 13 Qe2 Nxd3 14 cxd3!? Bxb3 15 Be3 was the course of no lesser game than M.Botvinnik-I.Boleslavsky, Sverdlovsk 1943, and now Botvinnik recommends 15...Qc6 16 axb3 d5 with counterplay.

TIP: Black can also generate reasonable counterplay against 9 f4 with 9...a5!? 10 a4 Nb4 11 Be3 Be6 (Diagram 5), hoping for the trap 12 Bf3? exf4 13 Bxf4 Nxc2! 14 Qxc2 Qb6+ which leaves him a pawn up after 15...Qxb3.

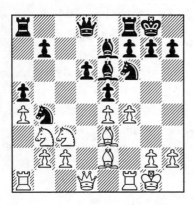

Diagram 5 (W)

White must be careful!

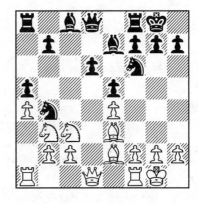

Diagram 6 (W)

The b4-knight is again a useful piece

9...a5

An advance of the a-pawn is a common way to gain counterplay in this variation. Black intends to break up White's queenside with the pawn, but he can also de-velop more classically: 9...Be6 10 Bf3 (playing for control of d5; instead 10 f4 exf4 11 Bxf4 sees White losing time with his dark-squared bishop and indeed he is here a tempo down on a line of the Scheveningen) 10...Na5 (10...a5 is again a decent alternative; for example, 11 Nd5 a4 12 Bb6 Qd7 13 Nc1 Bxd5 14 exd5 Nb4 15 c3?! Qb5! 16 cxb4 Qxb6 17 a3 e4 left White struggling in H.Deveau-M.Apicella, Saint Affrique 2005, and even the superior 15 c4 would have allowed Black good counterplay with 15...Rfc8 16 Be2 Bd8 17 Be3 b5!?) 11 Nxa5 Qxa5 12 Qd2 Rfc8 gives Black quite easy queenside counterplay and is clearly fine for him.

10 a4

Wisely holding Black up on the queenside. Instead a good example of the damage which the a-pawn can inflict was seen after 10 f4 in E.Kuipers-G.Bagaturov, Ghent 2005: 10...a4 11 Nd2 exf4 12 Rxf4 Ne5 13 Nc4 Nxc4 14 Bxc4 Be6 15 Bd5 Bxd5 16 exd5 a3 17 b3 Nd7 18 Bd4 Bf6 19 Bxf6 Nxf6 and Black had a good game. Note that the pawn on a3 remains a long-term thorn in such a position for White whose queenside will always be vulnerable.

Practice has also seen the slightly meek 10 Nd2 when 10...d5 11 exd5 Nxd5 12 Nxd5 Qxd5 13 Nc4 Qxd1 14 Rfxd1 Be6 15 c3 f5 16 Bb6 a4 is about equal, although we can understand that some readers may not like such an invasion of b6.. For those we recommend instead Tukmakov's much more dynamic 10...Be6 11 Nc4 b5!? with the idea that 12 Nxb5 Nxe4 13 f3 Nf6 14 Nbxd6 Nd5 15 Bc5 Nd4 (Ljubo-jevic) gives Black sufficient play for his pawn.

10...Nb4 (Diagram 6)

The logical continuation of Black's strategy as he aims to stymie White on the queenside. We will return to this unbalanced position in Game 5.

Theoretical Conclusion

Many decades of practice have shown that Black develops sufficient counterplay in this variation, especially with a timely advance of the a-pawn and by aiming to break with ...d5.

Illustrative Games

Game 4
☐ **L.Burijovich** ■ **S.Atalik**
Mar del Plata 2003

1 e4 c5 2 Nf3 Nc6 3 d4 cxd4 4 Nxd4 Nf6 5 Nc3 d6 6 Be2 e5 7 Nb3 Be7 8 0–0 0-0 9 Kh1 a5 10 a4

Just as in the main line White doesn't have to impede Black's a-pawn, but after 10 Be3 a4 11 Nd2 a3 **(Diagram 7)** Black gains good counterplay; for instance,12 Nc4 axb2 13 Rb1 b5!? 14 Nxb5 Rxa2 15 Bb6 Qd7 16 Ncxd6 Ba6 was promising in A.Zapata-D.Dunne, Lucerne 1982.

10...Nb4 11 f4 Qc7

Probably a simpler approach is 11...Bd7 (staying out of reach of White's f-pawn) 12 Bf3 Bc6 which is fine for Black, such as after 13 Qe2 Qc7 14 fxe5 dxe5 15 Be3 b6.

12 g4!?

Very sharp. A calmer alternative is 12 Be3 b6 13 Bf3, but after 13...Bb7 14 Qd2
Black has 14...d5!? 15 exd5 e4! 16 Nxe4 Nfxd5 with plenty of activity for the pawn.

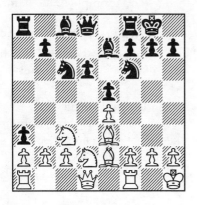

Diagram 7 (W)	**Diagram 8 (W)**
Undermining White's queenside	Thematically countering in the centre

 TIP: The ...d5 break is rarely a bad idea to be considering. Here it cost Black a pawn, but in return he activated all his pieces and found himself much better coordinated than White.

12...d5! (Diagram 8)

And a critical response. Atalik wants to use his slightly superior development to exploit White's weakened king position.

13 exd5?!

Not the best since now Black regains his pawn with a good position. Instead 13 fxe5 Nxe4 14 Nxd5 Qxe5 15 Nxe7+ Qxe7 cannot be bad for Black due to his far safer king and White should prefer 13 Nxd5!? Nfxd5 14 exd5 when Black must be precise: the tempting if greedy 14...Nxc2?! led to a massacre after 15 fxe5! Nxa1 16 d6 Qc6+ 17 Bf3 Qxa4? 18 dxe7 Re8 19 Nxa1 Qxa1 20 Bd5 Be6 21 Bxe6 fxe6 22 Qf3 h6 23 Bxh6! in S.Rahman-I.Hakki, Calcutta 2001. Much better is the alternative capture 14...Qxc2 and after 15 fxe5 Qe4+ 16 Bf3 Qxe5 the position is far from easy to assess, although again we quite like Black as his king will always be the safer.

13...Rd8 14 Nb5

Black also would have regained his pawn with a small advantage after 14 Bf3 e4! 15 Nxe4 Nfxd5 16 Nd4 Nxf4.

14...Qxc2 15 fxe5 Nfxd5 16 N3d4?!

Dropping a pawn. White had to keep her disadvantage within bounds with 16

Qxc2 Nxc2 17 Rb1 Bd7.

16...Qe4+ 17 Bf3 Qxe5 18 Qb3 Nc6 19 Bxd5 Nxd4!

Powerful play from Atalik and much stronger than 19...Rxd5?! 20 Nc3 Qxd4 21 Qxd5 when White would have been back in the game.

20 Bxf7+ Kh8 21 Nxd4 Rxd4 (Diagram 9)

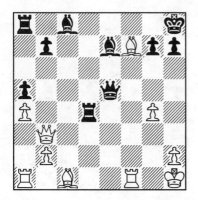

Diagram 9 (W)	**Diagram 10 (W)**
White's kingside is highly vulnerable	The attack is crushing

22 Qe3 Re4 23 Qg3 b6!?

Black understandably wants to get his bishop on the long diagonal, not that there was anything wrong with 23...Bxg4 and if 24 Bf4, then 24...Qf5 25 Bb8 Rxa4!? 26 Rae1 Qd7 with two extra pawns.

24 Bf4?

A horrible decision. Now White is torn apart by Black's raking bishops and again she had to get the queens off: 24 Qxe5 Rxe5 25 Kg2 Ba6 26 Rf2 would have retained a few chances to hold.

24...Rxf4! 25 Rxf4 Bb7+ 26 Kg1 Bc5+ (Diagram 10) 27 Kf1 Ba6+ 28 Bc4 Bxc4+ 29 Rxc4 Rf8+ 30 Kg2 Qxb2+ 0-1

Game 5
□ A.Caldeira ■ G.Milos
Sao Paulo 2002

---

1 e4 c5 2 Nf3 Nc6 3 d4 cxd4 4 Nxd4 Nf6 5 Nc3 d6 6 Be2 e5 7 Nb3 Be7 8 0-0 0-0 9 Be3 a5 10 a4 Nb4 11 Nd5

Now the hole on d5 vanishes, but White often feels the need to do something about the awkward knight on b4 and the possibility of a ...d5 break.

11...Nfxd5!

The correct recapture, retaining the active knight, whereas 11...Nbxd5 12 exd5 Bf5 is a little better for White after 13 f4.

12 exd5 Bf5 (Diagram 11)

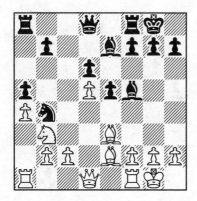
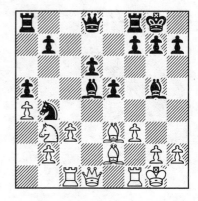

Diagram 11 (W)	**Diagram 12 (W)**
Awkward pressure against c2	There's a tactical problem on b3

13 Rc1 Be4!?

Milos wants to win against his lower-rated opponent, but already Black can exploit his queenside pressure to force a repetition with 13...Na2 14 Ra1 Nb4.

14 f3?!

A tactical oversight. Correct was 14 c4 and after 14...Bg5 15 Qd2 Bxe3 16 Qxe3 Bc2 17 Qc3 Bg6 the position is about equal.

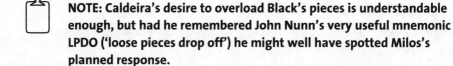

> **NOTE: Caldeira's desire to overload Black's pieces is understandable enough, but had he remembered John Nunn's very useful mnemonic LPDO ('loose pieces drop off') he might well have spotted Milos's planned response.**

14...Bxd5! 15 c3 Bg5 (Diagram 12) 16 f4?!

A sign of panic having presumably realized that 16 Bxg5 Qxg5 followed by ...Qe3 leaves Black better and especially in the case of 17 cxb4? Qe3+ 18 Kh1 Bxb3 19 Qe1 Rfc8.

16...exf4 17 Bxf4 Bxf4 18 Rxf4 Qg5 19 g3 Bxb3 20 Qxb3 Nd5 (Diagram 13) 21 Rff1 h5!?

Tempting, although there wasn't much wrong either with 21...Qe3+ 22 Kh1 Qxe2

23 Qxd5 Qxb2.

22 Qb5 Rae8! 23 Bf3 Re5 24 Bxd5 Rxd5 25 Qxb7 h4 26 Rce1 hxg3 27 Re8?

The final error. Instead White had to defend his king the best he could with 27 Re2 gxh2+ 28 Kh1, not that this would probably have saved him after 28...Rf5.

27...Rxe8 28 Qxf7+ Kh7 29 Qxe8 Re5 (Diagram 14) 30 Qc6 Qe3+ 31 Kh1 Rh5 0-1

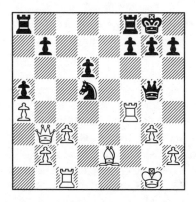

Diagram 13 (W)

White is in serious trouble

Diagram 14 (W)

White's king cannot survive

White Retreats to f3

1 e4 c5 2 Nf3 Nc6 3 d4 cxd4 4 Nxd4 Nf6 5 Nc3 d6 6 Be2 e5 7 Nf3 (Diagram 15)

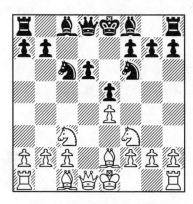

Diagram 15 (B)

White hopes for Bg5xf6

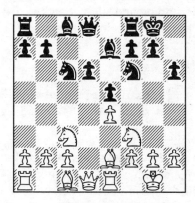

Diagram 16 (W)

White plays to prevent ...d5

A more positional continuation than 7 Nb3 as White gives up on the f4-plan and plays to restrict Black's active possibilities.

7...h6!

Wisely taking control of the g5-square.

 WARNING: Black must be aware that 7 Nf3 covers the g5-square, thereby making 7...Be7?! 8 Bg5 Nxe4?? impossible. Better is 8...0-0, although after 9 0-0 Be6 10 Bxf6 Bxf6 11 Nd5 White has a small but lasting advantage due to both his control of d5 and Black's lack of counterplay.

8 0-0 Be7 9 Re1 0-0 (Diagram 16) 10 h3

Consistent with the highly positional and restraining plan begun by White's last. Instead the immediate 10 Bf1 allows 10...Bg4 when 11 h3 Bh5 12 g4 Bg6 13 Nh4!? (Black isn't especially troubled by this, but neither is he in any case; for example, 13 Bg2 Rc8 begins queenside counterplay with ...Na5-c4 a likely follow-up) 13...Bxe4! 14 Nxe4 Nxe4 15 Nf5 d5 16 Bg2 Bb4!? (the safe choice, whereas 16...Nf6 17 g5 hxg5 18 Bxg5 gives White some initiative for his pawn) 17 c3 Bc5 18 Bxe4 dxe4 19 Qe2 Qd3 20 Qxe4 Rfd8 was fine for Black in D.Vargic-A.Jankovic, Djakovo 2005.

We should also note that 10 Bc4 is possible, but this does leave White a tempo down on a line of the fashionable variation 6 Bc4 e5 which will be analysed at the beginning of Chapter Three. Here 10...Be6 11 Nd5 Rc8 12 c3 Na5! 13 Nxf6 Bxf6 14 Bd5 Nc4 gave Black sufficient counterplay in G.Kuzmin-A.Kosten, Bratislava 1996.

10...Be6

Classical development is the best option. Instead 10...a6 11 Bf1 b5 runs into the undermining and slightly awkward 12 a4! and the regrouping 10...Re8 11 Bf1 Bf8 can be met by 12 Nh2! **(Diagram 17)** 12...a6 13 Ng4 Nxg4 14 hxg4 Be6 15 Nd5 which gave White an edge in I.Glek-A.Volzhin, Linares 1996.

11 Bf1

 NOTE: The point of White's play is that Black cannot liberate his position with ...d5 since the e5-pawn would hang.

11...Nb8!

The standard approach, rerouting the knight to the superior d7-square since it was doing little on c6. Black can now consider meeting Nd5 with ...Nxd5; exd5 Bf5, while the harmoniously-placed d7-knight will later emerge on c5, f6 or b6. Nevertheless, there is an intriguing alternative available in 11...Qd7!? 12 Nd5 Bd8 – see Game 6.

12 b3

Preparing to fianchetto. Practice has also seen the prophylactic space grab 12 a4

Nbd7 13 a5, but after 13...a6 14 Nd5 Nxd5! 15 exd5 Bf5 16 c4 Bg6 17 b4 Re8!? 18 Bb2 e4! 19 Nd2 Bg5 Black had sufficient counterplay in N.Guliev-A.Korotylev, Moscow 2006.

12...a6 13 Bb2 Nbd7 (Diagram 18)

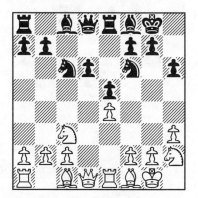

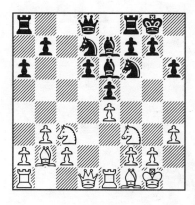

Diagram 17 (B)	Diagram 18 (W)
Ng4 will exchange a defender of d5	Black improves his queen's knight

Completing Black's regrouping and we will return to this strategically unbalanced position in Game 7.

Theoretical Conclusion

After the positional retreat to f3 play revolves around the d5-square. Black must remember to insert 7...h6 and shouldn't overly worry about Nd5 since an exchange on that square gives him kingside counterplay in the resulting unbalanced structure.

Illustrative Games

Game 6
☐ **D.Kononenko** ◼ **A.Kovalev**
Alushta 2003

1 e4 c5 2 Nf3 Nc6 3 d4 cxd4 4 Nxd4 Nf6 5 Nc3 d6 6 Be2 e5 7 Nf3 h6 8 0-0 Be7 9 Re1 0-0 10 h3 Be6 11 Bf1 Qd7 12 Nd5 Bd8

This both preserves the dark-squared bishop, without which d6 can become weak, and prepares to activate it.

TIP: After an exchange on d5 whether or not Black can activate his dark-squared bishop is often crucial to how well he stands.

13 c4 (Diagram 19)

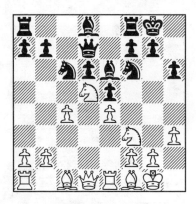
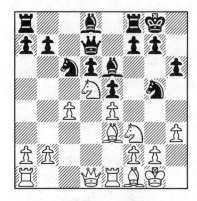

Diagram 19 (B)	**Diagram 20 (W)**
Black has a choice of plans	Gaining kingside counterplay

13...Nh7!?

Bearing in mind our last note Black might have considered the more straightforward 13...Bxd5 14 exd5 Ne7 with the idea of 15 b3 Bb6 16 Be3 Bxe3 17 Rxe3 Nf5 18 Re1 Rfe8, gaining comfortable equality.

14 Be3

Practice has also seen 14 b3 Ng5 15 Nxg5 hxg5 (15...Bxg5!? 16 Bb2 f5 is a reasonable alternative) 16 Be3 as in S.Iuldachev-T.Gelashvili, Baku 2005, and now we quite like 16...Ba5!? aiming to reach a good knight against bad bishop scenario after 17 Bd2 Bxd2 18 Qxd2 Bxd5! 19 cxd5 Nd4.

14...Ng5 (Diagram 20)

Completing Black's original plan. He is happy to see exchanges on g5 and to land up with a pawn there since he would then gain reasonable play on the kingside, especially with ...g4 in the offing.

15 Nd2 f5 16 exf5 Bxf5 17 c5!?

The sharpest counter. White might also have played more slowly and after 17 Be2 Ba5 18 a3 Ne7 19 Nxe7+ Qxe7 20 b4 Bb6 the position is dynamically balanced.

17...Nd4 18 Nc4?!

This allows a superb blow. Instead Kononenko had to find 18 Bxd4 exd4 19 Qb3 when anything might have happened after 19...Kh8 20 f4 Ne6.

18...Ngf3+!! (Diagram 21)

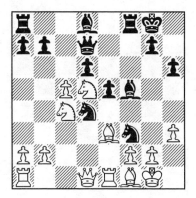

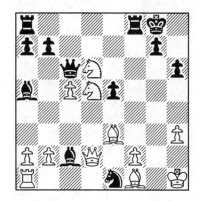

Diagram 21 (W)

Ripping open the white kingside

Diagram 22 (W)

Decoying White's queen away

Superb tactical awareness from Kovalev.

19 gxf3 Bc2 20 Qc1 Nxf3+ 21 Kh1 Nxe1 22 Nxd6!

The best defence; White needs to cover the e4-square.

22...Qc6 23 Qd2?!

However, this isn't the correct follow-up. White had to avoid 23 Bc4? b5! when Black is doing rather well in view of 24 Nxb5? Be4+, but 23 Qxe1 Qxd5+ 24 Bg2 wouldn't have been so bad for him: after 24...e4 25 Qb4 Bf6 (Kovalev) the strong d6-knight and the weakness of e4 allows White to fight on with only a small disadvantage.

23...Ba5! (Diagram 22) 24 Bg2?

The final error. Perhaps White hadn't realised that his knights would be skewered at the end of the exchanges. Better was 24 Qxa5 Qxd5+ 25 Kg1, although after 25...Nf3+ 26 Kh1 Nh4+ 27 Kh2 Bd3 28 Rd1 Rf6 Black would have found himself very much in the driving seat.

24...Bxd2 25 Ne7+ Kh7 26 Bxc6 Bxe3 27 Bxb7 Bxc5 0-1

Game 7
☐ **I.Yagupov** ■ **K.Aseev**
St Petersburg 1999

---

1 e4 c5 2 Nf3 Nc6 3 d4 cxd4 4 Nxd4 Nf6 5 Nc3 d6 6 Be2 e5 7 Nf3 h6 8 0-0 Be7 9 Re1 0-0 10 h3 Be6 11 Bf1 Nb8 12 b3 a6 13 Bb2 Nbd7 14 a4 Qc7 15 a5

A logical plan. White seizes space on the queenside both to prevent ...b5 and to help him after any future piece exchange on d5.

15...Rac8! (Diagram 23)

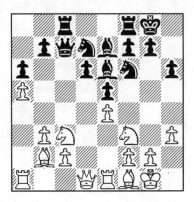

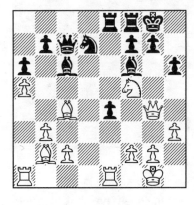

Diagram 23 (W)	Diagram 24 (B)
Holding up Nd5	White wisely forces a draw

Preventing Nd5 and now White has to resort to a different method to gain some play.

16 Nd2!? d5 17 exd5 Nxd5 18 Nxd5 Bxd5 19 Bc4

White can also attack e5 with 19 Nc4, but this doesn't change the view that Black has equalized: 19...Be6 20 Qh5 (or 20 Nxe5 Nxe5 21 Bxe5 Qxc2 22 Qf3 Qxb3 23 Qxb3 Bxb3 24 Bxg7 Kxg7 25 Rxe7 Bd5 with full equality) 20...f6 21 Ne3 Bc5 22 Ng4 Rf7! 23 Ra4 Nf8 saw Black keep his kingside well covered in V.Golod-K.Aseev, Beer-Sheva 1998.

19...Bc6 20 Qg4 Rce8

At first it might seem that White has some pressure here, but Aseev has everything covered and can play to break out with ...e4.

21 Nf3 Bf6 22 Nh4 e4!

Consistent, although we also wonder about 22...Kh7!? with the idea that 23 Ba3 e4 24 Bxf8 Rxf8 gives Black good compensation for the exchange: the a1-rook is en prise and ...Ne5 imminent.

23 Nf5! (Diagram 24) 23...Bxb2 24 Nxh6+ Kh7 25 Nxf7 g6

Now the game fizzles out to perpetual, just as it would have done after 25...Nf6 26 Qh4+ Kg6 27 Qg5+ Kh7.

26 Qh4+ Kg7 27 Qh6+ Kf6 28 Qh4+ Kg7 ½-½

Chapter Three

The Sharp 6 Bc4

▨ **Introduction**

▨ **The Benko Variation: 6...Qb6!?**

▨ **White Plays 7 Ndb5**

▨ **White Plays 7 Nb3**

Introduction

1 e4 c5 2 Nf3 Nc6 3 d4 cxd4 4 Nxd4 Nf6 5 Nc3 d6 6 Bc4 (Diagram 1)

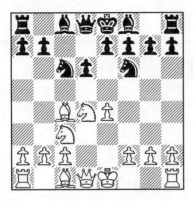

Diagram 1 (B)	**Diagram 2 (W)**
A great favourite of Fischer's	Not so bad for Black

This active development of the light-squared bishop is White's second main system against the Classical Sicilian. White hopes to attack the black king and indeed the struggle can quickly become rather sharp. That helps to explain why this system was such a favourite with Bobby Fischer whose successful use of it in the sixties brought 6 Bc4 fully into the limelight.

Black's main response is to blunt the bishop with 6...e6 after which White can either castle kingside (the Sozin Attack – Chapter Four) or even more aggressively opt to go long (the Velimirovic Attack – Chapter Five). In this chapter we will chiefly focus on Pal Benko's attempt to disrupt White's plans with the uncompromising 6...Qb6!?, but first we must examine Black's less common approaches:

a) The immediate attempt to transpose to the Dragon with 6...g6 has never had a good reputation according to theory because of 7 Nxc6 bxc6 8 e5!. Nevertheless, this position continues to occur quite often (for instance, even in the World Championship match between Schlechter and Lasker in 1910), quite possibly because White doesn't have such a big advantage after 8...Ng4! **(Diagram 2)**: for example, 9 Bf4 d5 10 Nxd5!? exd5 11 Bxd5 Bd7 12 Bxa8 Qxa8 leads to an extremely unclear situation. Perhaps White should prefer 9 exd6 Qxd6 10 Qxd6 exd6 when his superior structure gives him a small edge.

b) Many Classical Sicilian players are not after a transposition to the Dragon, but for those that are we should mention that 6...Bd7 first and only then ...g6 has been considered a more accurate way of transposing.

c) To play in the style of the Boleslavsky with 6...e5!? looks rather misguided here: Black helps rather than hinders the c4-bishop and also gives up control of the d5-square. However, as shown by the games of both Baklan and Epishin this untheoretical system is by no means so bad and the resulting positional struggle may well not appeal to many 6 Bc4 practitioners. After 6...e5, a move whose popularity may well grow after being endorsed in *Dangerous Weapons: The Sicilian*, White has three main options:

c1) 7 Nde2 Be6 8 Bb3 Be7 **(Diagram 3)** 9 Ng3 (focussing on the d5-square with 9 Bg5 is probably a better try for an edge) 9...0-0 10 0-0 Nd4 11 Bxe6 fxe6 12 Be3 Nc6 13 Qe2 a6 14 Rfd1 gave Black decent central control in G.Kuzmin-V.Baklan, Alushta 2004, and now we quite like Palliser's suggestion of 14...Qe8!? after which, for example, 15 Rd2 Qg6 16 Qc4 Ng4 begins counterplay.

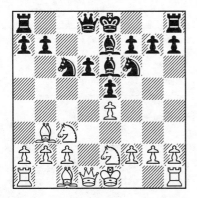

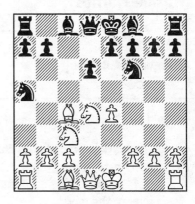

| **Diagram 3 (W)** | **Diagram 4 (W)** |
| Another under-rated black system | Forcing the bishop to commit |

c2) The sharp 7 Nf5!? will be seen in Game 8.

c3) 7 Nf3 Be6 8 Bb3 h6! 9 0-0 Be7 10 Re1 0-0 11 Nd5 Rc8 12 c3 Na5 13 Nxf6+ Bxf6 14 Bd5 Qc7 was very solid for Black, but a touch better for White in B.Damljanovic-V.Baklan, Vrnjacka Banja 1998.

> **NOTE: Black's 8th was a very important move in this last variation. Without it White would have followed up with Bg5 and Bxf6, thereby gaining a small but lasting advantage due to his control of the d5-square.**

d) 6...Na5!? **(Diagram 4)** looks a little primitive, but already forces White to make an important decision over his light-squared bishop: if it retreats to b3 the dangerous bishop can be exchanged at an appropriate moment, but if it withdraws instead to d3 or e2 Black has a reasonable choice between either a Dragon or a

Scheveningen-type set-up. The main advocate of 6...Na5 is our friend from Voronezh, GM Konstantin Chernyshov, and in Game 9 we'll see him dealing with the most critical response: 7 Bb5+!? Bd7 8 Qe2.

Theoretical Conclusion

In recent years the once condemned 6...e5 and 6...Na5 have been holding their own, and not just due to the element of surprise which usually accompanies them. We don't see any way for White to prove a real advantage against the former and neither does 7 Bb5+ Bd7 8 Qe2 bring one against the latter, especially if Black continues with the quiet 8...e6. Those who like to employ 6 Bc4 as White should expect to see much more of these two systems in the next few years.

Illustrative Games

Game 8
□ **T.Abergel** ■ **K.Bolding**
Val d'Isere 2004

1 e4 c5 2 Nf3 Nc6 3 d4 cxd4 4 Nxd4 Nf6 5 Nc3 d6 6 Bc4 e5 7 Nf5 Be6!

 TIP: Black should always challenge the a2-g8 diagonal in this variation. Instead the greedy 7...Bxf5?! 8 exf5 Qd7 is punished by 9 0-0! Qxf5 10 Nd5 Nxd5 11 Bxd5 Be7 12 f4 with a rather dangerous initiative for the pawn.

8 Bb3 (Diagram 5)

Diagram 5 (B)
Black doesn't have to play solidly

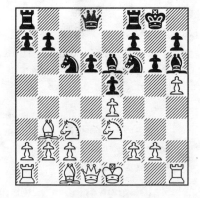

Diagram 6 (B)
Black can defend his kingside

8...g6

The safest move, driving back the white knight. We would also like to draw the reader's attention to Baklan and Vysochin's fascinating suggestion of 8...Nxe4!?, after which 9 Nxg7+ (or 9 Bxe6 Nxc3 10 Bxf7+ Kxf7 11 bxc3 d5 12 Rb1 Qd7 with an unclear situation; Black's central control compensates for his slightly problematic king position) 9...Bxg7 10 Nxe4 d5 11 Ng5 0-0 12 0-0 Nd4 13 c3 Nxb3 14 Qxb3 Qe7 is quite unbalanced but about equal.

9 Ne3 Bh6 10 h4!?

Abergel isn't interested in a positional struggle and instead injects some aggression into the position. However, 10 Ned5 is probably a better try and then 10...Bxc1 11 Rxc1 Bxd5 12 Bxd5 0-0 13 0-0 Nd4 14 Qd3 is a touch better for White due to his control of d5.

10...0-0!

Brave and correct.

11 h5 (Diagram 6) 11...Nxh5 12 g4

Perhaps White might have tried 12 Ncd5!? and after 12...Nd4 13 c3 Nxb3 14 axb3 Bg5 15 g3 he maintains some Sveshnikov-like compensation for the pawn.

12...Bxe3 13 gxh5

Black also wouldn't have had any problems after 13 Bxe3 Nf4 14 Bxf4 exf4 15 Qf3 Qg5! 16 Qh3 h6.

13...Bxc1 14 hxg6!

Correctly not rushing to recapture the piece since 14 Qxc1?! Bxb3 15 axb3 Nd4 16 Nd5 g5!? would have left Black with the upper hand.

14...Bxb3 15 Qh5 h6 16 Rxc1 Qg5! (Diagram 7)

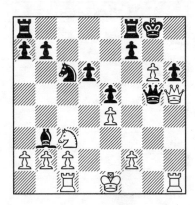

Diagram 7 (W)

Prudently trading queens

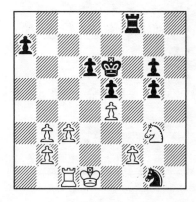

Diagram 8 (W)

Neither side can do much

Now the game rather fizzles out, but Bolding had to avoid 16...Qf6? 17 Qxh6 Qg7 when 18 Qh7+ Qxh7 19 gxh7+ Kg7 20 axb3 would have left White with all the chances.

17 Qxg5 hxg5 18 axb3 Nd4 19 Rh7 fxg6 20 Rxb7 Rf7

A decent alternative was 20...Rf4 and after 21 Nd5 Rxe4+ 22 Kf1 Rh4 23 Kg2 Rg4+ 24 Kh3 Rh4+ it's perpetual.

21 Rxf7 Kxf7 22 Ne2 Nf3+ 23 Kd1 Ke6

Perhaps Black might have tried 23...Rh8!?, although White should be able to maintain a rough balance after 24 Ng3 Rh2 25 Ke2 Nd4+ 26 Ke3.

24 c3 Rf8 25 Ng3 Ng1 (Diagram 8) 26 Ke1 Nh3 27 Rc2 a5 28 Nf1 g4 29 Re2 ½-½

Game 9
□ **D.Gross** ■ **K.Chernyshov**
Prague 2001

---

1 e4 c5 2 Nf3 Nc6 3 d4 cxd4 4 Nxd4 Nf6 5 Nc3 d6 6 Bc4 Na5 7 Bb5+ Bd7 8 Qe2 Rc8!?

The most ambitious move, but in view of White's sharp 11th, quite possibly not the best. Instead there doesn't seem to be anything wrong with the more solid 8...e6; for example, 9 Bg5 Be7 10 0-0-0 a6 11 Bxd7+ Nxd7 12 Bxe7 Qxe7 **(Diagram 9)** 13 Nb3 Nxb3+ 14 axb3 Rc8 15 Qd2 Rc6 didn't give one leading 6 Bc4 exponent any advantage in M.Golubev-D.Kryakvin, Odessa 2006. Indeed after his overly-ambitious 16 Nd5?! Golubev would have been a little worse had Black found 16...Nc5! based on the point that 17 Nxe7?! Nxb3+ 18 Kb1 Nxd2+ 19 Rxd2 Kxe7 wins a clear pawn.

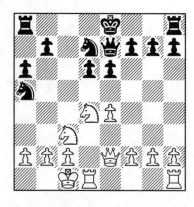

Diagram 9 (W)

Equalizing exchanges

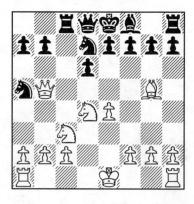

Diagram 10 (W)

A provocative approach

9 Bg5 Bxb5 10 Qxb5+ Nd7 (Diagram 10) 11 Nd5!?

The sharpest continuation, although we should note that it hasn't put Chernyshov off this pet variation of his. More recently he faced 11 Qe2 and after 11...Nc4 12 Nd5 Qa5+! 13 b4 Qa4 14 0-0 (14 a3!? would have been more prudent after which 14...e6 15 Nc3 Qa6 16 0-0 Qb6 remains quite unclear) 14...h6 15 Bh4 g5! 16 Bg3 e6 17 Ne3 Qxb4 18 Rab1 Qd2 Black was better in V.Varadi-K.Chernyshov, Harkany 2006.

11...Rc4!?

Making good use of the knight's position on a5, but quite possibly it's here that Black should look for an improvement.

12 Bd2

Somewhat more dangerous appears to be 12 Nb3!?, especially since 12...Rxe4+ 13 Be3 Nxb3 14 axb3 Qb8 15 0-0 a6 16 Qd3 leaves White with a dangerous lead in development and the black rook somewhat offside.

12...Rxd4 13 Bxa5 (Diagram 11)

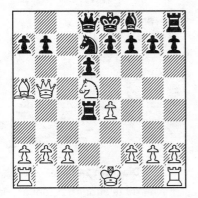

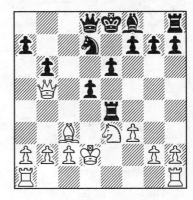

Diagram 11 (B)

Black has sufficient resources

Diagram 12 (B)

The rook needs careful handling

13...b6!?

Chernyshov wants to win! Instead he could have pretty much forced a draw with 13...Rxe4+ 14 Kf1 Qc8! when White has nothing better than to repeat with 15 Nc7+ Kd8 16 Ne6+ Ke8 17 Nc7+.

14 Bc3

Considering White's superior development, perhaps he might have given up two pieces for a rook, not that 14 Qc6!? Rxd5 15 exd5 bxa5 16 0-0 e5 17 dxe6 fxe6 18 Rfe1 Kf7 would have been at all clear.

14...Rxe4+ 15 Kd2?!

A strange decision. Surely 15 Ne3 e6 16 0-0-0 was correct, retaining reasonable compensation for the pawn after 16...Qc8?

15...e6 16 Ne3 d5 17 f3 (Diagram 12) 17...Rh4

The safest square for the rook, but 17...Rf4!? was even stronger since 18 g3 runs into 18...Rxf3! 19 Qe2 Rxe3 20 Qxe3 Bc5 21 Bd4 Bxd4 22 Qxd4 0-0 with more than enough for the exchange.

18 g3 Rh5 19 Rae1 a6 20 Qc6 Bc5 21 g4 Rh3?

In a very complex and unusual situation Black again fails to find the best square for his rook. Correct was 21...Rg5! when 22 f4! Bxe3+ 23 Rxe3 Rxg4 24 Rxe6+! fxe6 25 Qxe6+ Qe7 26 Qxg4 0-0 would have kept all three results very much open.

22 Bxg7! Rg8 23 Nf5 (Diagram 13)

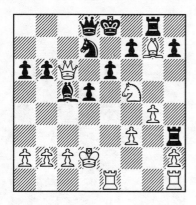

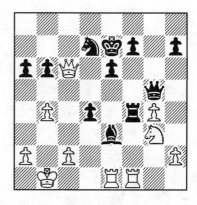

Diagram 13 (B)

Why is the f3-pawn taboo?

Diagram 14 (W)

Black hasn't quite enough compensation

23...Rxg7!

A fine recovery after realizing that 23...Rxf3?? was impossible on account of the brutal 24 Rxe6+! fxe6 25 Qxe6+ Be7 26 Nd6 mate.

24 Nxg7+ Kf8 25 Nh5 Rxf3 26 Kc1 Qg5+ 27 Kb1 Ke7 28 Ng3 Be3

Black is treading a tightrope around here, but Chernyshov impressively maintains his balance while avoiding lines like 28...Qxg4? 29 Qxd5 Bf2 30 Re4 Bxg3 31 hxg3 Qxg3? 32 Rd1 when White wins.

29 Qc3 Nc5 30 b4?!

Rather weakening. Instead 30 Rhf1 Rxf1 31 Rxf1 would have maintained some advantage in view of 31...a5? 32 Nf5+! exf5 33 Rxf5 Qg4 34 Qxe3+ Ne6 35 Rxd5.

30...Nd7 31 Rhf1 d4 32 Qc6 Rf4 (Diagram 14) 33 Rxf4 Qxf4 34 Rf1 Qe5

After many adventures White now decides to settle for a draw, but there was no need to abandon his winning hopes just yet.

35 Rxf7+?! Kxf7 36 Qxd7+ Kg6 37 h4 Qxg3 38 Qxe6+ Kg7 ½-½

The Benko Variation: 6...Qb6!?

1 e4 c5 2 Nf3 Nc6 3 d4 cxd4 4 Nxd4 Nf6 5 Nc3 d6 6 Bc4 Qb6!? (Diagram 15)

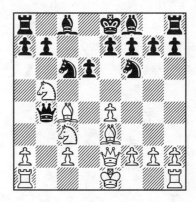

Diagram 15 (W)	Diagram 16 (B)
Disrupting White's plans	Black must be accurate

This attack with the queen was first played by Benko in 1957 and became quite popular after his games with Cardoso (Portoroz Interzonal 1958) and Fischer (Bled Candidates 1959). By deploying his queen so early Black aims to force the d4-knight to move after which White can rarely castle queenside in the manner of the Velimirovic Attack and instead a fairly positional struggle often ensues. Initially Black was also aiming to avoid all the theory of 6...e6 with this approach, but over time 6...Qb6 has acquired a sizable body of theory of its own due in no small part to its adoption by Kramnik in the nineties.

White's main options after 6...Qb6, 7 Ndb5 and 7 Nb3, will be considered respectively in the final two sections of this chapter, but we should note that he has no less than three reasonable alternatives:

a) 7 Be3!? is both the most aggressive and the most risky choice; something which isn't a surprise when one learns that it was first played by no less an attacker than the great Velimirovic. After 7...Qxb2 8 Ndb5 the only move is 8...Qb4, aiming to return home via a5. White should respond with Zaitsev's 9 Qe2 **(Diagram 16)** which is somewhat more dangerous than certain sources have suggested:

a1) 9...Qa5 10 Bd2 Qd8 11 Nd5 Nxd5 12 exd5 Ne5 13 Bb3 (we also wonder about the more direct 13 f4!? Bg4 14 Nxd6+! exd6 15 Bb5+) 13...a6 14 f4 Ng4 15 Na3 maintained quite reasonable compensation in A.Cela-J.Fedorowicz, New York 2004, and now Black should probably try Nogueiras's suggestion of 15...Nf6!?, intending the unclear 16 Bc3 Qc7 17 Bb2 Bg4 18 Qe3 Qc5.

a2) 9...Nxe4 is more critical when we will examine the equally critical response 10 Bxf7+! in Game 10. White should, though, avoid 10 Bd4?! because 10...Bf5! 11 a3 Nxd4 12 axb4 Nxe2 13 Nxe4 Bxe4 14 Nc7+ Kd7 15 Nxa8 Bxg2 favours Black.

a3) We should also draw the creative reader's eye to the rare but fascinating 9...Bg4!? 10 f3 Nxe4, although after 11 Bd4! **(Diagram 17)**

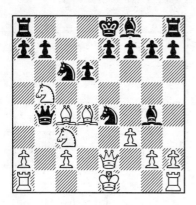

Diagram 17 (B)	Diagram 18 (B)
What's going on?	Another aggressive white option

11...Bf5!? (or 11...Nxd4 12 Qxe4 Nxc2+ 13 Kd2 Bf5!? 14 Qxf5 Qxc4 15 Kxc2 Rc8 16 Qd3 when Black probably doesn't have quite enough for the piece) 12 a3 Nxc3 13 Bxc3 Qc5 14 0-0-0! (but not 14 Nc7+?! Kd8 15 Nxa8 b5! 16 Rb1 Qxc4 17 Qxc4 bxc4 when the knight is trapped on a8 and Black is better) 14...Be6 15 Nc7+ Kd8 16 Nxe6+ fxe6 17 Kb2 White retains rather dangerous compensation.

b) 7 Nxc6 bxc6 8 0-0 **(Diagram 18)** received some attention from Topalov in the late nineties and raises a key question: is White's superior development more important than Black's strong centre?

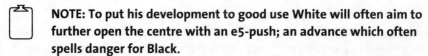

> **NOTE: To put his development to good use White will often aim to further open the centre with an e5-push; an advance which often spells danger for Black.**

After 8 0-0 Black must decide how to develop his kingside:

b1) 8...e6 9 Qe2 Be7 10 e5!? dxe5 11 Qxe5 0-0 12 Na4 Qb4 13 b3 Nd5! was rather complex in E.Sutovsky-D.Gross, Guarapuava 1995.

b2) 8...g6 is quite risky: 9 e5 (or 9 Be3 hoping for 9...Qxb2?! 10 Bd4 Qb7 11 Bxf6 exf6 12 Nd5! Bg7 13 Qf3 with some advantage; Black does better with 9...Qc7 when 10 f4 Bg7 11 Bd4 0-0 12 Kh1 Rb8 was S.Karjakin-E.Miroshnichenko, Kramatorsk 2001, and now the logical 13 e5!? Ne8 14 Bb3 dxe5 15 fxe5 Bxe5 16 Bxe5 Qxe5 17 Qf3 would have been a reasonable pawn sacrifice) 9...dxe5 10 Qe2 Qd4!? 11 Be3 Qd6 12 Rad1 Qc7 13 f4! Bg4 14 Qf2 e4! was dynamically balanced in V.Topalov-V.Kramnik, Novgorod 1997.

b3) We feel that the safest option is for once not to follow in Kramnik's footsteps, but rather to prevent e4-e5 once and for all with 8...e5. See Game 11 for details.

c) A more positional course is 7 Nde2 **(Diagram 19)**, intending either f4-f5 followed by Nf4 with pressure against e6 or Ng3-h5 exchanging an important kingside defender. This approach has been used by both Fischer and Golubev, but we are not that impressed by White's position after 7...e6 8 0-0 Be7 9 Bb3 0-0 (9...a6!? also deserves serious consideration; not least because 10 Bg5 Qc7 11 Ng3 b5 12 Kh1 h5! 13 Bxf6 gxf6 14 Nxh5 Bb7 gave Black good attacking chances for his pawn in G.Kasparov-J.Timman, Manila Olympiad 1992):

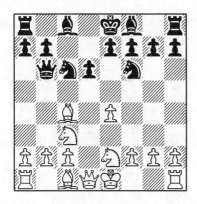

Diagram 19 (B)

The knight heads for the kingside

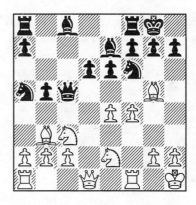

Diagram 20 (W)

Black has enough counterplay

c1) 10 Kh1 Na5 11 Bg5 Qc5!? 12 f4 b5 **(Diagram 20)** 13 Ng3 saw White massing on the kingside in R.Fischer-P.Benko, Bled 1959, but after the calm 13...Nxb3 14 axb3 Bb7 15 Nh5 Kh8 (Fischer) Black would have been fine.

c2) 10 Bg5 Qc7 11 Ng3 a6 12 Qd2 (or 12 Nh5 Nxh5 13 Bxe7 Qxe7 14 Qxh5 Nd4 15 Rad1 Nxb3 16 axb3 Bd7 with easy equality) 12...h6 13 Bxf6 Bxf6 14 Nh5 was M.Golubev-D.Kononenko, Alushta 2006, and now the solid 14...Be7 15 Rad1 Bd7 is a decent alternative to the game's 14...Bd4!?.

Theoretical Conclusion

Those who employ the Benko Variation must make sure that they are prepared for 7 Be3. We don't feel that 7...Qxb2 8 Ndb5 Qb4 9 Qe2 gives White more than enough compensation, but it does appear that theory has often underestimated this dangerous approach. As shown by Topalov, 7 Nxc6 bxc6 8 0-0 is another line not without its dangers, although all of 8...e6, 8...g6 and 8...e5 appear playable depending on Black's taste. Finally, 7 Nde2 does not appear too dangerous since Black both gains decent counterplay on the queenside and has sufficient resources on the kingside.

Illustrative Games

Game 10
□ **J.Hector** ■ **H.Stefansson**
Aarhus 2003

1 e4 c5 2 Nf3 Nc6 3 d4 cxd4 4 Nxd4 Nf6 5 Nc3 d6 6 Bc4 Qb6 7 Be3 Qxb2 8 Ndb5 Qb4 9 Qe2 Nxe4 10 Bxf7+! Kxf7! (Diagram 21)

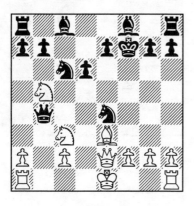
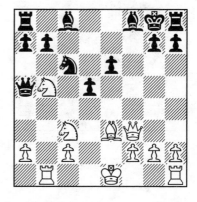

Diagram 21 (W)	Diagram 22 (W)
A complicated situation	White has sufficient compensation

Taking up the challenge. Black should respond thus, not least because 10...Kd8 fails to solve his problems: e.g., 11 a3 Nxc3 (or 11...Qb2 12 Rd1! Bg4! − 12...Nxc3?? fails to the aesthetic 13 Rxd6+! exd6 14 Bb6+! axb6 15 Qe8 mate − 13 Qxg4 Nxc3 14 Nxc3 Qxc3+ 15 Bd2 Qe5+ 16 Kf1!? g6 17 Be3 Kc7 18 Bd5 Bg7 19 h4 when White has the initiative according to Nisipeanu and Stoica) 12 axb4 Nxe2 13 Kxe2 e6 14 Rhd1 a6 15 Bh5 d5 16 Bb6+ Kd7 17 Nc7 Rb8 18 c4! Nxb4 19 cxd5 exd5 20 Rac1 gave White more than enough for his pawns in G.Szabo-E.Miroshnichenko, Istanbul 2005.

11 Rb1

The correct way of regaining the piece, whereas 11 Qh5+!? g6 12 Qd5+ Be6 13 Qxe4 leaves White in some trouble after 13...Bg7 14 Qxb4 Nxb4 15 Kd2 Rhc8.

11...Qa5

> **WARNING: Both sides must be very careful in this variation. Here it's Black's turn to have a plausible blunder with 11...Nxc3? 12 Qf3+ Kg8 13 Rxb4 Nxb4 which fails to 14 Nc7! Nxc2+ 15 Kd2 Nxe3 16 fxe3 Rb8 17 Rf1 when White wins.**

12 Qc4+ e6 13 Qxe4 d5 14 Qf3+ Kg8 (Diagram 22)

Finally the black king reaches relative safety, although there's still the small matter of the h8-rook to solve.

15 0-0

Quite possibly a better way to retain sufficient compensation is 15 Bf4!? a6 16 Bc7 b6 17 Nd6 Bxd6 18 Bxd6.

15...a6 16 Nxd5 axb5 17 Nb6 h5

Much more materialistic was 17...Rb8!? and after 18 Qe4 Kf7 19 Qf4+ Ke8 it's not clear whether White has quite enough for the piece.

18 Qe4!

White too isn't in a hurry to be materialistic. Indeed he is probably right not to be since 18 Nxa8 Qxa8 19 Rxb5 Qxa2 20 Rxh5 Rxh5 21 Qxh5 Qxc2 sees his initiative drying up and Black must be for preference after 22 Qe8 Ne7.

18...Nd8 (Diagram 23)

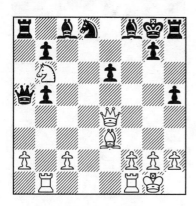

Diagram 23 (W)

Black keeps e6 covered

Diagram 24 (W)

The game begins to fizzle out

19 Qd3 Nf7 20 Rxb5 Qxa2 21 Bc5 e5!

Opening up the light-squared bishop and also preparing a path for the queen to retreat down.

22 Bxf8 Kxf8 23 Qc3

The game is roughly balanced after this and perhaps a more challenging approach was 23 Nxa8!? Qxa8 24 Rxe5!, not that Black should be worse after 24...Rh6!.

23...Be6 24 Nxa8 Qxa8 25 Rfb1 Qc8 26 Qd3 Bf5 27 Qa3+ Kg8 28 Rxb7 Qxc2 29 Rc1 Qd2 (Diagram 24) 30 h3 Rh6 31 Rcc7

Wisely doubling on the seventh and now Black isn't able to avoid a draw.

31...Rf6 32 Qa8+ Kh7 33 Rxf7 Qc1+ ½-½

Game 11
☐ **V.Topalov** ■ **V.Gavrikov**
Geneva (rapid) 1996

---

1 e4 c5 2 Nf3 Nc6 3 d4 cxd4 4 Nxd4 Nf6 5 Nc3 d6 6 Bc4 Qb6 7 Nxc6 bxc6 8 0-0 e5 9 Bg5!?

The sharpest approach. White is happy to offer a pawn to further his lead in development.

9...Qxb2!

Principled and correct, whereas 9...Qc5 10 Qd3 Be7 11 Be3 Qa5 12 a3! 0-0 13 b4 Qc7 14 Rad1 would have left White slightly better.

10 Qd3 Qb6 11 Bxf6 gxf6 12 Nd5! (Diagram 25)

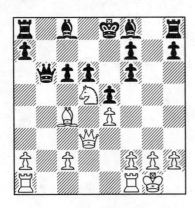

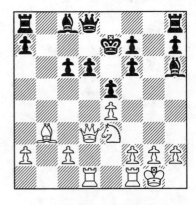

Diagram 25 (B)	Diagram 26 (B)
The knight cannot be touched	The tricky knight should be removed

12...Qd8

Wisely avoiding the vicious trap 12...cxd5? 13 Qxd5 Qb7 14 Rfb1!, winning the rook on a8.

13 Ne3

Perhaps White might have tried 13 Rab1!?, although after 13...Be7 14 Nxe7 Kxe7 15 Qa3 Qc7 we feel that Black can hold his own; for example, 16 Rfd1 Rb8 17 Rxd6 Qxd6 18 Qxd6+ Kxd6 19 Rxb8 Kc7 20 Rb1 Be6 sees a draw beckon.

13...Bh6

Now it's Black's turn to pass up a more enterprising option with 13...Rb8!? 14 Rab1 Rb6, keeping White fully at bay on the queenside.

14 Rad1 Ke7 15 Bb3 (Diagram 26) 15...Be6?

The black position is not that easy to handle in a rapidplay game, but a player of Gavrikov's experience should have realized the dangers posed by the white knight. Correct was 15...Bxe3! 16 fxe3 Be6 17 Qc3 Qd7 with rough equality.

16 Nc4!

Powerfully forcing the opening of the centre.

16...d5?

 WARNING: Always be very careful about opening the centre when your king resides there.

Bearing that in mind, Gavrikov should have tried 16...Qc7! when 17 Nxd6 removes an important pawn, but after 17...Rad8 18 Bxe6 Qxd6 19 Qxd6+ Rxd6 20 Rxd6 Kxd6 21 Bxf7 Black can most certainly fight on and has good chances to hold the endgame due to the presence of opposite-coloured bishops.

17 Ba4! Rc8

And not, of course, 17...dxc4? because of 18 Qa3+.

18 Qa3+ (Diagram 27) 18...c5 19 exd5 Bg4 20 f3 Bf5 21 d6+ Kf8 22 d7 Rc7 23 Rd5

Topalov might have already crowned his assault with 23 Nd6! and after 23...Be6 24 Ne8 Rxd7 25 Bxd7 Bxd7 26 Nxf6 Black's resistance is at an end.

23...Kg7?!

Now White wins down the d-file and Black might have instead struggled on with 23...Be6 since 24 Rfd1 Bxd5 25 Rxd5 Rg8 26 Na5 Kg7 27 Nc6 Rxc6 28 Bxc6 gives him some blockading chances on the dark squares.

24 Nd6! Bxd7 25 Rfd1 Qe7 26 Bxd7 Qxd7 27 Qd3 (Diagram 28) 27...Qe6 28 Qe4

The attack is overwhelming. Not only is White attacking with the legendary team of queen and knight, but his overall coordination is vastly superior to Black's.

28...Kg8 29 Nf5 1-0

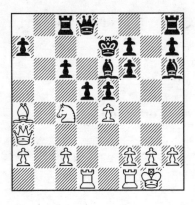

Diagram 27 (B)

Levering open the black position

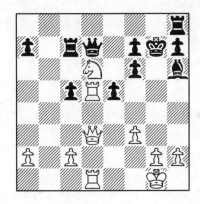

Diagram 28 (B)

There's no defence

White Plays 7 Ndb5

1 e4 c5 2 Nf3 Nc6 3 d4 cxd4 4 Nxd4 Nf6 5 Nc3 d6 6 Bc4 Qb6 7 Ndb5 (Diagram 29)

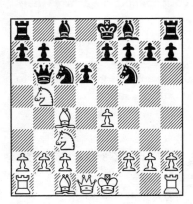

Diagram 29 (B)

Preparing Be3

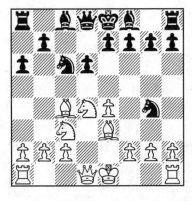

Diagram 30 (W)

Black avoids a Sozin transposition

This might be less aggressive than 7 Be3, but it is still quite a provocative approach, not to mention also a challenging one.

7...a6

The most natural, forcing the aggressively-placed knight backwards. However, there is a good alternative in 7...Bg4!?. After 8 f3 (8 Nd5!? is the non-Velimirovic approach, netting the bishop pair after 8...Nxd5 9 Qxg4; however, this is by no means the end of the world for Black and after 9...Nf6 10 Qe2 a6 11 Nc3 e6 12 Bb3 Qc7 13 Be3 Na5 14 0-0 Be7 15 Rfd1 0-0 16 f3 Rac8 the position was pretty level in G.Ginsburg-L.Gerzhoy, Ashdod 2003) 8...Bd7 9 Qe2 a6 10 Be3 Qa5 11 Nd4 e6 play has a reached a Velimirovic Attack with the additional moves f3 and ...Qa5 inserted: quite whom this favours is not clear.

8 Be3 Qa5

Staying true to the Benko Variation by declining to transpose to our next chapter with 8...Qd8 9 Nd4 e6 (which equates to 6...e6 7 Be3 a6). Another approach is to retreat to d8 and after 9 Nd4 to play 9...Ng4!? **(Diagram 30)**; for example, V.Ivanchuk-V.Kramnik, Linares 1998, continued 10 Nxc6 bxc6 11 Qf3 Ne5 12 Qe2 e6 13 0-0-0 Be7 14 Bd4 and here Ivanchuk recommends 14...Nxc4 15 Qxc4 Qc7 16 Bxg7 Rg8 17 Bh6 Rxg2 18 Rhg1 Rg6 with an unclear situation.

9 Nd4 e6

The most common reply.

 NOTE: The position is now the same as that which occurs after 6 Bc4 e6 7 Be3 a6 except that Black has gained the useful move ...Qa5.

The text is, though, by no means essential. For a start there is 9...Nxe4, a move which no less a 6 Bc4 authority than Fischer himself thought refuted 7 Ndb5. Practice has, however, shown that the pawn grab is rather risky and should probably even be adorned as '?!'; for example, 10 Qf3 f5 11 Nxc6 bxc6 12 0-0-0 **(Diagram 31)** 12...d5 (12...Rb8!? may improve and after 13 Nxe4 fxe4 14 Bf7+ Kd8 15 Qxe4 Qb4 Black at least has some counterchances) 13 Nxe4 fxe4 14 Qh5+ g6 15 Qe5 Rg8 16 Rxd5! cxd5 17 Bxd5 gave White a huge initiative in S.Kindermann-B.Zueger, Mendoza 1985; a game which was by no means an atypical disaster for Black after 9...Nxe4?!.

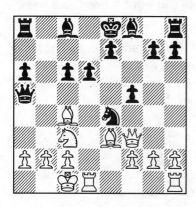

Diagram 31 (B)
White has some initiative

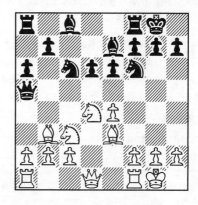

Diagram 32 (W)
Black has gained the move ...Qa5

Probably better attempts to avoid a Sozin-like position are both 9...Ne5!?, the subject of Game 12, and 9...Ng4!?, after which 10 Nxc6 bxc6 11 Bd2 g6 12 Be2 Ne5 13 f4 Nd7 14 Nd5 Qd8 15 Bc3 e5 16 Ne3 Nc5 17 Bf3 was the unbalanced continuation of S.Grigoryants-V.Baikov, Moscow 1999, and now Atalik recommends 17...Na4! 18 Qd2 Qb6 19 Nc4 Qc5 with counterplay.

10 0-0

It's not common for White to castle long in this variation because after 10 Qd2 Be7 11 0-0-0 Ng4! Black exchanges the strong bishop on e3; for example, 12 Kb1 Nxe3 13 fxe3 Qc7 14 Bb3 0-0 15 g4 Na5 16 h4 b5 17 g5 Bb7 left Black doing pretty well in A.Fedorov-H.Stefansson, Stockholm 1997.

10...Be7 11 Bb3 0-0 (Diagram 32)

This is a standard Sozin position, but for the extra move ...Qa5. In Game 13 we will examine Black's attempts to exploit this small gain.

Theoretical Conclusion

Those more at home in the Sozin than in the Velimirovic as White can consider 7 Ndb5 since this leads to Sozin-like positions. However, Black has a number of ways to respond and all bar the capture on e4 seem quite reasonable for him.

Illustrative Games

Game 12
□ **V.Topalov** ■ **V.Kramnik**
Belgrade 1995

1 e4 c5 2 Nf3 Nc6 3 d4 cxd4 4 Nxd4 Nf6 5 Nc3 d6 6 Bc4 Qb6 7 Ndb5 a6 8 Be3 Qa5 9 Nd4 Ne5!? (Diagram 33) 10 Bd3

NOTE: White can also first insert 10 Nb3 Qc7 and after 11 Bd3 e6 12 f4 Nc4 13 Bxc4 Qxc4 play has transposed to a position which more usually arises via 7 Nb3 e6 8 Bf4 Ne5 9 Be2 a6 10 Be3 Qc7 11 f4 Nc4 12 Bxc4 Qxc4 – see Game 14 in our next section for details.

10...Neg4

Continuing ambitiously, but perhaps this is too ambitious. Instead the calm 10...e6 11 f4 Nxd3+ 12 cxd3 Be7 13 0-0 0-0 14 Kh1 Bd7 15 Qb3 was seen in S.Kindermann-J.Fedorowicz, Dortmund 1986, and now Black might have arranged central counterplay with 15...Rae8!? and if 16 f5, then the other central break becomes possible with 16...d5!.

11 Bc1 g6 12 Nb3!

More precise than 12 f4 when 12...Qc5! 13 h3 e5 is fine for Black.

12...Qb6 13 Qe2 Bg7 14 f4 (Diagram 34) 14...Nh5!?

Diagram 33 (W)

Forcing the bishop backwards

Diagram 34 (B)

The g4-knight is rather offside

Determined not to have his knight driven backwards Kramnik plays very provocatively, but this is an extremely risky strategy. Nowadays Kramnik might have a rather unfair reputation as a boring strategist, but in his youth he was most certainly happy to mix it up with the best of them.

15 Nd5! Qd8 16 Bd2 e6 17 Ba5

The point of White's 15th. Black's position now hangs together rather precariously.

17...Qh4+ (Diagram 35)

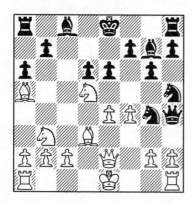

Diagram 35 (W)

Sacrificing material for counterplay

Diagram 36 (B)

Messy but good for White

18 g3 Nxg3 19 Nc7+!

Strong, although Topalov must have been tempted too by 19 hxg3!? Qxg3+ (and not 19...Qxh1+? 20 Kd2 Qh3 21 Nc7+ Kf8 22 Nxa8 Qxg3 23 Rf1 when Black hasn't anywhere near enough for a piece) 20 Kd2 exd5 21 Raf1 (threatening to trap Black's queen with 22 Rf3) 21...Nf6 22 exd5+ Kf8 23 Rf3 Qg4 24 Qf2 which would have left him with pretty reasonable play for the pawn.

19...Ke7 20 hxg3 Qxg3+ 21 Kd1 Nf2+ 22 Kd2

It wasn't easy to decide on the best square for the king, but subsequent analysis revealed that 22 Kc1! was correct and after 22...Nxh1 23 Nxa8 Qxf4+ 24 Bd2 Qe5 25 Qe1! **(Diagram 36)** White is clearly better.

22...Nxh1 23 Nxa8?!

Now Black gains good counterplay against White's exposed king. Topalov should have preferred 23 Rxh1 after which 23...Qxf4+ 24 Kd1 Rb8 25 Rf1 Qg3 26 Kc1, whilst not too clear, should be a little better for White.

23...Qxf4+ 24 Qe3 Qh2+ 25 Qe2 Qf4+ 26 Qe3 Qh2+ 27 Qe2 Bh6+ (Diagram 37)

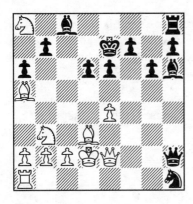
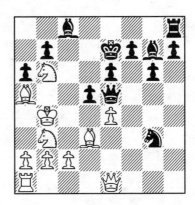

Diagram 37 (W)

Most players would repeat...

Diagram 38 (W)

...rather than have such a king

28 Kc3!?

An extremely ambitious attempt to avoid the repetition. White might also have done so with 28 Kd1, but then 28...Qg1+ 29 Qe1 (and not 29 Be1? e5! with the terrible threat of 30...Bg4) 29...Qg4+ 30 Be2 Qxe4 31 Nb6 Be3 32 Nd2 Qc6 would have offered Black plenty of pawns as well as reasonable activity for his piece.

28...Qe5+ 29 Kb4 Ng3 30 Qe1 Bg7!

Far stronger than 30...Qxb2?! 31 Rb1 Qe5 32 Nb6 when the knight returns from the corner to help White defend.

31 Nb6 d5! (Diagram 38) 32 Ka4?

Understandably a little concerned about his king position, Topalov errs. The correct path was 32 exd5! when 32...Qd6+ 33 Kc4 Qf4+ 34 Kc5 allows Black to either repeat or try 34...Bd7!?, not that he then appears to have anything better than the perpetual after 35 a4!.

32...Bd7+! 33 Nxd7 b5+

Perhaps Topalov missed this possibility which leaves him in severe trouble.

34 Kb4 Kxd7 35 Bb6

Neither would 35 Nc5+ Kc6 36 Rb1 have saved White in view of 36...Qd4+ 37 Ka3 Nxe4! 38 Bxe4 Qxc5+ 39 b4 Qc3+ 40 Qxc3+ Bxc3 when the pawns will stroll home.

35...Qxb2?

After such a complicated struggle we should not be surprised that both sides err in the time scramble. As Kramnik later pointed out the correct path was the decisive 35...Nxe4! 36 Bxe4 Qxb2! with the point that 37 Rb1 fails to 37...Rc8!! **(Diagram 39)** 38 Bc5 Bc3+! 39 Qxc3 a5+.

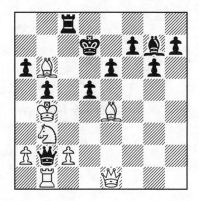

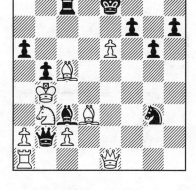

Diagram 39 (W)

Threatening 38...Rc4+ 39 Ka5 Ra4 mate

Diagram 40 (W)

Winning the queen

36 exd5 Rc8 37 dxe6+ Ke8! 38 Bc5?

White also had to avoid 38 c4? Ne4! 39 Rc1 Qxa2 and the correct approach was 38 Bxb5+! axb5 39 exf7+ Kxf7 40 Qxg3 after which Black has nothing better than 40...Qc3+ 41 Qxc3 Bxc3+ 42 Kxb5 Bxa1 43 Nxa1 h5 44 Nb3 h4 (Kramnik) with probably a small advantage in this rather unclear endgame.

38...Bc3+! (Diagram 40) 39 Qxc3 a5+ 40 Kxb5 Qxc3 0-1

Superb entertainment and a reminder that not only Topalov can excel at fighting chess.

Game 13
☐ N.De Firmian ■ I.Smirin
Antwerp 1994

1 e4 c5 2 Nf3 Nc6 3 d4 cxd4 4 Nxd4 Nf6 5 Nc3 d6 6 Bc4 Qb6 7 Ndb5 a6 8 Be3 Qa5 9 Nd4 e6 10 0-0 Be7 11 Bb3 0-0 12 f4 Bd7

Black can also use the position of his queen to counter in the centre with 12...Nxd4 13 Bxd4 e5 **(Diagram 41)** and after 14 fxe5 dxe5 15 Be3 Bc5 (but not the tempting 15...Ng4?! in view of 16 Qd5! Qxd5 17 Nxd5 Bd6 18 Bb6 Be6 19 Rad1 which brought White some advantage in F.Gobet-V.Hort, Biel 1982) 16 Qe2 Be6! Black has equalized.

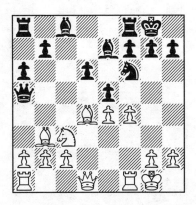

Diagram 41 (W)

Fighting back in the centre

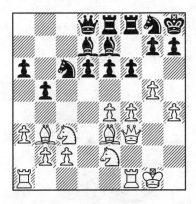

Diagram 42 (W)

There's no way into Black's position

> **NOTE: Black doesn't fear a doubling of his e-pawns here since that would leave him controlling a number of rather useful central squares and not least d5.**

13 f5

Increasing the pressure against e6 in a bid to induce the horribly weakening ...e5. White has also attacked on the kingside with 13 Qf3!? Rae8 14 Nde2 b5 15 a3 Kh8 16 g4, but after 16...Ng8! 17 g5 Qd8 18 h4 f6 **(Diagram 42)** Black's noteworthy re-grouping held everything together and also gave him some counterplay in S.Grigoriants-S.Kiselev, Moscow 1998.

13...Nxd4 14 Bxd4 Rac8

Black doesn't, of course, create weaknesses with 14...e5, but he can also employ 14...exf5 15 exf5 Bc6 after which, for example, 16 Qd3 Rae8 17 Rad1 Nd7 18 Qg3

Bf6! 19 Qxd6 Bxd4+ 20 Qxd4 Nf6 gave him enough for his pawn in N.Short-V.Kramnik, Novgorod 1996.

15 Qf3

Wisely not rushing forwards with 15 g4?! because of 15...e5 16 Be3 Rxc3! 17 bxc3 Bc6, gaining more than enough for the exchange.

 TIP: The exchange sacrifice on c3 is an important resource in most variations of the Sicilian. Never forget about it, especially if it exposes White's king after queenside castling or, like here, when it leads to the destruction of White's centre.

15...Kh8!?

A useful waiting move. Instead 15...b5? had to be avoided on account of 16 fxe6 Bxe6 (or 16...fxe6 17 Qh3 with extremely awkward pressure against e6) 17 Nd5 Bxd5 18 exd5 (Smirin) which would have left White in control.

16 Rad1 b5! (Diagram 43)

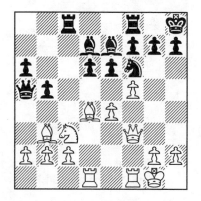 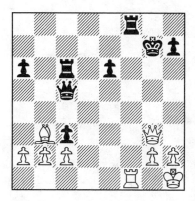

Diagram 43 (W)	Diagram 44 (B)
Black has calculated carefully	Perpetual looms

17 Bxf6 Bxf6 18 Rxd6 Bc6

Yet again we see Black happy to give up a pawn in return for good activity. Just look at those raking bishops! That said, White retains some sharp tactical trumps of his own and quite possibly Smirin had already seen as far as the finish when calculating his 16th!

19 fxe6 b4!

An essential intermezzo, whereas 19...fxe6? 20 Rxc6! Rxc6 21 e5 would have been a little embarrassing.

20 Rxc6! Rxc6 21 e5 Qc5+

Defending the rook and now the game fizzles out to a perpetual.

22 Kh1 bxc3 23 exf6 fxe6 24 fxg7+ Kxg7 25 Qg3+ (Diagram 44) 25...Kh8 26 Rxf8+ Qxf8 27 Qe5+ Qg7 28 Qb8+ ½-½

White Plays 7 Nb3

1 e4 c5 2 Nf3 Nc6 3 d4 cxd4 4 Nxd4 Nf6 5 Nc3 d6 6 Bc4 Qb6 7 Nb3 (Diagram 45)

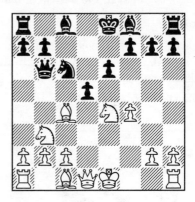

Diagram 45 (B)

Preparing to retreat the bishop

Diagram 46 (W)

A useful equalizing trick

This remains White's main reply to Benko's 6...Qb6. He will now retreat his light-squared bishop to d3 or e2 and play often develops along Scheveningen-type lines.

7...e6 8 0-0

Prudent. Instead 8 f4 is a little premature and after 8...Nxe4! 9 Nxe4 d5 **(Diagram 46)** 10 Bd3 (10 Bxd5 exd5 11 Qxd5? only serves to lead White intro trouble after 11...Nb4 12 Qc4 Bf5, but 10 Qe2!? deserves attention when 10...dxc4 11 Be3 Qb5 12 0-0 Be7 is approximately equal) 10...dxe4 11 Bxe4 Qb4+ 12 Nd2 f5! 13 Bxc6+ bxc6 14 Qf3 Bb7 15 Qb3 0-0-0! Black's bishop pair gave him the advantage in So.Polgar-V.Hort, London 1996.

A better alternative should White not want to play in classical Scheveningen style is Igor Zaitsev's straightforward attack on d6 with 8 Bf4!? which we will see in Game 14.

8...Be7

The most accurate move order, whereas 8...a6 weakens the b6-square and after the cramping 9 a4 Qc7 10 a5! Black faces some difficulties, especially because 10...Nxa5 11 Nxa5 b6 can be rebuffed by 12 e5! bxa5 (12...dxe5? 13 Qf3 wins material) 13 exf6 Qxc4 14 Qf3! Rb8 15 Ne4 g6 16 Qf4 Qc6 17 Ra3 which gave White a strong initiative in D.Vasiesiu-D.Solak, Bucharest 1997.

9 Be3

Now if White advances with 9 a4 0-0 10 a5 Black should be fine since he hasn't weakened b6 and will develop his light-squared bishop via d7; for example, 10...Qc7 11 Be2 Nb4! (stronger than 11...Rd8 when 12 Bf4 causes some problems with the development of the bishop from c8) 12 Bf4 Bd7 13 Qd2 Bc6 was about equal in M.Kodric-V.Tukmakov, Bled 1995.

Another possible approach is to try and double Black's pawns after 9 Bg5. Black can either respond in Richter-Rauzer style with 9...a6 10 Bxf6 gxf6, after which 11 Qh5 Bd7 12 Kh1 Ne5 13 Be2 0-0-0 gives both sides their chances, or sacrifice the d-pawn for control of the dark squares with 9...0-0!?: 10 Bxf6 Bxf6 11 Qxd6 Rd8 **(Diagram 47)** 12 Qg3 Be5 13 Qh3 Bd7 14 Kh1 Qb4 (a good alternative is 14...Na5!? 15 Bd3 Rac8 with queenside pressure) 15 Bd3 Bxc3 16 a3 Qe7 17 bxc3 e5 saw Black retain full compensation in L.Brunner-A.Khalifman, Lucerne 1993.

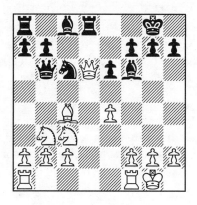

Diagram 47 (W)

Black has good compensation

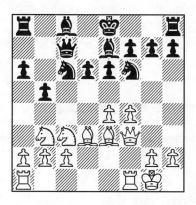

Diagram 48 (B)

White will attack on the kingside

9...Qc7 10 Bd3

Another way is 10 Be2 a6 11 f4 b5 12 Bf3 Bb7, transposing to a type of Classical Scheveningen and one in which Black has reasonable queenside counterplay.

NOTE: After 7 Nb3 Black must be prepared to play certain lines of the Classical Scheveningen, but this should not put him off 6...Qb6!?. The reason is that he does not need to know too much actual theory and he is also assured of quite standard Sicilian counterplay.

10...a6 11 f4

A less common approach is to prevent ...b5 with 11 a4 when Black should continue with 11...b6 followed by bringing his knight to the weakened b4-square.

11...b5 12 Qf3 (Diagram 48)

This position also arises quite commonly from both the Scheveningen and Paulsen variations. White's queen is heading to h3 and Black must decide what to do about the e4-e5 advance:

a) 12...0-0!? at first looks a little misguided, but it actually sets quite a fiendish trap: 13 e5?! dxe5 14 fxe5 Nxe5 15 Qxa8 Neg4! suddenly gives Black strong threats against both White's king and queen! Play might continue 16 Rxf6! (prudent whereas 16 Bf4? Qb6+ 17 Kh1 Bb7 18 Qxf8 Kxf8 19 h3 e5! leaves Black's extra queen superior to White's rooks) 16...Qxh2+ 17 Kf1 Nxe3+ 18 Ke2 Bxf6 19 Kxe3 b4 and this position might be unclear, but is certainly much easier to handle as Black.

b) 12...Rb8 hopes to avoid any problems down the long diagonal, but after 13 Rae1 Nb4 14 Kh1 0-0 White has 15 e5! since capturing on e5 loses material down the h2-b8 diagonal. However, this position is not so bad for Black and after the 15...Nxd3 16 cxd3 Nd7 17 Qg3 Bb7 18 Ne4 of S. Karjakin-Z.Kozul, Halkidiki 2002, the Ukrainian super-talent recommends 18...Bxe4 19 dxe4 dxe5 20 fxe5 Rbc8! with reasonable counterplay for Black.

c) Black's main move is 12...Bb7 after which White will look to play on the kingside, while Black will counter in the centre or on the queenside. Game 15 is a good example of how this common type of Sicilian struggle can unfold.

Theoretical Conclusion

Players with some Scheveningen experience as White often choose 7 Nb3 e6 8 0-0. Just as complex is 8 Bf4 and in both cases Black must be quite accurate in the complicated positions which typically arise.

Illustrative Games

Game 14
□ A.Cela ■ V.Kotronias
Ano Liosia 1997

1 e4 c5 2 Nf3 Nc6 3 d4 cxd4 4 Nxd4 Nf6 5 Nc3 d6 6 Bc4 Qb6 7 Nb3 e6 8 Bf4 Ne5 (Diagram 49)

Necessary to defend d6.

> **NOTE: Black doesn't fear the doubling of his pawns on e5. After 9 Bxe5?! dxe5 he controls not only the key d5-square, but also d4.**

9 Be2

White's usual choice, although he can also consider 9 Bb5+ after which 9...Bd7 10 Bxd7+ Nfxd7 11 Qe2 a6 12 0-0 Qc7 13 Rae1 Be7 14 Bc1 g5!? saw Black cement his strong knight on e5 in G.Milos-A.Yermolinsky, Groningen 1996.

Diagram 49 (W)

Keeping White's bishops at bay

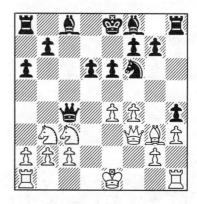

Diagram 50 (W)

White is stymied on the kingside

9...a6

The most accurate move order.

WARNING: Black should avoid 9...Be7 10 Be3 Qc7 11 f4 when he must retreat to c6 and accept a small disadvantage because 11...Nc4?! runs into the nasty 12 Bxa7! Bd7 (or 12...Nxb2 13 Nb5 Qc6 14 Qd4 with some advantage) 13 Bxc4 Qxc4 14 Bd4 leaving White a pawn ahead.

10 Be3

White can also try and force through e4-e5 with 10 Bg3, but after the precise 10...h5! (10...Qc7 11 f4 Nc4 12 e5! dxe5 13 fxe5 Nxe5 14 Qd4 Nfd7 15 0-0-0 Be7 16 Rhe1 gives White some initiative for his pawn) 11 h3 Qc7 12 f4 Nc4 13 Bxc4 Qxc4 14 Qf3 h4 **(Diagram 50)** 15 Bh2 Bd7 16 0-0-0 Rc8 17 Rhe1 b5 Black had good counterplay in V.Ivanchuk-V.Kramnik, Linares 1993.

10...Qc7 11 f4 Nc4 12 Bxc4 Qxc4 13 Qf3

The most challenging approach. Instead 13 Qd3 Qxd3 14 cxd3 Bd7 15 0-0 Be7 gives Black easy equality.

13...Qc7 14 0-0-0!? b5 15 a3 Bb7 (Diagram 51)

16 f5 Rc8!

Correctly allowing White to open the centre rather than see d5 become terribly weak after 16...e5?! 17 Bg5 Rc8 18 Bxf6 gxf6 19 Qf2 Bh6+ 20 Kb1 0-0 21 Nd5.

17 fxe6 fxe6 18 Nd4 Qd7 19 Qh3!

Consistent and best, whereas 19 Bg5 Be7 20 Rhe1 Rc5! 21 Bxf6 0-0! would have favoured Black due to his bishops and superior activity.

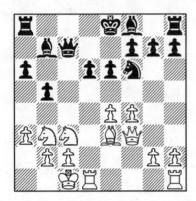

Diagram 51 (W)

Counterplay against e4

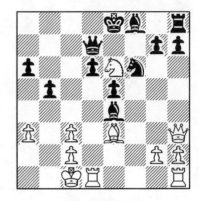

Diagram 52 (W)

White's centre has been destroyed

19...e5

Now it's time for this because Black has a powerful follow-up. Instead 19...Nxe4 would have been rather greedy and after 20 Nxe4 Bxe4 21 Rd2 Bd5 22 Re1 White enjoys good pressure for the pawn.

20 Ne6 Rxc3! 21 bxc3 Bxe4 (Diagram 52) 22 Bc5?

No doubt stung by Black's powerful exchange sacrifice, Cela fails to find the only way to fight on: 22 Rhf1! Ke7 (22...d5 23 Bc5 Bxc5 24 Nxc5 sees the knight escape) 23 Rxd6! Kxd6 24 Bc5+ Kc6 25 Bxf8 Rxf8! 26 Nxf8 Qxh3 27 gxh3 Kd6 28 Re1! would have reached a rather unclear endgame.

22...Bd5 23 Rxd5 Nxd5 24 Rd1 Nf4

Quite promising too was 24...Nxc3!? and after 25 Rd3 Ne2+ 26 Kb2 Nf4 27 Nxf4 Qxh3 28 Rxh3 exf4 White doesn't have enough for the two pawn deficit.

25 Nxf4 Qxh3 26 Nxh3 dxc5 27 Rd5 Be7 28 Rxe5 Kd7 (Diagram 53)

Black enjoys both the better structure and the superior minor piece in this endgame. Indeed he is probably already winning and Kotronias now converts with some ease:

29 Ng5 c4 30 Kb2 Re8 31 Nf3 Bf6! 32 Rh5

Alternatively, 32 Rxe8 Kxe8 33 g4 h6 34 h4 Kf7 35 g5 hxg5 36 hxg5 Be7 37 a4 bxa4

38 Ne5+ Ke6 39 Nxc4 Bxg5 and the g-pawn will carry the day.

32...h6 33 Nd4 Re5 34 Rh3 Rg5 35 g3 Re5 36 g4 Re4 37 Rh5 Rxg4 (Diagram 54) 38 Rd5+ Ke7 39 a4 bxa4 40 Nc6+ Kf7 41 Ra5 Rh4 0-1

Black's kingside pawns will decide.

Diagram 53 (W)
The open board suits the bishop

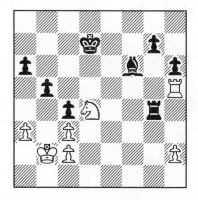

Diagram 54 (W)
White's pawns begin to fall

Game 15
☐ **P.Negi** ■ **N.Mamedov**
Dubai 2004

---

1 e4 c5 2 Nf3 Nc6 3 d4 cxd4 4 Nxd4 Nf6 5 Nc3 d6 6 Bc4 Qb6 7 Nb3 e6 8 0-0 Be7 9 Be3 Qc7 10 Bd3 a6 11 f4 b5 12 Qf3 Bb7 13 Qh3

Taking aim at h7. Practice has also seen 13 Rae1 0-0 14 g4 and after 14...b4 15 Ne2 d5! **(Diagram 55)** 16 e5 Ne4 17 Ng3 Nxg3 18 Qxg3 d4!? 19 Bd2 (or 19 Nxd4 Nxd4 20 Bxd4 Rfd8 21 c3 bxc3 22 bxc3 Rab8 with enough for the pawn; ...Bc5 is next up) 19...Rfe8 20 g5 Na5 21 f5 exf5 22 Rxf5 Nxb3 23 cxb3 Bd5 Black was holding his own in I.Zaitsev-V.Tukmakov, Riga 1970.

13...Nb4

A more radical attempt is Sofia Polgar's 13...h5!? 14 Kh1 Ng4 and after 15 Bg1 we quite like 15...Bf6! 16 a3 g6 with a reasonable position for Black.

14 a3 Nxd3 15 cxd3 Rc8 16 Rac1 Qd8 17 Nd4 0-0 (Diagram 56) 18 g4

Both sides have played pretty logically so far and now Negi decides that it's time to attack. A previous game had seen instead 18 Nf3 when 18...d5 19 e5 d4! 20 Nxd4 Nd5 21 Nxd5 Qxd5 was a promising pawn sacrifice in T.Nedev-J.Lautier, Halkidiki 2002.

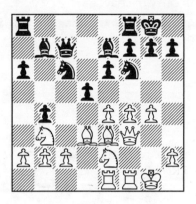

Diagram 55 (W)

Black frees his position

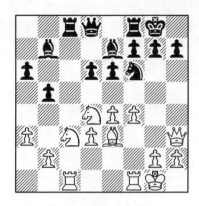

Diagram 56 (W)

Black has quite a solid position

 TIP: Freeing Black's position with ...d5 and if e5 then ...d4 is quite a common ploy in these Scheveningen positions. Here Black both opens up his light-squared bishop and gains good pressure down the d-file.

18...Nd7 19 b4

Prophylaxis against ...Nc5 and indeed 19 g5?! Nc5 20 Rfd1 e5! would have been a bit awkward for White.

19...Bf6 20 Nce2 Rxc1 21 Rxc1 (Diagram 57)

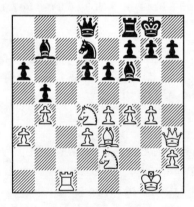

Diagram 57 (B)

The cramping g4-g5 is threatened

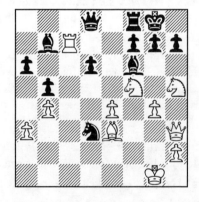

Diagram 58 (B)

There's no defence

21...e5

Perhaps a better approach was to hold up g5 with 21...h6!? and after 22 Nc6 Qa8 23 Na5 Rc8 24 g5 Rxc1+ 25 Bxc1 hxg5 26 fxg5 Bd8 Black maintains approximate equality.

22 Nf5 exf4 23 Nxf4!?

Somewhat more ambitious than settling for a tiny edge with 23 Bxf4 Be5 24 Qh4 Qxh4 25 Nxh4.

23...Ne5 24 Nh5! Nxd3?

Mamedov misses a powerful tactical shot. Instead he had to defend with 24...Bg5! 25 Nhxg7 Kh8 after which, for example, 26 Nh5 Rg8 27 Rf1 Nxg4 28 Bd4+ Ne5 gives Black enough counterplay.

25 Rc7! (Diagram 58) 25...Bxe4

Now the queen is lost, but there wasn't anything better in view of 25...Qxc7? 26 Nxf6+ gxf6 27 Qh6 followed by mate on g7.

26 Rc8! Qxc8 27 Nxf6+ gxf6 28 Ne7+ Kh8 29 Nxc8 Rxc8 30 Qh4 Kg8 31 Qxf6 Rc2 32 Qd8+ Kg7 33 Bd4+ Ne5 34 Qxd6 1-0

Chapter Four

The Sozin Attack

 **Introduction**

 **Flexible Approaches**

 **White Castles Quickly**

Introduction

1 e4 c5 2 Nf3 Nc6 3 d4 cxd4 4 Nxd4 Nf6 5 Nc3 d6 6 Bc4 e6 (Diagram 1)

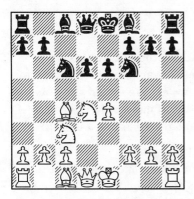

Diagram 1 (W)

Blunting the dangerous bishop

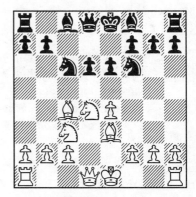

Diagram 2 (B)

Where will White castle?

Black closes the dangerous a2-g8 diagonal and forces White to play pretty actively if he wants to continue making good use of his light-squared bishop. In this chapter we will consider the Sozin Variation, named after the Soviet master Veniamin Sozin, which is generally associated with kingside castling by White, often linked to an advance of the f-pawn. Should White prefer to castle queenside he usually if not always does so with the move order 7 Be3, 8 Qe2 and 9 0-0-0 which leads to the theoretical and fascinating Velimirovic Attack – the subject of our next chapter.

One problem with studying both the Sozin and Velimirovic Attacks is the large number of early transpositional possibilities which occur. We will try to point these out as we go along, especially in our next section which is devoted to White playing 7 Be3 and then not hurrying to castle.

Flexible Approaches

1 e4 c5 2 Nf3 Nc6 3 d4 cxd4 4 Nxd4 Nf6 5 Nc3 d6 6 Bc4 e6 7 Be3 (Diagram 2) 7...a6

As we will examine in our next chapter this is quite a popular anti-Velimirovic move order. Should Black, however, wish to contest the main lines of that aggressive system he should instead begin with 7...Be7 followed by a quick ...0-0. White does indeed usually respond with 8 Qe2 and 0-0-0 (see the next chapter for details), partly because 8 Bb3 0-0 9 f4 runs into 9...Nxd4 10 Bxd4 (or 10 Qxd4 Ng4!

with good counterplay due to Vera's discovery of 11 Bd2 d5! 12 exd5 Bf6) 10...b5!? when practice has shown that Black has sufficient counterchances after 11 e5 dxe5 12 fxe5 Nd7.

8 Bb3

Prophylactically retreating the bishop to a safer square, while keeping both castling options fully open.

> **NOTE:** Another common way of reaching this position is via a prophylactic 7 Bb3 and then 7...a6 8 Be3. Always keep an eye open for transpositional possibilities after 6 Bc4 e6! We should also note that this position can be reached via a Najdorf move order: 1 e4 c5 2 Nf3 d6 3 d4 cxd4 4 Nxd4 Nf6 5 Nc3 a6 and then 6 Bc4 e6 7 Bb3 Nc6 8 Be3.

Instead 8 Qe2 is consistent with the Velimirovic Attack and will be considered in the final section of our next chapter. White might also opt for 8 0-0 when 8...Be7 9 Be3 0-0 transposes to the main line of the next section of this chapter.

8...Qc7 (Diagram 3)

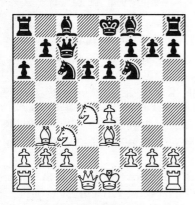

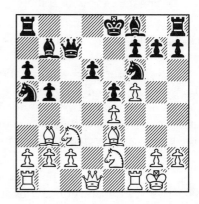

Diagram 3 (W)	Diagram 4 (W)
Black prepares ...b5	White can't maintain control of d5

Another approach is to exchange the potentially dangerous bishop with 8...Na5, but after 9 f4! Black must be careful since he has lost some central control.

> **WARNING:** 9...b5?! is best avoided in view of 10 e5! dxe5 11 fxe5 Nxb3 12 axb3 Nd5 13 Qf3 when White seizes the initiative and Black is struggling after 13...Bb7 14 0-0 Qc7 15 Nxd5 Bxd5 16 Qf2!.

Much better is 9...Qc7! which holds up e4-e5. White usually thus prefers 10 f5 when 10...Nc4!? (this might at first appear a little strange, but the problem with 10...e5 11 Nde2 Nxb3 is 12 cxb3! after which White can cause some problems down the c-file; an idea worth remembering) 11 Bxc4 Qxc4 12 Qf3 e5 13 Nb3 b5 14 0-0-0 a5 15 Bg5 b4 16 Nd2 Qc7 was unclear but roughly balanced in S.Voitsekhovsky-A.Kharlov, Tula 2001.

We should also mention the sharp continuation 8...Be7 9 f4 (9 Qe2 leads to the next chapter) 9...0-0 10 Qf3 Nxd4 (10...Qc7 transposes to our main line) 11 Bxd4 b5!? which entails a very complicated piece sacrifice: 12 Bxf6 Bxf6 13 e5 Bh4+ 14 g3 Rb8 15 gxh4 Bb7 16 Ne4 dxe5 17 Rg1 g6 and Black had reasonable practical compensation in N.Short-G.Kasparov, World Championship (Game 12), London 1993.

9 f4

Attacking with f4-f5 is a common way to try and make good use of the position of White's light-squared bishop. He can also prepare to castle queenside with 9 Qe2 (see the notes to White's 9th in the final section of Chapter Five) or go short at once. After 9 0-0 Na5 Black has an improved version of our last note, not least because 10 f4 b5 11 f5 e5! 12 Nde2 Bb7 **(Diagram 4)** supplies good central counterplay:

a) 13 Ng3?! sees White aiming to taking control of d5 after Bg5, but 13...Nc4 14 Qf3!? (or 14 Bxc4 Qxc4 15 Qf3 h5! 16 h4 Be7 and having forced the weakening h4 Black is better; note here Black's energetic play against e4) 14...Nxb2 15 Nd5 Bxd5 16 Bxd5 Rc8 17 Nh5 Nxd5 18 exd5 f6! kept him at bay on the kingside and didn't offer him enough for his pawn in A.Onischuk-Y.Pelletier, Biel 1999.

b) 13 Nd5 Nxd5 14 Bxd5 is a safer approach, but White is still unable to maintain piece control of d5 after 14...Nc4; for example, 15 Qc1 Bxd5 16 exd5 Rc8 17 Nc3 Nxe3 (much safer than getting involved in 17...Nxb2?! 18 Nxb5! Qxc2 19 Na7 Qxc1 20 Raxc1 Rxc1 21 Rxc1) 18 Qxe3 Qc5 19 Qxc5 Rxc5 20 a3 Be7 saw Black comfortably equalize in G.Ginsburg-Y.Pelletier, German League 2003.

9...Be7

A sharper approach is 9...b5!? 10 f5!? (safer is 10 Nxc6 Qxc6 11 f5 when 11...b4?? loses the queen to 12 Ba4; instead 11...Be7 12 0-0 0-0! – 12...Nxe4? leads to a catastrophe after 13 fxe6 Bxe6 14 Bxe6 fxe6 15 Qf3 – 13 fxe6 Bxe6 14 Nd5 Bxd5 15 exd5 Qb7 16 a4 Nd7 left Black close to equality in M.Golubev-A.Murariu, Bucharest 1996) 10...b4 **(Diagram 5)** and now:

a) 11 Na4 e5 12 Nf3 should be met not by 12...Nxe4?! 13 Nb6 Rb8 14 Nxc8 Rxc8 15 0-0 when White's superior development promises him good compensation, but rather the safer 12...Rb8, after which, for example, 13 Qd3 Be7 14 0-0-0 Na5 15 Bg5 was G.Hernandez-G.Serper, Los Angeles 1996, and now 15...Bb7 16 Rhe1 Nxb3 17 axb3 0-0 18 Bxf6 gxf6 19 Kb1 Bc6 followed by ...Rfd8 and ...d5 would have given Black good counterplay.

b) White players who prefer obscure complications might do well to investigate the still rather uncharted 11 fxe6!? bxc3 12 exf7+ Kd8 13 bxc3.

10 Qf3

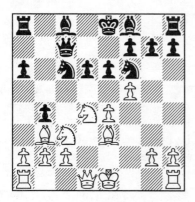

Diagram 5 (W)

The struggle quickly flares up

Diagram 6 (W)

An unbalanced situation

Continuing to flexibly delay castling. Quite common too is 10 0-0 when leading Sozin expert, Mikhail Golubev, feels that the standard manoeuvre 10...Na5 doesn't equalize after 11 f5!; for example, 11...Nc4 12 Bxc4 Qxc4 13 Qf3 0-0 14 Rad1 Rb8?! (better is Kaidanov's suggestion of 14...Nd7!?) 15 g4! b5 16 g5 Nd7 (M.Golubev-E.Knoppert, Belgian League 2002) 17 Qh5! b4 18 f6! gxf6 19 Nd5! exd5 20 Nf5 gives White a typical and extremely dangerous sacrificial attack. Thus Black should probably meet 10 0-0 with 10...0-0 when 11 Qf3 transposes to Game 17.

10...0-0 (Diagram 6)

It's finally time for White to castle. We will now consider 11 0-0-0 in Game 16 and 11 0-0 in Game 17. He might also try and delay the decision with 11 f5, but then the standard manoeuvre 11...Nxd4 12 Bxd4 b5 gives Black reasonable counterplay.

Theoretical Conclusion

Delaying castling in favour of an early Be3 and f4 remains quite a popular approach and leads to some rather rich and unbalanced positions. However, Black should be able to acquire quite reasonable counterplay whichever side White lands up castling.

Illustrative Games

Game 16
☐ **D.Reinderman** ■ **G.Kasparov**
Wijk aan Zee 1999

1 e4 c5 2 Nf3 Nc6 3 d4 cxd4 4 Nxd4 Nf6 5 Nc3 d6 6 Bc4 e6 7 Bb3 a6 8 Be3 Qc7 9 f4

Be7 10 Qf3 0-0 11 0-0-0 (Diagram 7)

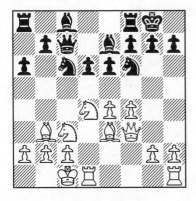

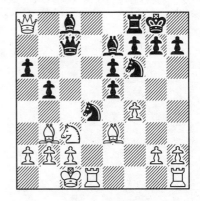

Diagram 7 (B)	**Diagram 8 (W)**
A race situation unfolds	An intriguing exchange sacrifice

11...Nxd4

Black's main way of beginning counterplay. The alternatives are:

a) 11...Na5 12 g4 b5 13 g5 Nxb3+ (or 13...Nd7 14 Bxe6! fxe6 15 Nxe6 Qc4 16 Nxf8 Bxf8 17 g6!? which sees White seizing the initiative) 14 axb3 Nd7 is a common method of gaining counterplay against the Velimirovic, but here White is well advanced on the kingside and Black appears to be a little slow: for example, 15 f5 b4 16 Na4 exf5 17 Nxf5 Ne5 18 Qg2 Rb8 19 Bb6! Qb7 20 Nxd6 Qc6 21 Nxc8 Rfxc8 22 Be3 Nc4 23 Bf4 didn't give Black enough for his pawn in S.Voitsekhovsky-I.Lutsko, Minsk 2000.

b) 11...b5!? 12 e5 (taking up the challenge; instead 12 g4 b4 13 Nce2 Nxd4 14 Bxd4 a5 gives Black good counterplay, such as with 15 g5 Nd7 16 Ba4 e5 17 Be3 Nc5 18 Bxc5 Qxc5) 12...Nxd4 13 Qxa8 dxe5 **(Diagram 8)** is an extremely interesting exchange sacrifice and after14 fxe5 Bb7 15 Qa7 Nc6 16 Qb6 Qxb6 17 Bxb6 Nxe5 (Ionov) Black has a pawn and the superior minor pieces for the exchange.

12 Rxd4

Quite possibly a better approach is 12 Bxd4, not worrying about 12...e5 (and not 12...b5? 13 Bxf6! Bxf6 14 e5 Bb7 due to 15 Bd5! Bxd5 16 Nxd5 exd5 17 exf6 Rac8 18 Rd2 gxf6 19 Qxd5 which left White much better in W.Wittmann-S.Ovsejevitsch, Budapest 2003) on account of 13 fxe5 dxe5 14 Qg3 Bd6 15 Be3 with good chances to gain a small advantage, as indeed White obtained after 15...Be6 16 Bh6 Ne8 17 Nd5 Bxd5 18 Rxd5 in N.De Firmian-D.Gurevich, Denver 1998.

12...b5 13 g4 (Diagram 9) 13...e5!

As ever Kasparov is both well prepared and ready to take up the challenge. Instead 13...b4?! 14 Rxb4 d5 15 Rd4 doesn't convince for Black and after 15...dxe4 (or 15...Bc5 16 exd5! Bxd4 17 Bxd4 with superb play for the exchange, as pointed out by Anand) 16 Qe2 a5 17 g5 Nd7 18 Nxe4 White was better in V.Anand-J.Piket, Amsterdam 1990.

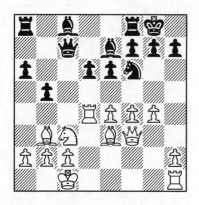

Diagram 9 (B)

Black should counter in the centre

Diagram 10 (B)

White is in control

14 Nd5 Nxd5 15 Rxd5 b4!

 NOTE: Exchange sacrifices to gain control of the position are a common ploy of White's in this sharp variation.

Thus Black should avoid 15...Be6?! on account of 16 f5! Bxd5 17 Bxd5 Rac8 18 Qg2 b4 19 g5 **(Diagram 10)** when White enjoys good attacking prospects.

16 f5 a5 17 Ba4

A sharp alternative was 17 Rd2!? and after 17...a4 18 Bd5 Bb7 19 Bxb7 Qxb7 20 g5 b3 21 a3 bxc2 both sides have their chances in this rather unclear position.

17...Bb7 18 g5 Rfc8 19 Qg2!

Wisely avoiding 19 g6? on account of 19...b3! 20 Bxb3 Bxd5 when 21 Qh5 fails to 21...h6 22 gxf7+ Kf8 23 Bxh6 Bf6 24 exd5 a4 (Kasparov).

19...Bxd5 20 exd5

Once again we see White giving up the exchange for control of the light squares, but here Kasparov is just in time to activate his queen as he retains good counterplay.

20...Qc4! 21 Kb1 Qh4!? 22 Bc6 a4 (Diagram 11) 23 Rf1?

Reinderman's desire not to regain the exchange is understandable, but now he runs into trouble on the queenside. Better was 23 Bxa8 Rxa8 24 Rg1! and after

24...Qc4 25 g6 hxg6 26 fxg6 Rf8 anything might have happened.

23...Qc4! 24 Rg1

Black would also have enjoyed the upper hand in the event of 24 Bxa8 Rxa8 25 f6 Bd8 26 Rf2 b3 27 a3 Rc8 with good attacking prospects.

24...b3 25 a3 Rxc6

Tempting, but quite possibly even better was 25...Rab8!? 26 f6 Bd8 27 Rc1 Bb6 bringing Black's final piece into play with some advantage.

26 dxc6 Rc8 27 Rd1 Rxc6 (Diagram 12) 28 cxb3?

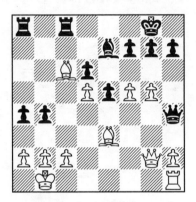

Diagram 11 (W)

A tricky situation

Diagram 12 (W)

White is under pressure

The decisive error. After 28 c3 f6 29 h4 Rc8 White wouldn't have had enough for his pawn, but he had to keep the queenside closed thus.

28...axb3 29 Ka1 e4 30 Qd2 f6?!

A surprisingly pedestrian move from Kasparov just when one would have expected him to finish the game off with the energetic 30...Qc2! 31 Qxc2 bxc2 32 Re1 d5 33 b4 d4.

31 h4 Kf7! 32 Qd5+

The ending is rather advantageous for Black, but after 32 g6+ hxg6 33 fxg6+ Kxg6 34 Qg2+ Kf7 35 h5 Bf8 36 Qg6+ Kg8 37 h6 the counterattack with 37...Qc2 38 Rg1 Ra6! (Kasparov) would also have decided the game in Black's favour.

32...Qxd5 33 Rxd5 g6 34 fxg6+ Kxg6 35 Rb5 fxg5 36 hxg5 (Diagram 13) 36...Rc2

Now the position becomes a little messy and Black could have maintained control with 36...d5! 37 Rxd5 Rd6 after which 38 Rxd6+ Bxd6 39 Kb1 Kf5 40 Kc1 Kg4 41 Kd2 Kf3 leaves White defenceless in the bishop ending.

WARNING: Try to avoid having your pawns stuck on the same colour as your bishop in an endgame, unless of course it's an opposite-coloured bishop endgame.

37 Kb1 Rg2 38 Rxb3 Bxg5 39 Bxg5 Kxg5 40 a4

Black's further advanced central pawns now romp home. Instead 40 Rb7 would have required Kasparov to be more accurate, although the instructive 40...Kf4! 41 Rf7+ Ke3 42 Rd7 h5! 43 Rxd6 h4 44 Rh6 Kd3! 45 Rxh4 Rg1+ 46 Ka2 e3 does the job easily enough.

40...Kf4 41 Rb7 e3 42 Re7 Kf3 43 Kc1 d5 44 a5 d4 (Diagram 14) 45 Rxh7 d3 46 Rh1 Rc2+ 47 Kb1 e2 48 a6 Rc8 0-1

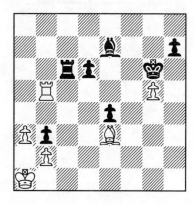

Diagram 13 (B)
Always look for ways to simplify!

Diagram 14 (W)
There's no stopping Black

Game 17
☐ **S.Rublevsky** ■ **A.Lugovoi**
Sochi 2004

---

1 e4 c5 2 Nf3 Nc6 3 d4 cxd4 4 Nxd4 Nf6 5 Nc3 d6 6 Bc4 e6 7 Bb3 a6 8 Be3 Qc7 9 f4 Be7 10 Qf3 0-0 11 0-0 b5!?

The sharp and critical approach. Black might also develop more slowly with 11...Bd7 12 Rad1 Rac8, but then 13 f5! e5 14 Nde2 Na5 15 g4 Nxb3 16 axb3 Bc6 17 g5! **(Diagram 15)** 17...Ne8 (or 17...Nxe4 18 Nxe4 d5 19 f6 dxe4 20 Qf5 Bd8 21 fxg7 Kxg7 22 Ng3 when Black's king becomes a little exposed) 18 Ng3 Bd8 19 f6 has been known to favour White ever since the instructive game P.Keres-G.Palmason, Amsterdam 1954.

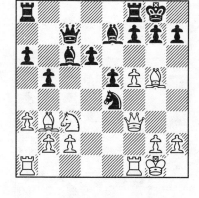

Diagram 15 (B)

White seizes the initiative

Diagram 16 (W)

An equalizing trick

12 e5!?

The ever well-prepared Rublevsky is up for the challenge. Instead 12 a3 Nxd4 13 Bxd4 Bb7 14 f5 e5 15 Be3 Bc6! gives Black sufficient counterplay: ...a5 is one plan, the other being to meet 16 Bg5 with 16...Nxe4! **(Diagram 16)**, after which 17 Bxe7 Nf6 (but not the greedy 17...Nd2? because of 18 Qg4 Qxe7 19 f6 Qa7+ 20 Rf2 g6 21 Qg5 and wins) 18 Nd5 Nxd5 19 Bxf8 Nf4 20 Qe3 Rxf8 21 Rxf4 exf4 22 Qxf4 Qe7 fizzled out to equality in Y.Balashov-A.Khalifman, Samara 1998.

12...Nxd4 13 Bxd4 dxe5

> WARNING: Black should avoid 13...Bb7?! on account of a powerful sacrifice: 14 exf6! Bxf3 15 fxe7 Qxe7 16 Rxf3 d5 17 f5 Rad8 18 f6 Qb4 19 Rd1 gives White both the initiative and more than enough for the queen.

14 fxe5 (Diagram 17) 14...Nd7

Perhaps Black should prefer 14...Bb7!? when 15 exf6!? Bxf3 16 fxe7 Qxe7 17 Rxf3 Rad8 isn't at all easy to assess; maybe White is a tiny bit better after 18 Bb6 Rd7 19 Raf1 Qd6 20 Be3, but anything could happen in such an unbalanced situation.

15 Bxe6!

Now White gains a tiny edge and this improves over 15 Rae1 Bb7 16 Qg4 Nc5 17 Re3 Rad8 18 Rg3 g6 when Black both defends on the kingside and has good counterplay.

15...fxe6 16 Qxa8 Bb7 17 Rxf8+ Nxf8

It might appear better to play 17...Bxf8!? 18 Qe8 Qc6, but then Rublevsky points out that 19 Kf2 Qxg2+ 20 Ke1! should retain the advantage; for example, his

20...Qh1+ 21 Kd2 Qxh2+ 22 Ne2 Nxe5 23 Qxe6+ Nf7 24 Rf1 leaves White somewhat better.

18 Qe8 Bc5 (Diagram 18) 19 Ne2!

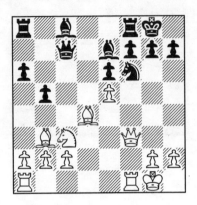 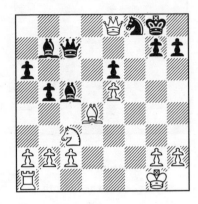

Diagram 17 (B)

A critical juncture

Diagram 18 (W)

Black hasn't quite enough compensation

The only way to retain the advantage, whereas 19 Bxc5 Qxc5+ 20 Kh1 Qf2 21 Rg1 Bxg2+! 22 Rxg2 Qf1+ would have forced perpetual.

19...Qxe5 20 Rf1 Bxd4+ 21 Nxd4 Qxd4+ 22 Kh1 Bxg2+! 23 Kxg2 Qd2+ 24 Kf3 g5!?

Ambitious, but Lugovoi was certainly right to avoid 24...Qxh2? on account of 25 Ke3 Qg3+ 26 Ke2 Qg2+ 27 Ke1 Qg3+ 28 Kd1 Qd6+ 29 Kc1 hiding the king and winning.

25 Qa8 Kg7 26 Kg3 Ng6 27 Qb7+ Kh6 28 Qe4 e5

Quite possibly 28...Qd6+ 29 Kg2 Nf4+ 30 Kh1 Kg7 was the way to go as Black when it would have been far from easy for White to make progress.

29 Rf6 Qc1 30 Kg2 Kg7 31 Rxa6 (Diagram 19) 31...Nf4+?

Too ambitious and now the advance of White's king causes severe problems. Correct was 31...Qxb2 after which 32 a4 bxa4 33 Qxa4 Qc1 34 Qd7+ Kh6 35 Qf5 sees both White retain a small advantage and Black good chances to hold.

32 Kf2 Qd2+ 33 Kg3 Nh5+ 34 Kg4! Qd7+

Neither would 34...Nf6+ have saved Black because of 35 Rxf6! Kxf6 36 Qf5+ Ke7 37 Qxg5+ Qxg5+ 38 Kxg5 with an easy win in the pawn ending.

35 Kxg5 h6+ 36 Kh4 Qd8+ 37 Kh3 Nf4+ 38 Kg3 Qg5+ 39 Kf2 (Diagram 20) 39...Qh4+ 40 Kf1 Qh3+ 41 Ke1 Qh4+ 42 Kd1 1-0

The checks run out after 42...Qg4+ 43 Kd2 when White's extra exchange and safer king quickly decide.

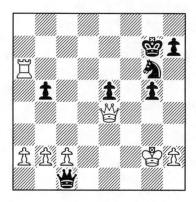

Diagram 19 (B)

Both kings are exposed

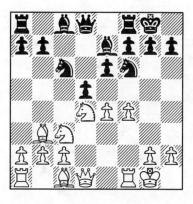

Diagram 20 (B)

White's king will run away

White Castles Quickly

1 e4 c5 2 Nf3 Nc6 3 d4 cxd4 4 Nxd4 Nf6 5 Nc3 d6 6 Bc4 e6 7 0-0 (Diagram 21)

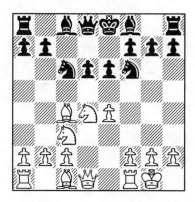

Diagram 21 (B)

White wants to advance his f-pawn

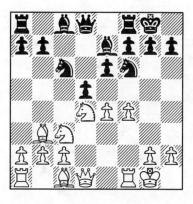

Diagram 22 (W)

Black fights for the initiative

White declares a lack of interest in the more ambitious and risky lines involving queenside castling, preferring to rush his king to safety and use his king's rook to support an advance of the f-pawn.

7...Be7

If the f-pawn is going to be launched, it makes sense too for Black to quickly evacuate his king from the centre.

8 Bb3

Sometimes White prefers 8 a3 to give his light-squared bishop a retreat square out of reach of Black's pieces. That does, though, come a cost in time and Black is able to develop sufficient counterplay; for example, 8...0-0 9 Ba2 Nxd4! (the simplest equalizer) 10 Qxd4 b6 11 Qd3 (and not 11 f4? which weakens the g1-a7 diagonal and after 11...d5! 12 Qd3 dxe4 13 Nxe4 Qxd3 14 cxd3 Black is better due to his superior structure) 11...Bb7 12 Bf4 Qc8 13 Rfe1 Rd8 14 Rad1 a6 15 a4 b5! gave Black a good game in S.Dvoirys-V.Zvjaginsev, Samara 1998.

8...0-0 9 Be3

Covering the a1-g7 diagonal in preparation for playing f4 and White can also prepare that advance with the careful 9 Kh1, the subject of Game 18.

> **TIP: Always look out for the chance to meet an early f4 by countering in the centre with ...d5.**

Thus after the immediate 9 f4 we can again recommend 9...d5!? **(Diagram 22)** and then:

a) 10 e5 Nxd4 11 Qxd4 b6 12 Kh1 Bc5 13 Qd3 Ng4 14 Qg3 h5 gives Black the initiative.

b) White does better with 10 exd5 exd5 11 Kh1, although after 11...Bc5 12 Be3 Qa5 Black has plenty of activity to offset his IQP.

We should also mention that it's possible to delay ...d5 after 9 f4; for example, 9...Nxd4 10 Qxd4 b6 11 Kh1 Ba6 was the famous game R.Fischer-E.Geller, Curacao 1962, in which the ambitious 12 Rf3 was strongly met by 12...d5! 13 exd5 Bc5 14 Qa4 Bb7.

9...a6 (Diagram 23)

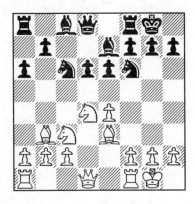

Diagram 23 (W)

Wisely preparing counterplay

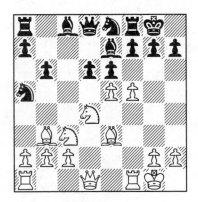

Diagram 24 (B)

Black must be very careful

The modern preference. Instead 9...Bd7 was popular in the fifties and sixties until Fischer demonstrated that 10 f4 Nxd4 11 Bxd4 Bc6 12 Qe2 b5 doesn't quite equalize on account of 13 Nxb5!; for example, 13...Bxb5 14 Qxb5 Nxe4 15 f5 Bf6 (Balogh's 15...e5!? is probably a better try) 16 Qd3 d5 17 Bxf6 Nxf6 18 c4! (Kasparov and Nikitin) gives White an edge.

Once again Black might also consider exchanging off the annoying bishop with 9...Na5, but after 10 f4 b6 11 e5! we don't feel that he can equalize:

a) 11...Ne8 12 f5! **(Diagram 24)** 12...dxe5 (even worse is 12...exf5?! 13 e6! Nxb3 14 Nc6! winning the queen for insufficient compensation on account of 14...Qc7? 15 Nd5!) 13 fxe6 Nxb3 (Black was flattened after 13...f6? in E.Geller-J.Vatnikov, Kiev 1950: 14 Nf5! Nxb3 15 Nd5! Nd4 16 Ndxe7+ Kh8 17 Ng6+! 1-0) 14 Nc6 Qd6 15 Qxd6 Bxd6 16 axb3 Bxe6 17 Nxa7 was a little better for White in R.Fischer-V.Korchnoi, Curacao 1962.

b) 11...dxe5 12 fxe5 Ne8 (and not 12...Nd7?! because of 13 Rxf7! Nxe5 14 Rxf8+ Bxf8 15 Bxe6+ Bxe6 16 Nxe6 Qxd1+ 17 Rxd1; never underestimate the power of White's light-squared bishop after 6 Bc4) 13 Qh5 (13 Qf3 Bb7 14 Qg3 is also promising) 13...g6 14 Qg4 Qc7 15 Bh6 Ng7 16 Rae1 Nxb3 17 axb3 gave White a pull in P.Kotsur-R.Scherbakov, Ekaterinburg 1999.

Returning to 9...a6:

10 f4 Nxd4!?

The sharpest approach.

> **NOTE: Instead 10...Qc7 leaves White with nothing better than 11 Qf3 when we're back in Game 17.**

11 Bxd4 b5 (Diagram 25)

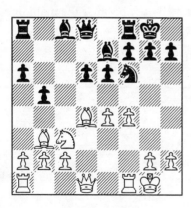

Diagram 25 (W)

Forcing White to open the centre

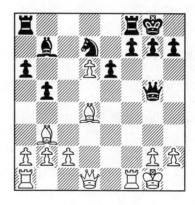

Diagram 26 (W)

It's rather unbalanced

12 e5

White should counter actively. Indeed 12 a3 fails to hold Black up on the queen-side since 12...Bb7 13 Qd3 a5! gives him good play: for example, 14 e5 (or 14 f5 b4 15 axb4 axb4 16 Qb5 Rxa1 17 Rxa1 bxc3! 18 Qxb7 cxb2 19 Bxb2 d5 fully freeing Black's pieces) 14...dxe5 15 fxe5 Nd7 16 Nxb5 Nc5 17 Bxc5 Bxc5+ 18 Kh1 Qg5!? gave Black promising activity for the pawn in no less a game than R.Fischer-B.Spassky, World Championship (Game 4), Reykjavik 1972.

12...dxe5 13 fxe5 Nd7 14 Ne4

It's probably more challenging to invade d6 than to try and attack with 14 Qg4 since then 14...Nc5 15 Be3 Nxb3 16 axb3 Qc7 17 Nxb5 Qxc2 18 Nd4 Qc7 19 Qg3 f5! gives Black sufficient counterplay.

14...Bb7 15 Nd6

Once again the tempting 15 Qg4 doesn't lead anywhere for White in view of the exchanging 15...Bxe4! 16 Qxe4 Nc5.

15...Bxd6 16 exd6 Qg5! (Diagram 26)

The logical outcome of the forcing play begun by Black on move 10. White has a strong passed d-pawn and the bishop pair, but must find a way to deal with Black's activity and his mobile e- and f-pawns. We will return to this exceptionally complex position in Game 19.

Theoretical Conclusion

A study of Fischer's games remains quite useful to understanding this variation. Since his retirement the concept of early castling followed by an advance of the f-pawn has generally not been so popular, although it did have a revival in the mid-nineties after Nigel Short's use of it in his match with Kasparov. It might even again return to the limelight in the next few years if only because the main line leads to such a fascinating and complicated struggle.

Illustrative Games

Game 18
☐ **G.Kaidanov** ■ **G.Serper**
Asheville 1997

1 e4 c5 2 Nf3 Nc6 3 d4 cxd4 4 Nxd4 Nf6 5 Nc3 d6 6 Bc4 e6 7 0-0 Be7 8 Bb3 0-0 9 Kh1 a6

Black's main move, but he has two interesting alternatives in response to White's slightly slow 9th:

a) 9...Nxd4!? 10 Qxd4 b6 11 Bg5 Bb7 gives Black quite a harmonious set-up; for example, 12 f4 Rc8 13 Rad1 Rxc3! 14 Qxc3 Nxe4 **(Diagram 27)** 15 Qf3 Bxg5 16 fxg5 d5 destroys White's centre and offers excellent play for the exchange.

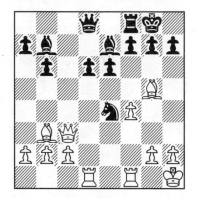

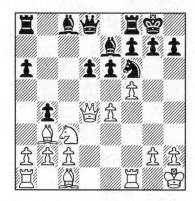

Diagram 27 (W)	Diagram 28 (W)
Thematic and effective	A useful temporary sacrifice

b) 9...Na5 10 f4 b6!? (provocatively tempting the white pawns forward) 11 f5 (or 11 e5!? Ne8 12 Qg4 h5!? 13 Qxh5 dxe5 14 Nf3 exf4 15 Bxf4 Nf6 with a rather unclear situation) 11...e5 12 Nde2 Nxb3 13 axb3 Bb7 gave Black good central counterplay in F.Ljubicic-I.Morovic, Pula 2000.

10 f4 Qc7

Holding up e4-e5, but probably this is not essential. Instead Black can play as in the main line with 10...Nxd4 11 Qxd4 b5 when 12 f5 b4! **(Diagram 28)** 13 Qxb4 d5 14 Qd4 dxe4 15 Qxd8 Rxd8 16 fxe6 Bxe6 saw him equalize in A.Volokitin-C.Lutz, German League 2004.

11 f5 Nxd4 12 Qxd4 b5 13 fxe6

The most challenging, whereas 13 a4 again allows the strong temporary pawn sacrifice 13...b4!? after which 14 Qxb4 d5 15 Qd4 Bc5 16 Qd3 dxe4 17 Nxe4 Nxe4 18 Qxe4 exf5! gave Black quite interesting counterplay in V.Ivanchuk-V.Salov, Linares 1991.

13...Bxe6 14 Bg5 (Diagram 29)

White might also attack d6 and after 14 Bf4!? Qc5 15 Rad1 Rad8 16 Qd3 Bc4 17 Bxc4 bxc4 18 Qd4! he has an edge.

14...Ng4

The best way of breaking the pin, whereas 14...h6?! would have been rather risky on account of the thematic 15 Bxf6 Bxf6 16 Rxf6! gxf6 17 Qxf6 (Serper) with good attacking chances for the exchange.

15 Nd5 Bxd5 16 Qxd5 Ne5

Neither would 16...Bxg5 have fully equalized because of 17 Rxf7! Rxf7 18 Qxa8+ Bd8 19 Be6! (but not 19 Rf1?? d5! with a vicious double attack) 19...Nf6 20 Rd1.

17 Bf4 Rad8 18 a4! (Diagram 30) 18...b4 19 a5 Bf6 20 Be3

Diagram 29 (B)

White has some pressure

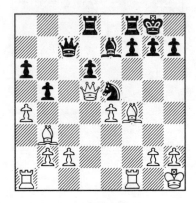

Diagram 30 (B)

Opening lines for the bishops

Another idea was to insert 20 Rad1!? Rd7 after which 21 Be3 Qc6 22 Bb6 retains an edge.

20...Nd7 21 Bc4 Nc5 22 Rf5

Serper has regrouped well, although we wonder whether White might have tried 22 Rxf6!? gxf6 23 Qf5 with quite promising play for the exchange, such as after 23...Rfe8 24 Bd5 Nd7 25 Bd4.

22...Rde8 23 Raf1 Nxe4 24 Bb6 Qc8 25 R5f4!?

Keeping up the threats, but quite possibly it was better to pick up the a6-pawn with 25 Qd3, thereby gaining a last advantage.

25...Re5 26 Qd3 Qe8 27 Bd4 Nc5 28 Qd1 (Diagram 31) 28...Rg5?

In a tricky situation Serper errs. Instead it was essential to give up the exchange with 28...Qd8!, not that White should probably accept since 29 Bxe5 dxe5 30 Rg4 Qxd1 31 Rxd1 h5 32 Rg3 e4 gives Black quite reasonable compensation.

29 Bxf6 gxf6 30 Rxf6

Not bad, but even stronger would have been 30 Qxd6 Qa8 31 R1f3! when Black's position is on the verge of collapse.

30...Qe4 31 Qe2?

Presumably Kaidanov underestimated Black's reply, although in any case White should have been looking to attack and 31 Qd2 Rg7 32 R6f4 Qb7 33 R1f3 would have left him with some advantage.

31...d5! (Diagram 32) 32 Bxa6

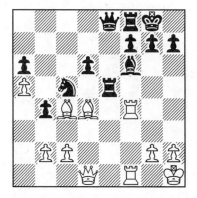

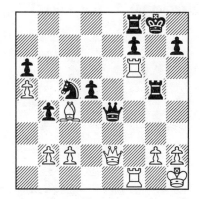

Diagram 31 (B)	**Diagram 32 (W)**
The rook must stay on e5	At last Black gets some counterplay

White might still have tried 32 Qd2, although now 32...Qe5! 33 Bd3 Ne4 34 Bxe4 dxe4 35 Rxa6 e3 36 Qe2 Qe4 would have given Black some awkward counterplay.

32...Nxa6 33 Qxe4 dxe4 34 Rxa6 Rc8 35 Rb6 Rxa5 36 Rxb4 Rxc2 ½-½

There's nothing left to play for because 37 Rxe4 Rxb2 38 Re8+ Kg7 39 Re7 can be met by 39...Rf5!.

Game 19
□ **M.Illescas** ■ **J.Polgar**
Dos Hermanas 1997

---

1 e4 c5 2 Nf3 Nc6 3 d4 cxd4 4 Nxd4 Nf6 5 Nc3 d6 6 Bc4 e6 7 0-0 Be7 8 Bb3 0-0 9 Be3 a6 10 f4 Nxd4 11 Bxd4 b5 12 e5 dxe5 13 fxe5 Nd7 14 Ne4 Bb7 15 Nd6 Bxd6 16 exd6 Qg5 17 Qe2

A major alternative is 17 Rf2 when 17...a5! **(Diagram 33)** is the best way to pursue counterplay: 18 a4 (or 18 Qe2!? Ra6! 19 Bc3 Rxd6 20 Bxa5 Nc5!? offering a pawn in the name of activity) 18...Ra6 19 axb5 Rxd6 20 Qd2 Qxb5! 21 Rxa5 Qc6 22 Qf4 e5 23 Bxf7+ Kh8 24 Rxe5! was the highly unclear course of F.Peredy-J.Gal, Szeged 1997, and now 24...Rf6! (24...Nxe5? 25 Qxe5 Rf6 26 Qe7 was the venomous course of the game) 25 Rg5 R8xf7 26 Bxf6 Rxf6 27 Qd4 Qe6 28 Rxf6 Nxf6 would have remained rather unclear and about equal.

17...Kh8

Black can also begin to advance his pawns straight away and 17...e5 18 Bc3 Qg6 19

Rad1 Kh8 20 Bd5! Bxd5 21 Rxd5 Qe6 22 Rfd1 Rfc8 23 Ba5 Rc6 24 b3 Rac8 25 Bc7 was the positional continuation of N.Short-G.Kasparov, World Championship (Game 14), London 1993, when Kasparov recommends 25...f5!? 26 c4 bxc4 27 bxc4 e4 **(Diagram 34)** 28 Rf1 Rf8 29 g4 f4! with decent counterplay.

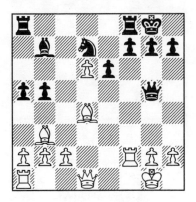

Diagram 33 (W)

18 a4 Ra6 is the idea

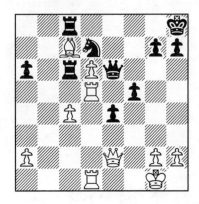

Diagram 34 (W)

Both sides have their trumps

18 Rad1 Qg6 19 c4

White can also take aim at g7, but after 19 Rd3?! e5 20 Rg3 Qxd6 21 Bc3 f6 22 Qg4 g6 Black's kingside defences are holding.

19...bxc4 20 Bxc4 f5 21 Bc3 (Diagram 35)

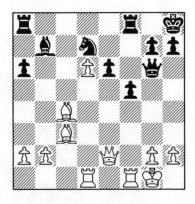

Diagram 35 (B)

Black relies on his mobile central pawns

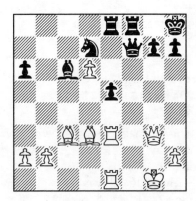

Diagram 36 (W)

The e-pawn is taboo, but why?

21...f4!?

Characteristically Polgar wants to attack. Another principled approach was 21...e5 after which 22 Bd5 Bxd5 (but not the tempting 22...Qxd6? 23 Bxb7 Qb6+ 24 Kh1 Qxb7 due to 25 Qd3 Rf7 26 Rxf5 Rxf5 27 Qxf5 regaining the pawn with a large advantage) 23 Rxd5 f4 is once again far from clear.

22 Bd3 f3 23 Qf2 Qh5 24 Qg3 e5!

Bringing up the rear pawn in a bid to force White to capture on f3. Instead 24...f2+? 25 Kh1 e5 would have been somewhat less effective on account of 26 h3! Rf6 27 Rd2 Raf8 28 Bc2 when White would have been in total control.

25 gxf3 Bxf3 26 Rde1 Rae8 27 Re3 Bc6 28 Rfe1

It was by no means impossible to capture with 28 Bxa6!? when Polgar intended 28...Rxf1+ 29 Bxf1 Rf8 when the idea of 30...Qd1 maintains good counterplay.

28...Qf7 (Diagram 36) 29 Bxe5??

After such a complex struggle, Illescas was already low on time and now badly miscalculates. Instead 29 Qh4 would have remained far from easy to assess after 29...g5!?, although one quite plausible line does run 30 Qg3 Qd5 31 Be4 Qxd6 32 Bxc6 Qxc6 33 Bxe5+ Nxe5 34 Rxe5 Qb6+ 35 Kh1 Qc6+ when the game ends in a repetition.

29...Nxe5 30 Rxe5 Qa7+ 31 R5e3

Now White loses a rook and the game. Neither, though, would 31 R1e3 have saved him on account of 31...Rxe5 32 Qxe5 Re8 and presumably Illescas had missed that 31 Qe3 can be decisively met by 31...Rxe5! with the point of 32 Qxa7 Rxe1+ 33 Bf1 Rfxf1 mate.

31...Rf3 32 Qh4 h6 0-1

Chapter Five

The Velimirovic Attack

- ▨ **Introduction**
- ▨ **Black Castles Quickly**
- ▨ **Black Delays Castling**

Introduction

1 e4 c5 2 Nf3 Nc6 3 d4 cxd4 4 Nxd4 Nf6 5 Nc3 d6 6 Bc4 e6 7 Be3 (Diagram 1)

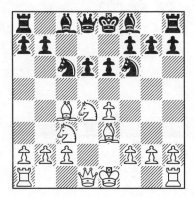

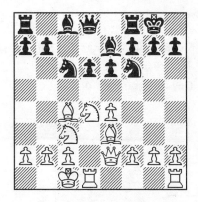

Diagram 1 (B)

A very sharp system

Diagram 2 (B)

Black must play for ...b5

This development of the queen's bishop when followed up by the aggressive moves Qe2 and 0-0-0 signifies the Velimirovic Attack. Black, for his part, must strive to gain counterplay which usually involves playing for a queenside counterattack. Traditionally Black castled and only then looked to the queenside, but nowadays it is quite popular to delay castling.

> **NOTE: By delaying castling Black both removes a target for White's forces, which are ready to attack on the kingside, and is able to accelerate his queenside counterplay.**

Black Castles Quickly

1 e4 c5 2 Nf3 Nc6 3 d4 cxd4 4 Nxd4 Nf6 5 Nc3 d6 6 Bc4 e6 7 Be3 Be7 8 Qe2 0-0 9 0-0-0 (Diagram 2) 9...a6

Black logically prepares ...Qc7 and ...b5. He can also opt for the move order 9...Qc7 10 Bb3 a6, but we should note that the central break 9...d5?! is misguided here in view of White's superior development: 10 Nf3! (an idea of Boleslavsky's; White maintains the central tension which causes Black problems completing his development) 10...Nxe4 11 Nxe4 Qa5+ 12 Bd2 Qa4 13 Bd3 dxe4 14 Qxe4 Qxe4 15 Bxe4 f6 (or 15...Bd7 16 Bg5!) 16 Bxc6 bxc6 17 Nd4 Bc5 18 Be3 Bxd4 19 Rxd4 e5 20 Rd6 was the instructive continuation of M.Hawelko-J.Bielczyk, Jachranka 1987, in which despite the opposite-coloured bishops, it was very hard for Black to reach a draw.

Black might also play on the queenside with 9...Qa5 (see Game 20; a Velimirovic classic), but that is nowadays seldom seen. So too is 9...Bd7, this time in view of the energetic 10 f4!, preparing both e5 and f5.

10 Bb3

A useful prophylactic measure. Instead 10 Rhg1 gives Black easy counterplay after 10...Nxd4 11 Bxd4 b5 12 Bb3 b4 13 Na4; for example, 13...Bd7!? 14 Nb6 Bb5 15 Qf3 Rb8 16 Nc4 a5!? with good play.

10...Qc7 (Diagram 3)

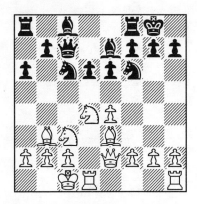

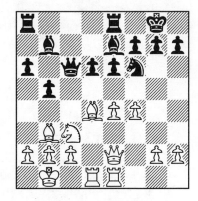

Diagram 3 (W)	**Diagram 4 (B)**
A pawn race is imminent	g2-g4 is not White's only plan

Black's main move, continuing the queenside plan, but there are alternatives:

a) 10...Qe8!? was first employed by Beliavsky with the idea of preventing 11 g4 in view of 11...Nxd4 12 Rxd4 e5 when Black wins the g-pawn (with the queen on c7, 13 Rc4 would be possible). White must this prepare the advance of his g-pawn and after 11 Rhg1 Nd7 12 g4 Nc5 13 g5 b5 14 Qh5!? b4 15 Nxc6 Nxb3+ 16 axb3 Qxc6 play has transposed to the main line (see Game 22).

b) A common plan is ...Nf6-d7-c5, knocking out the b3-bishop. Thus Black has tried 10...Nd7 and after 11 g4 Nc5 12 Rhg1 Nxb3+ 13 axb3 Nb4 14 Rg3 Qa5 he has excellent counterplay. However, White should not continue in such stereotyped vein. Instead 11 f4! Nc5 12 Nxc6 Nxb3+ 13 cxb3! is somewhat more awkward and after 13...bxc6 14 e5 Qc7 15 exd6 Bxd6 16 Qf2 Black's position becomes vulnerable.

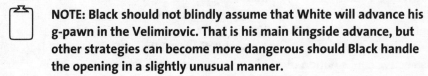

NOTE: Black should not blindly assume that White will advance his g-pawn in the Velimirovic. That is his main kingside advance, but other strategies can become more dangerous should Black handle the opening in a slightly unusual manner.

11 g4

Wasting no time on the kingside, but again there are alternatives:

a) 11 f4 is a little slow here: for example, 11...Nxd4 12 Rxd4 (12 Bxd4? e5 12 fxe5 dxe5 14 Be3 Bg4 wins the exchange) 12...b5 13 f5! exf5 14 exf5 Bxf5 15 g4 Be6 16 g5 Nd7 17 Qh5 (A.Lukin-Shirov, Daugavpils 1989) 17...Ne5 18 Rg1 gives White some compensation for his pawn, but no more than that.

b) 11 Kb1 was tried by Velimirovic himself. White's plan is not to attack with his pawns, but rather to begin by centralizing his pieces and once again the position rapidly becomes quite unclear: for example, 11...b5 12 Nxc6 Qxc6 13 Bd4 Bb7 14 Rhe1 Rfe8 15 f4 **(Diagram 4)** 15...Rad8 16 Rd3 a5 17 Rg3 a4 18 Bd5! exd5 19 Nxd5 saw typically aggressive play from White in M.Hawelko-S.Dejkalo, Swidnica 1986, and now it was necessary to return the piece to maintain a rough balance with 19...Qd7! 20 Nxf6+ Bxf6 21 Bxf6 Bxe4 22 Rxg7+ Kf8.

c) 11 Rhg1!? is a non-essential preparatory move, but still a quite dangerous one as we'll see in Game 21.

11...Nd7

> **TIP: Not only does White's light-squared bishop support a number of dangerous piece sacrifices on d5, but it can also be a good defensive piece. Thus Black should always consider exchanging it with ...Nf6-d7-c5; a manoeuvre which became popular after Larsen successfully employed it against Fischer.**

The text is by no means essential, but Black should be aware that 11...b5? 12 g5 Nd7? is not recommended in view of the typical tactical device 13 Nd5! exd5 14 Nxc6 Qxc6 15 Bxd5. Black does better with 12...Nxd4 13 Bxd4 Nd7, but after 14 Qh5 **(Diagram 5)** 14...Nc5 (preventing a rook swing with Rd1-d3-h3...) 15 Rhg1 (...but the king's rook can swing too) 15...Nxb3+ 16 axb3 Qd8 17 Rd3 White has a very dangerous attack.

A much better alternative is 11...Nxd4!? 12 Rxd4 Nd7; for example, 13 g5 b5 14 f4 (14 Qh5 is less threatening in this particular position and 14...g6! 15 Qh6 Re8 16 f4 Bf8 17 Qh4 Nc5 18 Rg1 Rb8 19 Rg3 b4 20 Ne2 e5 gave Black reasonable counter-play in A.Fedulov-R.Scherbakov, Smolensk 2000) 14...Nc5 15 f5 exf5 16 Bd5 Rb8 17 exf5 sees White's pieces aggressively placed, but the situation is objectively no more than unclear, such as after 17..Bxf5 18 Rf1 Qd7 19 Rdf4 Be6.

12 g5

Consistent, but by no means essential. Black must also be ready for Velimirovic's sacrificial 12 Nf5!? exf5 13 Nd5 Qd8 14 gxf5 **(Diagram 6)**, gaining an open g-file and a dominant knight on d5 for the piece. Black has often struggled here, but we believe that the situation is by no means so bad. Velimirovic has now analysed 14...Na5 15 Rhg1 Nxb3+ 16 axb3 Kh8 17 Bd4 f6 18 Qg4 Rg8 19 Nxf4 Ne5 20 Bxe5 fxe5 21 Ng6+! hxg6 22 Qh3+ Bh4 23 Rxd6 Qe7 24 Rdxg6 with a strong attack, but Black has the major improvement 20...g5! when White has nothing more than perpetual check with 21 Qh5 fxe5 22 Ng6+ Rxg6 23 fxg6 Qg8 24 Rxg5 Bxg5 25 Qxg5 Qxg6 26 Qd8+ Qg8 27 Qf6+.

Diagram 5 (B)	Diagram 6 (B)
A powerful rook lift beckons	A dangerous sacrifice

 WARNING: Castling against the Velimirovic leads to some very rich and fascinating positions, but Black must make sure that he is pretty well prepared before contesting them.

Another critical test which Black must be ready for is a modification of Velimirovic's idea, namely 12 Rhg1 Nc5 13 Nf5!?. Now 13...exf5?! cannot be recommended in view of 14 gxf5 Bf6 15 Nd5 Qd8 16 Qh5 Kh8 17 Rg3 followed by Rh3. Much better is 13...b5! 14 Bd5! Bb7 (14...exd5?! 15 Nxd5 Qb7 16 e5! gives White the initiative) 15 g5 when Black must again know what he's doing **(Diagram 7)**:

a) 15...exf5 was refuted in the game A.Sokolov-V.Salov, Nikolaev 1983: 16 g6! hxg6 17 Rxg6 Ne5 18 Rxg7+! Kxg7 19 Rg1+ Ng6 20 exf5 Rh8 21 Bd4+ Bf6 22 fxg6 fxg6 23 Qg4 and Black was blown away.

b) Sokolov points out that 15...b4? fails due to 16 Qh5! bxc3 17 Rg3! exd5 18 g6!.

c) The best move is the calm 15...Rfc8!, both preparing counterplay down the c-file and introducing the key defensive option of ...Bf8. Following 16 Rg3 b4 (16...Bf8!? is also possible when I.Rogers-Z.Lanka, Linz 1996, ended in perpetual after 17 Qh5 g6 18 Nh6+ Kh8 19 Qh4 b4 20 Rh3! bxc3 21 Nf4 f5! 22 Nf6 h6 23 Qxh6+ Bxh6 24 Rxh6+ Kg7 25 Rh7+) 17 Nxg7!? Kxg7 18 Qh5 Rg8! 19 Bxe6! A.Fedorov-M.Kobalia, Maikop 1999, would have remained extremely unclear had Black found 19...Nxe6! 20 Nd5 Qd8 21 f4 (Fedorov).

After that lengthy but essential discussion, we return to White's main move, 12 g5:

12...Nc5 13 Rhg1

Preparing Rg3-h3 and Qh5. Instead the pawn-storm has been known to be inaccurate ever since the classic game R.Fischer-B.Larsen, Palma de Mallorca 1970: 13 h4 b5 14 f3? (too slow; 14 h5 b4 15 Na4 Nxe4 16 g6 is both a much better try and far from clear) 14...Bd7 15 Qg2 b4 16 Nce2 Nxb3+ 17 axb3 a5 18 g6 fxg6 19 h5 Nxd4 20 Nxd4 g5! 21 Bxg5 Bxg5+ 22 Qxg5 h6 23 Qg4 Rf7! and having kept White at bay on the kingside, Black's queenside attack carried the day.

13...b5 (Diagram 8)

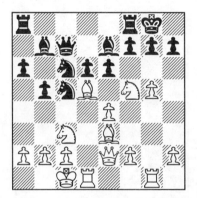

Diagram 7 (B)	Diagram 8 (W)
Both pieces should not be touched	Another very theoretical line

Black finally gets his own pawns underway. We will return to this very critical situation in Game 22, but we should mention for those who prefer a slightly less theoretical life that 13...Bd7!? 14 Rg3 Rfc8 is probably a safer option.

Theoretical Conclusion

Theory and practice have proved that in many lines of the Velimirovic Black gains sufficient counterplay, but he really does need to know his theory. Just one slip and the dangerous white attack can crash home which helps to explain the popularity of our next system.

Illustrative Games

Game 20
□ **R.Fischer** ■ **E.Geller**
Skopje 1967

1 e4 c5 2 Nf3 Nc6 3 d4 cxd4 4 Nxd4 Nf6 5 Nc3 d6 6 Bc4 e6 7 Be3 Be7 8 Qe2 0-0 9

0-0-0 Qa5 10 Bb3

At some point the bishop was going to become a target on the c-file and so Fischer prudently retreats it.

10...Nxd4

Black doesn't have to follow up his quite rare 9th move thus, but after 10...Bd7 11 Ndb5 Ne8 12 Bf4! e5 13 Be3 a6 14 Na3 b5 15 Nd5 White's control of d5 gives him a pleasant advantage.

11 Bxd4 (Diagram 9)

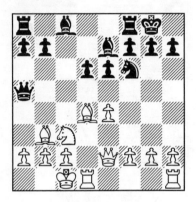

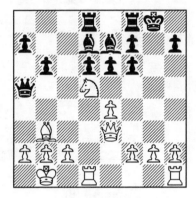

Diagram 9 (B)	**Diagram 10 (B)**
White develops harmoniously	A thematic and strong sacrifice

11...Bd7

Naturally Black shouldn't hurry to grab a pawn: 11...Qg5+? 12 Kb1 Qxg2 13 Rhg1 Qxh2 14 Rh1 Qf4 15 Rdg1 gives White a huge attack, as pointed out by Fischer.

 WARNING: Always be very careful when opening lines for your opponent's attack, even if doing so involves winning material.

12 Kb1!?

Not strictly necessary, but earlier in the same event Fischer had won a convincing victory after this further prophylactic move.

12...Bc6

That earlier game (R.Fischer-J.Sofrevsky) had seen 12...Rad8 13 Qe3 b6?! (Fischer himself pointed out the improvement 13...b5!? 14 a3 b4 15 axb4 Qxb4 16 Bxa7 after which we actually quite like Black's position following 16...Ra8!? 17 Qb6 Qc5! 18 Qxc5 dxc5 19 Bb6 Bc6) 14 Bxf6 gxf6? (hideous; 14...Bxf6 15 Rxd6 Bc8 16 Rhd1 would have kept White's advantage within bounds) 15 Nd5! **(Diagram 10)**

15...Rfe8 (White's attack is overwhelming in the event of 15...exd5 16 Rxd5 Qa6 17 Rh5 Bg4 18 Qg3 Qe2 19 h3) 16 Nxe7+ Rxe7 17 Rxd6 Rc8 18 Qd4 Be8 19 Qxf6 1-0.

13 f4 Rad8?!

Too slow. White can afford to centralize in this line, but Black needs the destabilizing option of ...b4 to gain counterplay. Thus it was again time for 13...b5!? and if 14 e5, then 14...dxe5 15 Qxe5 Rad8 maintaining rough equality.

14 Rhf1 b5 (Diagram 11)

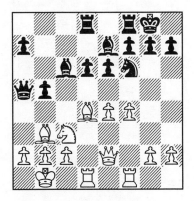 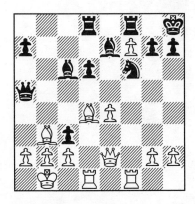

Diagram 11 (W)

White's mobile centre menaces

Diagram 12 (W)

The f-pawn clogs up Black's defences

15 f5

Having brought all his pieces to good squares, Fischer decides to open the f-file. Another tempting option was 15 e5!? especially since 15...dxe5 16 fxe5 Nd7 17 Qg4 Qc7 18 Rxf7!? Kxf7 19 Bxe6+ Ke8 20 Qxg7 gives White a rather dangerous attack.

15...b4 16 fxe6!

Not the usual way of sacrificing a piece in the Velimirovic, but here 16 Nd5? was insufficient on account of 16...exd5 17 exd5 Nxd5 18 Bxd5 Bxd5 19 Qxe7 Qxa2+ 20 Kc1 Rc8! 21 Qxa7 Qc4! (Geller) when it would have been Black enjoying a monstrous attack.

16...bxc3 17 exf7+ Kh8 (Diagram 12) 18 Rf5 Qb4 19 Qf1 Nxe4

The knight had to move since 19...Bxe4? would have failed to the attractive 20 Rxf6 Bxf6? 21 Qxf6! and if 21...gxf6, then 22 Bxf6 mate. Geller might have preferred 19...Ng4, but Fischer was ready with 20 Bxc3 Qb7 21 Qf4 after which White would have enjoyed promising compensation for the piece.

20 a3?

Weakening his defences down the b-file and throwing away all White's hard-won advantage. Instead 20 Qf4! cxb2 (or 20...Nd2+ 21 Rxd2 cxd2 22 c3! leaving Black defenceless in view of 22...Qxb3? 23 Bxg7+! Kxg7 24 Qg4+ Kh8 25 Qd4+ Bf6 26 Qxf6 mate) 21 Rh5 Nf6 22 Rh6! **(Diagram 13)** would have maintained a vicious attack; for instance, 22...Ne4 23 Qf5! Ng5 fails to 24 Qg4 Be4 25 h4.

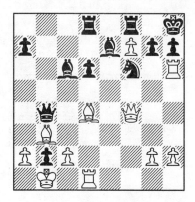

Diagram 13 (B)	Diagram 14 (W)
The pressure mounts	There's no defence down the b-file

20...Qb7 21 Qf4?

Another slip as Fischer completely underestimates the coming counterattack, whereas 21 Rh5! Ng5!? (White forces a draw after 21...Nd2+ 22 Rxd2 cxd2 with 23 Rxh7+! Kxh7 24 Qf5+ Kh6 25 Qe6+) 22 h4! Rxf7 23 Rxg5! Rdf8 24 Rg3 would have remained extremely unclear.

21...Ba4! (Diagram 14) 22 Qg4 Bf6 23 Rxf6 Bxb3 0-1

Wisely avoiding 23...gxf6?? 24 Qxe4! when it's White who wins, preferring to threaten the decisive 24...Ba2+ to which there's no decent defence.

Game 21
□ **K.Movsziszian** ■ **K.Spraggett**
Tarragona 2006

---

1 e4 c5 2 Nf3 Nc6 3 d4 cxd4 4 Nxd4 Nf6 5 Nc3 d6 6 Bc4 e6 7 Be3 Be7 8 Qe2 0-0 9 0-0-0 a6 10 Bb3 Qc7 11 Rhg1 b5 12 g4 (Diagram 15) 12...b4 13 Nxc6

Against Black's consistent advance of the b-pawn, White might like to sacrifice immediately, but following 13 Nd5 Nxd5! 14 Nxc6 Nxe3 15 Nxe7+ Qxe7 16 Qxe3 a5 17 Ba4 Bd7! all the exchanges favour Black, as pointed out by Scherbakov.

13...Qxc6

The correct recapture, whereas 13...bxc3 14 Nxe7+ Qxe7 15 Bd4 cxb2+ 16 Bxb2 Bb7

17 e5 dxe5 18 Qxe5 leaves White's bishop pair looking rather menacing.

 TIP: Try not to concede the bishop pair on an open board. Here White's unopposed dark-squared bishop is especially hard for Black to contain.

14 Nd5!? exd5

The main theoretical continuation, but if Black wishes to avoid the coming piece sacrifice he should prefer 14...Nxd5!? 15 exd5 Qb7 after which 16 dxe6 fxe6 17 Bd4 d5 18 g5 Rf5 was rather unclear in G.Ginsburg-Z.Lanka, Austrian League 2005.

15 g5 Nxe4 16 Bxd5 Qa4 (Diagram 16) 17 Bd4!?

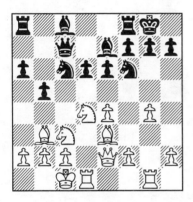

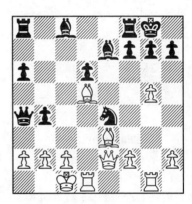

Diagram 15 (B)

White hopes for g5 and Rg3-h3

Diagram 16 (W)

An important tabiya

The most ambitious continuation, but by no means the only one:

a) 17 Bxa8 looks a little greedy, but after 17...Nc3 18 bxc3 Be6 19 Bd4 bxc3 20 Bxc3 Rxa8 21 g6! the game fizzles out to a level ending following 21...hxg6 22 Rxg6 Qf4+ 23 Rd2 fxg6 24 Qxe6+ Qf7 (Pelletier).

b) 17 Bxe4 Be6 18 Bd4 g6! (and not 18...Qxa2? on account of 19 Qh5 g6 20 Qh6 f6 21 Bxg6!) 19 Bxa8 Rxa8 20 a3 bxa3 21 b3 Qc6 isn't easy to assess, but we quite like Black's compensation for the exchange.

17...Bf5 18 Bxe4 Bxe4 19 Qxe4 Qxa2!?

A critical novelty in place of the earlier 19...Rfe8 20 Kb1 Bf8 21 Qd3 Qc6 22 h4 Qe4 23 h5 Rac8 24 Be3 Re6 25 Qxe4 Rxe4 26 Rd5 which gave White an edge in A.Fedorov-I.Lutsko, Minsk 2005.

20 Qxe7 Rae8 21 Qc7 Re4! 22 Be3

White must give up b2 since 22 Qb6?? would have failed to 22...Re2 when 23 b3 only accelerates the forthcoming mate.

22...Rc4! 23 Qxd6 b3 24 Kd2 Rxc2+?

Now White's king slips away. In this unbalanced position Black should prefer 24...Qxb2 25 Qd3 bxc2! 26 Rc1 Rfc8 **(Diagram 17)** reaching a rather unbalanced and unclear position which could really do with some testing.

Diagram 17 (W)	Diagram 18 (B)
A future battleground	Mate will follow

25 Ke1 Qxb2 26 Qd3 a5 27 Rg4 Rc3 28 Qe4 Qa3

White would have had the upper hand too in the event of 28...Rcc8 29 Kf1 Rfe8 30 Qf5.

29 Rh4 g6 30 Bd4 Rc1?

Now White's attack decides. Instead Black would have retained some chances to confuse the issue with 30...Qb4 31 Bxc3 Qxc3+ 32 Kf1 b2 33 Qb7 Qc1 34 Rhd4 a4.

31 Rxh7! (Diagram 18)

There's no defence down the h-file.

31...Qb4+ 32 Ke2 Rc2+ 33 Kf3 Qxd4 34 Rxd4 Kxh7 1-0

Game 22
☐ **J.Howell** ■ **M.Wahls**
Gausdal 1986

---

1 e4 c5 2 Nf3 Nc6 3 d4 cxd4 4 Nxd4 Nf6 5 Nc3 d6 6 Bc4 e6 7 Be3 Be7 8 Qe2 0-0 9 0-0-0 a6 10 Bb3 Qc7 11 g4 Nd7 12 g5 Nc5 13 Rhg1 b5 14 Nxc6

White's main move, but we should also mention:

a) 14 Bd5!? Bd7! (but not 14...Nxd4 15 Bxd4 exd5? on account of 16 Nxd5 Qb7 17

Nf6+! Bxf6 18 gxf6 Ne6 19 Rxg7+! Nxg7 20 Rg1 when White wins in some style) 15 Nxc6 Bxc6 16 Bxc5 dxc5 17 Bxc6 Qxc6 18 e5 Rfd8 sees Black equalize.

b) 14 Qh5 b4! 15 Nxc6 Nxb3+ 16 axb3 Qxc6 transposes to our main game.

14...Nxb3+ 15 axb3 Qxc6 16 Qh5 b4 (Diagram 19)

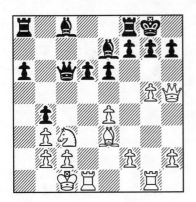 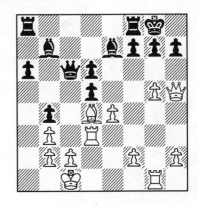

Diagram 19 (W)	Diagram 20 (B)
How best to sacrifice?	Black's queen can't aid his defence

17 Bd4

In the early days of the Velimirovic White tried to make 17 Nd5!? exd5 18 Bd4 work, but after 18...Be6!? we haven't been able to find anything clear for him, not least because 19 Qh6? fails to 19...Qxc2+! 20 Kxc2 Rfc8+ 21 Kb1 gxh6 22 gxh6+ Kf8.

17...Bb7?!

At the time of this game it was known that 17...bxc3? 18 Qh6! cxb2+ 19 Kxb2 e5 20 Bxe5 left White somewhat better, but only after it did Black find the correct path: 17...Bd7! 18 Rg4! (18 Nd5? now fails as Black covers the h3-square with 18...exd5 and 19 Qh6!? is foiled by the desperado 19...Qxc2+! 20 Kxc2 Rfc8+ and 21...gxh6) 18...bxc3 19 Rh4 Bxg5+ 20 Qxg5 cxb2+ 21 Bxb2 e5! 22 Rg1 g6 23 Qh6 Rfc8 24 c4 Be6 25 Qxh7+ Kf8 gave Black enough counterplay down the c-file in P.Roth-N.Stanec, Austrian League 1994; an impressive and theoretically very important line.

18 Nd5!

A strong improvement of Howell's over 18 Rg4 bxc3 19 Rh4 cxb2+ 20 Bxb2 Qxe4! 21 Rxe4 Bxe4 22 Ba3 Rfc8 23 Rd2 Rab8 which had given Black excellent counterplay in M.Chandler-L.Yudasin, Minsk 1982.

18...exd5 19 Rd3 (Diagram 20) 19...Rfc8 20 c3 dxe4

The alternative is 20...bxc3, but after 21 Rf3! cxb2+ 22 Kxb2 Qc2+ 23 Ka3 Rf8 24 Rh3 Qxe4 25 g6! fxg6 26 Qxh7+ Kf7 27 Bxg7! (Macieja) White enjoys a dangerous attack.

NOTE: Having sacrificed a piece and said 'A', White must usually be prepared to say 'B' in the Velimirovic. Only by putting further wood on the fire does his attack generally succeed.

21 Rh3 Kf8 22 g6! (Diagram 21)

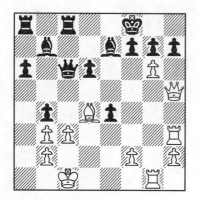 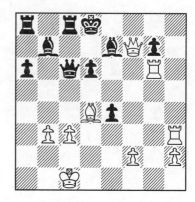

Diagram 21 (B)

The kingside is ripped open

Diagram 22 (W)

Spot the mate in four!

22...fxg6

Neither would 22...h6 23 gxf7 Bf6 have helped in view of 24 Bxf6 gxf6 25 Qg6 Ke7 26 Rxh6 d5 27 f8Q+! Rxf8 28 Rh7+ Kd8 29 Rf7!, as again later analysed by Macieja.

23 Qxh7 Ke8 24 Rxg6 bxc3 25 Qg8+ Kd7 26 Qe6+ Kd8 27 bxc3 Bf8

White mates in style after this, but the more mundane 27...Kc7 28 Qxe7+ Qd7 29 Bb6+ Kc6 30 Qe5 would also have forced resignation.

28 Qf7! Be7 (Diagram 22) 29 Qxe7+! Kxe7 30 Rxg7+ 1-0

Mate follows after both 30...Ke6 31 Rh6+ Kd5 (or 31...Kf5 32 Rf6) 32 Rg5 and 30...Kd8 31 Bf6+ Ke8 32 Rh8.

Black Delays Castling

1 e4 c5 2 Nf3 Nc6 3 d4 cxd4 4 Nxd4 Nf6 5 Nc3 d6 6 Bc4 e6 7 Be3 a6 (Diagram 23)

Black doesn't touch his kingside for the time being, preferring to make a start on the queenside.

8 Qe2 Qc7

NOTE: The queen is well placed on c7 should Black not be in a hurry to castle. She both supports an early ...b5 and helps to generate some pressure down the c-file.

Black's last can also be seen as a useful semi-waiting move. Black would like to immediately advance on the queenside, but needs White to castle first. The reason can be seen in the variation 8...Na5 9 Bd3 b5 10 b4!? Nb7?! 11 0-0 when it's White who seizes the queenside initiative by following up with the a4-break. Here Black does better with 10...Nc4! 11 Bxc4 bxc4 when White should reject the pawn in favour of 12 0-0! Bb7 13 Bg5 Be7 14 Rad1 which brought him an edge in A.Danin-A.Lugovoi, St Petersburg 2004.

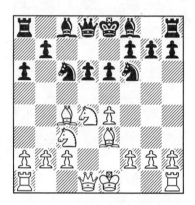

Diagram 23 (W)

Prioritizing queenside counterplay

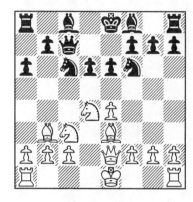

Diagram 24 (B)

White delays castling

9 0-0-0

Consistent with White's play in the main line of the Velimirovic (see our last section), but more challenging might possibly be 9 Bb3!? **(Diagram 24)**, followed by a swift advance of the g-pawn. After 9...Na5 10 g4 b5 11 g5 Nd7 White has a number of tempting options, but none seem to bring any advantage:

a) 12 Nxe6 fxe6 13 Bxe6 hopes to exploit the fact that the black king is still in the centre, but Black defends with 13...Nb6! (taking control of the d5-square) 14 Bxb6 Qxb6 15 Qg4 Qc5.

b) 12 Bxe6!? fxe6 13 Nxe6 has similar designs and forces Black to return some material: 13...Qc4! 14 Qxc4 Nxc4 15 Nc7+ Kd8 16 Nxa8 Nxe3 17 fxe3 Bb7 18 a4 b4 19 Nd5 Bxa8 gave White a rook and two pawns for the minor pieces, but not the advantage in O.Brendel-D.Shengelia, Werther 2004.

c) The only other independent plan is to organize a pawn storm against e6, but after the instructive variation 12 f4 b4 13 Na4 Bb7 14 f5 e5! 15 Ne6! fxe6 16 fxe6 Nc5 17 Nxc5 dxc5 18 Bd5 0-0-0 we agree with Kasparov and Nikitin that the situation is rather unclear and about even.

9...Be7

Black might not be in a hurry to castle, but at some point doing so might well be wise. Furthermore, this useful developing move prevents 10 g4 on account of an exchange on d4 followed by ...e5 and ...Bxg4. Another popular approach is to begin immediate counterplay with 9...Na5!? **(Diagram 25)**:

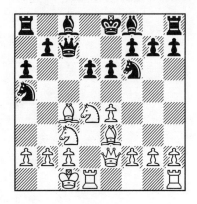

Diagram 25 (W)	**Diagram 26 (B)**
Wasting no time on the queenside	White attacks in the centre

a) 10 Bb3 is a little too routine and 10...b5 11 g4 b4 12 g5 bxc3 13 gxf6 cxb2+ 14 Kxb2 gxf6 while fairly unclear gave Black quite reasonable counterplay in G.Szabo-V.Nevednichy, Bucharest 2005.

b) 10 Bd3 b5 11 Bg5 (combining active piece play with an advance of the f-pawn looks like the way to go; instead 11 g4 b4 12 Nb1 Bb7 13 Nd2 d5! gives Black good counterplay as did 11 a3 Rb8 12 g4 Nd7 13 f4 Nc5 14 g5 Nxd3+ 15 Rxd3 Nc4 16 h4 b4 17 axb4 Rxb4 in D.Petrosian-Y.Dembo, Moscow 2004) 11...Be7 (prudent, whereas 11...b4 is rather risky on account of 12 Nd5!? exd5 13 exd5+: both 13...Be7 14 Bxf6 gxf6 15 Rhe1 Ra7 16 Qh5 and 13...Kd8 14 Bxf6+ gxf6 15 Rhe1 give White good compensation for the piece) 12 a3 Bb7 (probably better is Rublevsky's suggestion of 12...Bd7!? 13 f4 Nc4 14 Qe1 0-0 15 Bxc4 Qxc4 16 e5 dxe5 17 fxe5 Nd5 18 Bxe7 Nxe7 which seems fairly satisfactory for Black) 13 f4 **(Diagram 26)** 13...Rc8 14 Bxf6! gxf6 (White gains more than enough for the piece after 14...Bxf6?! 15 Bxb5+! axb5 16 Ndxb5 Qb6 17 Nxd6+ Kf8 18 Nxc8 Bxc8 19 e5 Be7 20 Qb5) 15 Qh5 Qd7 and now 16 Nd5 was a pretty dangerous sacrifice in D.Yevseev-E.Alekseev, St Petersburg 2002, and 16 f5 e5 17 Ne6! also looks rather effective.

Returning to 9...Be7:

10 Bb3

Another way of preparing g4 is 10 Rhg1!? when Black remains advised to keep his king in the centre; for example, 10...Na5 11 Bd3 b5 12 g4 Bb7 13 g5 Nd7 14 Qh5 g6 15 Qh6 b4 16 Qg7 Rf8 17 Nce2 Nc5 **(Diagram 27)** 18 Kb1 Rc8 gave Black good queenside counterplay in D.Stellwagen-J.Van Der Wiel, Leeuwarden 2004.

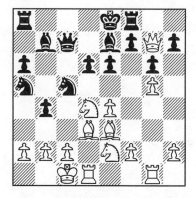

Diagram 27 (W)

Black's king is fairly safe on e8

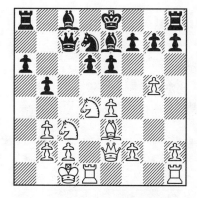

Diagram 28 (W)

Black hopes to undermine e4

10...Na5

Another possible move order is 10...b5 11 g4 (11 Nxc6!? Qxc6 12 Bd4 Bb7 13 Rhe1 is an independent centralizing plan, but 13...Qc7! 14 e5 dxe5 15 Bxe5 Qa5 seems acceptable enough for Black) 11...Na5, transposing. Indeed Black must either get on with things on the queenside or accept a transposition to our last section with 10...0-0.

11 g4 b5 12 g5 Nxb3+

> **WARNING: By delaying castling Black avoids much of the theory associated with the main line Velimirovic, but he must still be careful. Here the immediate 12...Nd7?! should be avoided on account of 13 Bxe6! fxe6 14 Nxe6 Qc4 15 Nxg7+ Kf8 16 Nf5 netting three good pawns and the initiative for the piece.**

13 axb3 Nd7 (Diagram 28)

Now Black's plan is to attack the e4-pawn, thereby restricting White's options, before finally castling on the kingside. White, for his part, must either continue his kingside pawn-storm (as we'll consider in Game 23) or try another fascinating piece sacrifice with the 14 Nf5!? of Game 24.

Theoretical Conclusion

Keeping his king in the centre is not such an easy ride for Black, but both theory and practice show that doing so gives him good chances to neutralize White's initiative and then to counterattack. Indeed we can recommend this system to Black, especially if he doesn't like memorizing too many long theoretical lines, although it is important to be aware that ...Na5 must not be played too quickly.

Illustrative Games

Game 23
□ **G.Rechlis** ■ **J.Piket**
Gausdal 1986

1 e4 c5 2 Nf3 Nc6 3 d4 cxd4 4 Nxd4 Nf6 5 Nc3 d6 6 Bc4 e6 7 Be3 a6 8 Qe2 Qc7 9 0-0-0 Be7 10 Bb3 Na5 11 g4 b5 12 g5 Nxb3+ 13 axb3 Nd7 14 h4 b4 (Diagram 29)

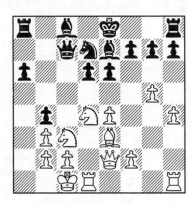
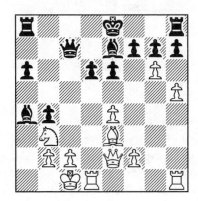

Diagram 29 (W)	**Diagram 30 (W)**
Both sides launch their pawns	White's pawns appear menacing

Black might also attack e4 straight away and after 14...Bb7!? 15 f3 b4 16 Na4 g6 17 h5 Rg8 18 Qh2 Rc8, as analysed by Nisipeanu and Stoica, a rather unclear situation arises.

15 Na4

White doesn't want to have his knight sidelined. More ambitious might be 15 Na2!? a5 16 Nb5 Qb8 17 Qd3 and after 17...Bb7 18 Nxd6+ Qxd6 19 Qxd6 Bxd6 20 Rxd6 Bxe4 21 Rhd1 Rc8! 22 c3 Ne5 the position is about equal.

15...Nc5 16 h5 Bd7

The main theoretical move, but we also wonder about 16...Nxe4!? with the idea of meeting 17 g6 with 17...Bf6 18 gxf7+ Kxf7 19 Bf4 Bb7 20 f3 e5 21 fxe4 exf4 22 Rhf1 Be5 after which Black's bishop pair gives him the upper hand.

17 g6!

White should be prepared to give up a pawn to further his kingside initiative.

17...Nxb3+ 18 Nxb3 Bxa4 (Diagram 30) 19 h6!?

This doesn't promise any advantage, but is probably better than 19 gxf7+ Kxf7 20 Kb1 Rhc8 21 Rhg1 Bf6 22 Bg5 Qc4 23 Qxc4 Rxc4 24 Rxd6 Rxe4 which gave Black the better ending in R.Webb-P.Wells, Portsmouth 2002.

19...fxg6 20 Nd4 e5 21 Ne6 Qc6 22 hxg7 Rg8 23 Rxh7 Bb3!

Correctly trying to dislodge the strong knight, whereas in the later game A.Szieberth-N.Hjelm, Budapest 1993, Black got into serious difficulties after 23...Rc8? 24 Bc5! Qb5 25 Qg4.

24 Rd5! Rc8 25 Rh8 (Diagram 31)

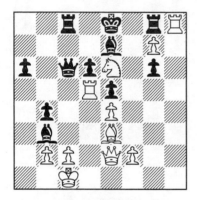

Diagram 31 (B)

Black's resources are sufficient

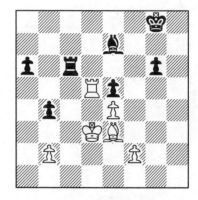

Diagram 32 (W)

White has enough activity to draw

25...Kf7!?

Piket wants to win. Instead he could have steered the game towards a draw with 25...Qxc2+ 26 Qxc2 Rxc2+ 27 Kb1 Kf7 28 Rxg8 Kxg8 29 Rd3 Rxb2+! 30 Kxb2 Bxe6 (Szieberth).

26 Nc5! dxc5!

Both sides are up to the challenge, whereas 26...Bxd5? 27 Qf3+! Kxg7 28 exd5 would have left Black struggling in view of 28...Qe8? 29 Ne6+ Kxh8 30 Qh3+ followed by mate.

27 cxb3 c4 28 bxc4 Qxc4+ 29 Qxc4 Rxc4+ 30 Kd2 Kxg7 31 Rxg8+ Kxg8 32 Kd3 Rc6 (Diagram 32) 33 Rd7

Probably an even simpler way to draw was 33 Rxe5!? Bf6 34 Rc5 Rxc5 35 Bxc5 Bxb2 36 Bxb4.

33...Kf7 34 Bg5 Rd6+ 35 Rxd6 Bxd6 36 Kc4 Ke6 37 Bd2 a5 38 Kb5 Bc7 39 b3 Bd8 40

Be3 Kd7 41 Kc5 Be7+ 42 Kd5 Bd6 43 f3 Bb8 ½-½

White's active king continues to fully compensate for Black's extra pawn.

Game 24
☐ **D.Fernando** ■ **N.De Firmian**
Lisbon 2000

---

1 e4 c5 2 Nf3 Nc6 3 d4 cxd4 4 Nxd4 Nf6 5 Nc3 d6 6 Bc4 e6 7 Be3 a6 8 Qe2 Qc7 9 0-0-0 Be7 10 Bb3 Na5 11 g4 b5 12 g5 Nxb3+ 13 axb3 Nd7 14 Nf5!? (Diagram 33)

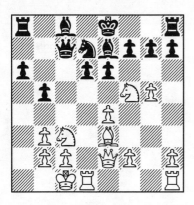

Diagram 33 (B)

White wants to open the e-file

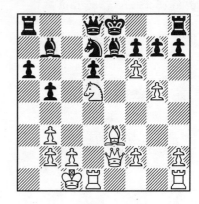

Diagram 34 (B)

Black must be calm and careful

As chucking his kingside pawns up the board doesn't seem to promise any advantage (see our last illustrative game), White has begun to reconsider this old sacrificial idea of Velimirovic's.

14...exf5

It's probably best to accept the offer since 14...b4 15 Nxe7 Kxe7 16 Na4 a5 17 Rd2 Ba6 18 Qg4 Bb5 19 Bf4! e5 20 Be3 leaves White with a small but stable advantage.

15 Nd5 Qd8 16 exf5 Bb7

The e-file might be open, but it's been long known that Black must keep his king on it: 16...0-0? 17 f6! gxf6 18 Bd4 Ne5 19 gxf6 Bxf6 20 Rhg1+ Bg7 (or 20...Kh8 21 Qh5! with the decisive threat of 22 Bb6) 21 Bxe5! dxe5 22 Qxe5 f6 23 Ne7+ Kf7 24 Qh5+ and 1-0 brought a crushing victory for the man himself in D.Velimirovic-J.Sofrevski, Titograd 1965.

17 f6! (Diagram 34) 17...gxf6

Another option is 17...Bxd5!? and after 18 fxg7 Rg8 19 Rxd5 Rxg7 20 f4 Kf8 21 h4 f6

22 Re1 Qc7 anything might happen.

18 Rhe1 Bxd5

> **WARNING: Once again Black needs to know his stuff and that he
> shouldn't castle: 18...0-0? being punished by the brutal 19 gxf6 Bxf6
> 20 Qg4+ Kh8 21 Nxf6 Nxf6 22 Bd4 Rg8 23 Re8! Rxe8 24 Qg5 (Velimi-
> rovic).**

19 Rxd5 Rg8 20 gxf6

White has also tried 20 Bf4 Kf8 21 Qd2, but after 21...Rxg5! 22 Bxg5 fxg5 23 h4 a5!
24 hxg5 a4 25 b4 a3 it was Black who enjoyed good attacking chances in J.Hector-
A.Fishbein, Stavanger 1997.

20...Nxf6 21 Rf5 Ng4! (Diagram 35)

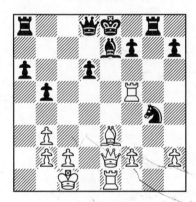

Diagram 35 (W)
White has sufficient compensation

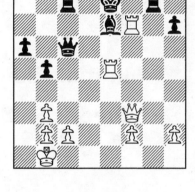

Diagram 36 (B)
It's perpetual

22 Bd4?!

A little imprecise: 22 Bg5 Ne5 23 Bxe7 Qxe7 24 f4 Nd3+ 25 cxd3 Qxe2 26 Rxe2+ is a
better way of maintaining the balance.

22...Qd7?!

De Firmian returns the favour immediately, whereas 22...Rg6! 23 Qf3 Ne5 24 Qd5
f6 would have left White beginning to struggle.

23 Qf3 Rc8 24 Rxf7 Ne5 25 Bxe5 dxe5 26 Kb1 Qc6

Now White gets to sacrifice to force perpetual. Black might have risked 26...Rf8!?,
but after 27 Rxf8+ Bxf8 28 Rxe5+ Be7 29 Qe4 it's clear that White retains some
awkward pressure for the piece.

27 Rxe5! (Diagram 36) 27...Qxf3 28 Rexe7+ Kd8 ½-½

6 Bg5: The Richter-Rauzer

▨ **Introduction**

▨ **Dreev's 6...Bd7!?**

Introduction

1 e4 c5 2 Nf3 Nc6 3 d4 cxd4 4 Nxd4 Nf6 5 Nc3 d6 6 Bg5 (Diagram 1)

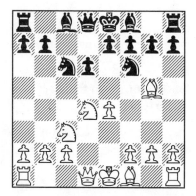

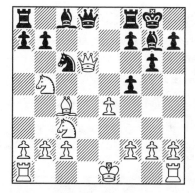

Diagram 1 (B)

White's most popular choice

Diagram 2 (W)

Black hasn't enough compensation

Developed by the German Kurt Richter and the Soviet Vsevolod Rauzer in the 1930s, this is the Richter-Rauzer Attack. It has been popular with white players since the middle of the 20th Century and remains very much White's main weapon against the Classical.

 WARNING: Not only does White actively deploy his bishop with 6 Bg5, but he also hinders a number of Black's possible development schemes.

One set-up prevented by 6 Bg5 is a Dragon-type response. Admittedly 6...g6 is still seen occasionally, but Black's quick development and bishop pair does not compensate for the damage to his structure. The recent game A.Volokitin-M.Carlsen, Biel 2006, was a good example of this: 6...g6?! 7 Bxf6 exf6 8 Bc4 Bg7 9 Ndb5 0-0 10 Qxd6 f5 **(Diagram 2)** 11 0-0-0 Qa5 (weaker is winning back the pawn: 11...Qg5+ 12 f4 Qxg2 13 e5! Qg4 14 Rhf1 Bxe5 15 Bxf7+! Rxf7 16 fxe5 with a clear advantage for White) 12 Qc7 fxe4 13 Qxa5 Nxa5 14 Bd5 Bg4 15 Rde1 Rad8? (better was 15...a6 16 Nd6 e3 17 f3! Bf5 18 Rd1 Be5 19 Nxf5 gxf5 with some chances to equalize) 16 Rxe4 Bf5 17 Ra4 b6 18 Rd1 a6 19 Nd4 Bd7 20 Rb4 b5 21 Nf3 and Black lacked sufficient compensation.

As we've seen in the Classical Sicilian 6...e5 usually works, but the exception is against the Richter-Rauzer. Here 6...e5?! 7 Bxf6 gxf6 (even worse is 7...Qxf6? because of 8 Nd5 Qd8 9 Nb5) 8 Nf5! Bxf5 9 exf5 gives White some advantage, such as after 9...Nd4 10 Qxd4!? exd4 11 Bb5+ Qd7 (it's mate after 11...Ke7?? 12 Nd5) 12 Bxd7+ Kxd7 13 Ne2 Re8 14 Kd2.

Another move which we cannot recommend for Black is 6...Qa5?!. White has a comfortable advantage after both 7 Bxf6 gxf6 8 Nb3 Qg5 9 Nd5 and 7 Bb5!? Bd7 8 Nb3.

In a moment we will turn to Black's only really good alternative to the main line with 6...e6, namely 6...Bd7!?, but first we must note that sometimes 6...Qb6!? is seen. This is the best of Black's rare responses to the Richter-Rauzer.

NOTE: After 6...Qb6 play often transposes into one of the main lines following 7 Nb3 e6 8 Qd2 Be7 9 0-0-0 0-0 (see Game 28).

Against 6...Qb6 White also has the interesting response 7 Be3!? **(Diagram 3)** and after 7...Qxb2 8 Ndb5 Qb4 9 Bd2 Black has to avoid a fiendish trap.

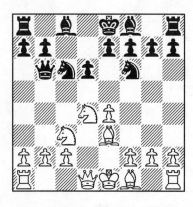

Diagram 3 (B)
A dangerous gambit

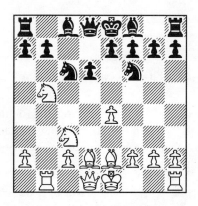

Diagram 4 (W)
White retains fair compensation

WARNING: 9...Nxe4?? 10 a3 forced resignation in the game Y.Yemelin-B.Jobava, Abu Dhabi 2003, in view of the decisive 10...Nxc3 11 axb4 Nxd1 12 Nc7+ Kd8 13 Nxa8 Nb2 14 Bc3.

Baadur Jobava might be a world-class player and theoretician, but we hope that none of our readers will follow in his footsteps! Black should prefer 9...Qc5 10 Be2! (it's an early draw after 10 Nc7+ Kd8 11 Nxa8 Ng4 12 Qf3 Nd4 13 Qd1 Nc6) 10...Qb6 11 Rb1 (A.Balashov-Petrienko, Voronezh 1987), and now we feel that 11...Qd8! **(Diagram 4)** is best, although after 12 Nd5 Nxd5 13 exd5 Ne5 14 0-0 White's lead in development gives him decent compensation for the pawn.

Dreev's 6...Bd7!?

1 e4 c5 2 Nf3 Nc6 3 d4 cxd4 4 Nxd4 Nf6 5 Nc3 d6 5 Nc3 d6 6 Bg5 Bd7 (Diagram 5)

Diagram 5 (W)

Rapid queenside development

Diagram 6 (W)

A positionally-complex situation

This plan was first applied by no less a player than Bogoljubow against Richter (!) in 1937. It is currently a fairly popular alternative to 6...e6, due in no small part to being a key part of Alexei Dreev's repertoire.

 NOTE: With 6...Bd7 Black ignores the potential destruction of his pawn structure, preferring to strive for rapid queenside counterplay with ...Rc8 and ...Qa5.

7 Qd2

As usual in the Richter-Rauzer White prepares to castle queenside. A principled alternative is to exchange on f6 which can be done either immediately or after 7 Be2 Qa5 **(Diagram 6)**, as we'll examine further in Game 25.

It should be noted too that preventing ...Qa5 with 7 Nb3 is not especially challenging for Black who developed good counterplay with 7...a6 8 f4 e6 9 Qd2 b5 10 0-0-0 b4! (hoping for 11 Ne2?! Nxe4!) 11 Bxf6 gxf6 12 Ne2 a5 13 Nbd4 Qb6 in R.Popov-I.Doukhine (Moscow 2006).

7...Rc8

Dreev's preference. Black intends to exchange on d4 and then play ...Qa5, but perhaps the text isn't necessary and we wonder if the older 7...Nxd4!? 8 Qxd4 Qa5 9 f4 e6 is really so bad at all.

8 0-0-0

A critical alternative is the sharp 8 f4!? **(Diagram 7)**.

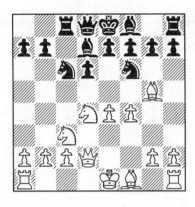

Diagram 7 (B)

Will Black be over-run?

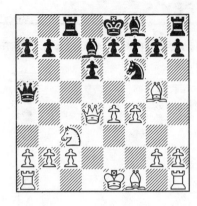

Diagram 8 (W)

Boldly provoking e4-e5

Black must now decide whether or not to continue his plan:

a) 8...h6 9 Bh4 (or 9 Bxf6 gxf6 when 10 0-0-0 Nxd4 11 Qxd4 Qa5 transposes to a position which we'll consider after 8 0-0-0 Nxd4 9 Qxd4 Qa5 10 f4 h6 11 Bxf6 gxf6, while 10 Nf5!? Qa5 11 Bd3 Nb4 12 0-0 Nxd3 13 Qxd3 Qb6+ leads to a very unclear situation according to Ivanchuk) 9...g5!? (a dangerous way of activating the king-side) 10 fxg5 hxg5 11 Bxg5 Bg7 12 0-0-0 Nxd4 13 Qxd4 Qa5 14 Bd2 was the under-rated course of S.Karjakin-C.Balogh, Khanty-Mansyisk 2005, and now we recommend the typical exchange sacrifice 14...Rxc3!? 15 a3 Bh6! 16 Bxh6 Rxh6 17 bxc3 Qxa3+ 18 Kd2 e5 with good compensation; for example, 19 Qb4 Qxb4 20 cxb4 Nxe4+ 21 Ke1 Ng3 22 Rg1 Rxh2 most certainly cannot be worse for Black.

b) 8...Nxd4 9 Qxd4 Qa5 **(Diagram 8)** 10 e5 dxe5 (and not 10...Ne4? 11 b4!) 11 fxe5 e6 (correctly maintaining the pin along the fifth and again Black must be careful: 11...Bc6?? 12 b4 Qa3 13 Bc1 would not be the way to go) 12 0-0-0 Bc6 13 Nb5 (13 Bb5 Nd5 14 Nxd5 Bxb5 15 Qxa7!? is a fiendish trick, hoping for 15...Qxa7?? 16 Nc7+! Rxc7 17 Rd8 mate, but after the correct 15...Bb4! 16 Qxb7 0-0 Black has good counterplay) 13...Bxb5 14 exf6 Bc6 15 h4 g6 16 Bc4 Bc5! 17 Qe5 (or 17 Qg4 h5 18 Qe2 0-0 19 Kb1 b5 20 Bb3 Qb4 when Black's a-pawn is ready and the situation is again unclear) 17...Bb6 18 Qe2 0-0 was rather unclear in K.Asrian-A.Dreev, Stepanakert 2005.

Thus Black seems to have two fully playable responses to 8 f4, but the situation is rather sharp in either case and Black must be well prepared here!

8...Nxd4 9 Qxd4 Qa5 10 f4

Once again White hopes to blow open the centre in a bid to exploit his superior development. Alternatively, 10 Bxf6 gxf6 11 Kb1 Qc5 12 Qd2 f5 **(Diagram 9)** 13 exf5 Bxf5 14 Bb5+ Kd8 gave Black reasonable counterplay in E.Bacrot-G.Sosonko,

Antwerp 1996, and 10 Bd2!? (guarding against the typical exchange sacrifice on c3) 10...e5!? (10...a6 11 Kb1 Qc5 12 Qxc5 Rxc5 13 f3 has been shown to give White a small edge) 11 Qd3 a6 (it's too early to sacrifice: 11...Rxc3?! 12 Bxc3 Qxa2 13 f3 g6 14 Kd2 and White's king is quite safe on d2) 12 a3 reaches a fascinating situation in which we quite like Baklan's suggested queen sacrifice: 12...Ng4!? 13 Qe2 Qc5 14 f3 Nf2 15 Be3 Nxd1 16 Bxc5 Nxc3 17 bxc3 Rxc5 which really deserves some tests.

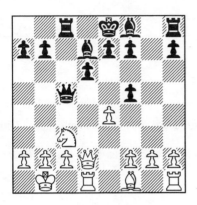

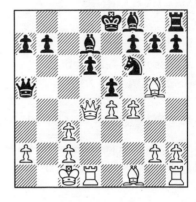

Diagram 9 (W)
Opening up Black's bishops

Diagram 10 (W)
Another critical position

10...Rxc3

> **TIP: After playing 6...Bd7, Black is usually on the look-out for such an exchange sacrifice: he both destroys White's structure and picks up a useful central pawn.**

We should note that Black isn't forced to give up material and instead after 10...e6 11 e5 dxe5 12 fxe5 play has transposed to note 'b' to White's 8th move. There's also 10...h6 11 Bxf6 gxf6 when it might look like Black has just lost a tempo, but the situation actually remains quite unclear: 12 Kb1 (12 f5 h5! prepares to activate the dark-squared bishop) 12...Qc5 13 Qd3 Bg7 14 Be2 a6 15 g4 f5! 16 e5 fxg4 17,Rhg1 h5 18 h3 Be6 19 hxg4 h4 was most certainly very complicated in R.Ponomariov-V.Milov, Ohrid 2001.

11 bxc3

A clubplayer might prefer to get the queens off, but 11 Qxc3 Qxc3 12 bxc3 Ne4 is actually rather pleasant for Black — White needs to keep the queens on to pose Black any problems.

11...e5! (Diagram 10)

Wisely preventing e5 from White, while fixing the weakness on e4. We will return to this fascinating and critical situation in Game 26.

Theoretical Conclusion

6...Bd7 is currently quite an attractive option. There are some sharp lines and Black must be careful with his king stranded in the centre, but there is much less to study here than after 6...e6.

Illustrative Games

Game 25
□ **P.Carlsson** ■ **A.Kogan**
Bajada de la Virgen 2005

1 e4 c5 2 Nf3 Nc6 3 d4 cxd4 4 Nxd4 Nf6 5 Nc3 d6 6 Bg5 Bd7 7 Bxf6 gxf6 8 Be2 Qa5

 NOTE: Remember that this position frequently arises too from 7 Be2 Qa5 8 Bxf6 gxf6.

9 0-0

White has also opted to keep the knights on with 9 Nb3, as in the high-level game A.Morozevich-A.Dreev, Moscow 2004: 9...Qg5 10 g3 f5! 11 f4 Qh6!? 12 Qd2 Bg7 13 0-0-0 fxe4 14 Nxe4 a5 **(Diagram 11)** 15 Qe3 (at first the aggressive 15 Nbc5? looks like a better try, but Dreev was ready with 15...Bh3! 16 Nxb7 0-0 after which the white knight finds itself embarrassingly trapped on b7) 15...0-0 16 a3 Qe6 17 Qd3 h6 18 Kb1 a4 19 Nc1 Nd4 20 Nc3 Rfc8 when there was no doubt that Black enjoyed a strong initiative.

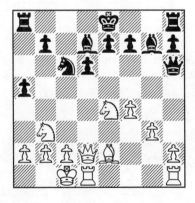

Diagram 11 (W)
White comes under some pressure

Diagram 12 (W)
White needs a plan

WARNING: In the 6...Bd7 variation White can't afford to sit still. He must strive to gain some central pressure before Black seizes the initiative.

9...Nxd4

We wonder about the attempt to exploit the half-open g-file with 9...Rg8!?. One sample line then runs 10 Nd5 Bh3 11 Bf3 Ne5 12 Ne3 Bh6! 13 Ndf5 Bxe3 14 Nxe3 0-0-0 15 Kh1 Be6 when Black will follow up with ...Kb8 and ...Rc8 with quite a reasonable position.

10 Qxd4 Rc8 (Diagram 12) 11 a4!

Not so much to hold up ...b5, but as part of a plan to play actively on the queenside.

11...Qc5 12 Qd2 a6 13 Nd5 f5?!

It's both thematic and tempting to open lines for the dark-squared bishop like this, but now White gains a dangerous initiative. Instead it was time to be brave and take the plunge: 13...Qxc2! 14 Qe3 Bh6 15 Qxh6 Qxe2 16 Qg7 (or 16 Nb6 Rg8! 17 Nxc8 Rxg2+! 18 Kxg2 Qg4+ with perpetual) 16...Rf8 17 Rac1 Rxc1 18 Rxc1 Bc6 19 Nc7+ Kd7 20 Qxf8 Qxe4 21 Qg8 Kxc7 and after a number of forced moves, J.Magem Badals-E.Ubilava, San Sebastian 1992, remained unbalanced and about equal.

14 c4

Bearing in mind the position of the black king, White might also consider 14 exf5!? Bxf5 15 Rfe1 Be6 (and not 15...Qxc2?! 16 Qb4! Qc6? in view of the devastating 17 Nf6+! Kd8 18 Qa5+) 16 c4 a5 17 Ra3 with some initiative.

14...fxe4 15 b4 Qa7 16 c5 Qb8 (Diagram 13)

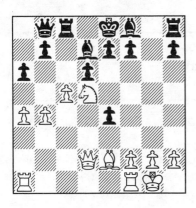

Diagram 13 (W)
An unhappy black queen

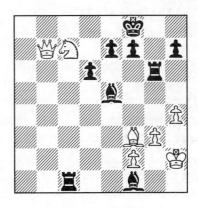

Diagram 14 (B)
Both sides want to attack!

17 Qd4 Rg8 18 Qxe4 Bc6 19 Bf3

It is clear that things have gone wrong for Black: he is cramped and struggling to coordinate his forces.

19...Rg6 20 b5!? axb5 21 axb5 Bxb5 22 Nb6 Rxc5 23 Ra8?!

The logical culmination of White's aggressive queenside play, but probably not best. Instead it was better to reject the queen in favour of 23 Rfb1! f5 24 Qh4 Rh6 25 Qf4 Ba6 26 Nd7! Kxd7 27 Rxa6 retaining a rather dangerous initiative.

23...Qxa8 24 Nxa8 Bxf1 25 h4

Maybe Carlsson initially intended 25 Qxb7?!, but after 25...Bxg2! 26 Qb8+ Kd7 27 Qb7+ Ke6 28 Qb3+ Kf6 29 Qb2+ e5 30 Bxg2 Bh6 only Black can be better.

25...Rc1!?

Now it's Kogan's turn to become ambitious. He could have instead forced a draw with 25...Ba6 26 Qa4+ Kd8 27 Nb6 Rc7 28 Qa5 Rc5 29 Qa4 Rc7.

26 Kh2 Bg7 27 Qxb7 Be5+ 28 g3 Kf8 29 Nc7 (Diagram 14) 29...Rc4?!

Losing the thread, albeit in a likely time scramble. Instead the prudent 29...Rxc7!? 30 Qxc7 Rf6 would have retained excellent chances to hold.

30 h5 Rg5 31 Nd5?!

Now the game fizzles out to a perpetual, but with 31 h6! e6 32 Nd5! White would have posed serious difficulties: 32...Bxg3+ 33 fxg3 Rc2+ 34 Kh1 exd5 35 Qd7! Re5 36 Bxd5 being most certainly in his favour.

 TIP: Always be very careful about allowing an enemy pawn to cramp your king from h6 (or h3 when White): the resulting back-rank difficulties have cost many a game.

31...Kg7 32 Qxe7 Rf5 33 Ne3! Rxf3 ½-½

Game 26
□ **Y.Solodovnichenko** ■ **E.Miroshnichenko**
Alushta 2001

---

1 e4 c5 2 Nf3 Nc6 3 d4 cxd4 4 Nxd4 Nf6 5 Nc3 d6 6 Bg5 Bd7 7 Qd2 Rc8 8 0-0-0 Nxd4 9 Qxd4 Qa5 10 f4 Rxc3 11 bxc3 e5 12 Qc4?!

Having induced ...e5, now is a much better moment than the previous move for White to exchange queens and 12 Qb4 Qxb4 13 cxb4 Nxe4 **(Diagram 15)** reaches a rather unclear situation in which White has a number of aggressive tries:

a) 14 Bc4 Nf2 15 fxe5 Nxh1 16 exd6 f6 17 Be3 b6 18 b5 h5 19 a4 Bg4! 20 Rxh1 Bxd6 sees Black fully solving his difficulties.

b) 14 Bh4 g5 15 Bd3 (the simpler 15 fxg5!? looks like a better try, gaining an edge after 15...Be7 16 Re1 Nxg5 17 Bc4) 15...Nc3 16 Bxg5 Nxd1 17 Rxd1 Be7 18 Bh6 Rg8! 19 g3 f5 was about equal in N.Draoui-E.Miroshnichenko, Paris 2001.

c) 14 Rd5!? h6 15 Bh4 g5 16 fxg5 hxg5 17 Be1 Be7 18 Ra5 a6 19 b5! Bd8 20 bxa6 Bxa5 21 a7 Ke7 22 Bxa5 Bc6 23 Bb6 was far from easy to assess in A.Volokitin-A.Motylev, Bermuda 2003: White's strong pawn on a7 being counterbalanced by Black's excellent central control.

12...d5! (Diagram 16)

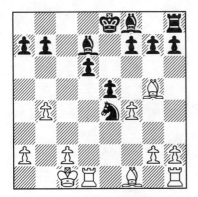

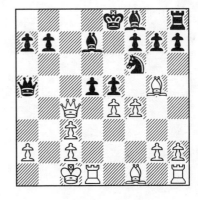

Diagram 15 (W)
Not an easy position to handle

Diagram 16 (W)
Blasting open the position

 TIP: After ...e5, never forget that ...d5 is the thematic freeing break to aim for.

13 exd5?!

Badly underestimating the danger against his king. Instead it was essential for White to return the exchange to reach a roughly level position after 13 Rxd5! Nxd5 14 Qxd5 Qxd5 15 exd5 f6 16 Bh4 exf4 17 Bf2 b6.

13...Ba3+ 14 Kd2

Sadly forced. Instead 14 Kb1? Ne4! 15 Bd3 Nc5! would have been extremely strong since 16 Ka1 b5 traps the white queen.

14...Nxd5 15 Re1?

Another horribly ambitious move, although even after the superior 15 Rb1 Black would have retained the initiative with 15...Nb6 16 Qe4 f6 17 Bh4 (17 Qxb7? fails to 17...fxg5! 18 Qb8+ Kf7 19 Qxh8? Qd5+ 20 Ke1 Qe4+ 21 Kd2 Nd5 with a mating attack) 17...Bc6 18 Qf5 Qd5+ 19 Qd3 Qxa2.

15...f6 (Diagram 17) 16 Rb1

Desperation in view of lines like 16 Bh4 Nxc3! 17 Ke3 g5 with an overwhelming attack.

16...0-0?!

Miroshnichenko later pointed out that he could have won a miniature with 16...fxg5, especially since 17 Rxb7 Nxc3! 18 Qxc3 Bc1+! terminates proceedings.

17 Rxb7 Rc8?

A tactical slip, whereas 17...Be6! 18 f5 Bf7 would have retained far more than enough compensation for the exchange.

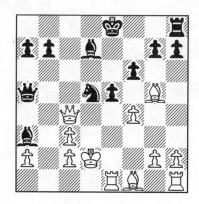

Diagram 17 (W)

White's king will do well to survive

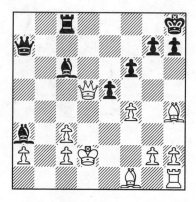

Diagram 18 (W)

The open d-file is decisive

 WARNING: While it's good to attack with all the pieces, always beware making too many methodical moves without checking first for any tricky tactics.

18 Rxa7?

After this White is quickly blown away, but matters would have been somewhat different after 18 Rb5! Qxc3+ 19 Qxc3 Nxc3 20 Rb3 (the point): for example, 20...fxg5 21 Ba6 Ne4+ 22 Ke3 exf4+ 23 Kxe4 Bc6+ 24 Kf5 Rf8+ 25 Kg4 leaves Black with nothing than more than perpetual in the shape of 25...Bd7+ 26 Kf3 Bc6+.

18...Qxa7 19 Qxd5+ Kh8 20 Bh4 Bc6 (Diagram 18) 21 Qe6 Bc1+!?

Good enough, but even simpler would have been 21...Rd8+ 22 Bd3 Bd5 23 Qf5 e4 24 Re1 exd3 with the idea of 25 Qxd5 Qb8!.

22 Ke1

A tougher defence was 22 Kxc1!? Qe3+ 23 Kb2 Rb8+ 24 Qb3 Rxb3+ 25 axb3, although Black's extra queen and initiative should decide after 25...exf4 26 Bd3 g5 27 Re1 Qb6.

22...Qe3+ 23 Be2 Rd8 24 Bf2

Allowing a pretty finish, but it was also mate after 24 Kf1 Qxf4+ 25 Bf2 Be3.

24...Rd1+! 0-1

Chapter Seven

The Traditional 6...e6
7 Qd2 Be7

▨ **Introduction**

▨ **White Plays 7 Qd2**

▨ **The Old Main Line with 9 Nb3**

▨ **The Old Main Line with 9 f4**

Introduction

1 e4 c5 2 Nf3 Nc6 3 d4 cxd4 4 Nxd4 Nf6 5 Nc3 d6 6 Bg5 e6 (Diagram 1)

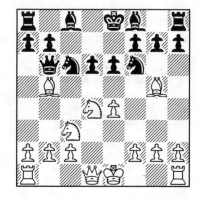

Diagram 1 (W)
The main line

Diagram 2 (W)
Black provokes Be3

Black's main choice against the Richter-Rauzer. Please note that after this section we will focus exclusively on 7 Qd2 which is by far White's most popular response, but he does have some alternatives.

7 Bb5

Developing and the most important alternative to 7 Qd2. Lesser options being:

a) 7 Qd3 was sometimes used by Paul Keres and should probably be followed up by short castling: 7...Be7 8 Rd1 (8 0-0-0 0-0 9 Nb3 d5! 10 exd5 Nb4 gives Black easy equality) 8...0-0 9 Be2 h6!? (9...d5 10 exd5 Nxd5 11 Bxe7 Qxe7 is also possible) 10 Bc1!? e5!? 11 Nxc6 bxc6 12 0-0 Be6 13 Qg3 Kh8 reaches a surprisingly complex position.

b) 7 Be2 is another old-fashioned approach. After 7...Be7 8 0-0 0-0 9 Kh1 a6 10 a4 h6 11 Be3 (hoping for a Scheveningen...) 11...e5!? (...but Black prefers to play in the spirit of the Boleslavsky) 12 Nb3 Be6 13 f4 exf4 14 Bxf4 d5! 15 exd5 Nxd5 16 Nxd5 Qxd5 17 Qxd5 Bxd5 Black had full equality in V.Meijers-A.Kharlov, Cappelle la Grande 2004.

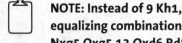

> **NOTE: Instead of 9 Kh1, 9 Qd2 looks logical, but allows a typical equalizing combination: 9...Nxe4!? 10 Nxe4 Nxd4 11 Qxd4 Bxg5 12 Nxg5 Qxg5 13 Qxd6 Rd8.**

c) Back in the 1930s Richter often preferred 7 Nxc6 bxc6 8 e5, but practice has shown that after 8...dxe5 9 Qf3 Be7 and 8...Qa5 Black gets an excellent position.

7...Bd7

In 1994 Kramnik and Khalifman introduced the ambitious move 7...Qb6!? **(Diagram 2)**, with the idea of 8 Be3 Qc7 after which Black has a good version of the Scheveningen since White's bishop is misplaced on b5 (...a6 will come with tempo). The evaluation of this ambitious idea depends on the typical Sicilian sacrifice 8 Bxf6 gxf6 9 Nd5!?, but after 9...exd5 10 exd5 a6 White needs a good move:

a) The attempt to regain the material leads to a catastrophe after 11 Ba4? Qa5+ 12 c3 Qxd5 13 Nxc6 Qe4+! 14 Qe2 Qxe2+ 15 Kxe2 Bd7.

b) 11 Bxc6+ bxc6 12 Qe2+ correctly sees White playing for the initiative. After 12...Be6! 13 Nxe6 (13 Nxc6? Kd7!) 13...fxe6 14 Qxe6+ Be7 15 0-0-0!? White has two pawns and the initiative for his piece, but still we feel that here a draw would be a good outcome for him.

c) 11 Qe2+ Kd8 12 Nxc6+ Kc7! 13 Qe8 bxc6 14 Bxc6 Ra7 15 0-0 Kb8 **(Diagram 3)** 16 Rfe1 f5! (taking away the e4-square from white queen) 17 a4 Bg7 18 Qe2 Bb7 was D.Harris-A.Yermolinsky, Asheville 2002, and according to Yermolinsky after 19 Ra3 Bxc6 20 Rb3 Bb5 21 axb5 a5! White hasn't full compensation for the piece.

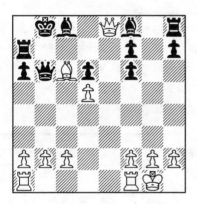

Diagram 3 (W)
Black's king reaches safety

Diagram 4 (B)
A critical divide after 7 Bb5

8 Bxc6 bxc6

It's quite rare for Black not to keep the bishop pair, but we believe that Jobava's 8...Bxc6 9 Nxc6 bxc6 and if 10 e5!?, then 10...dxe5 11 Qf3 e4!, wisely returning the pawn, is a sensible alternative.

9 Qf3 (Diagram 4) 9...Qb6

As once played by Shirov, but Black has two decent alternatives:

a) 9...c5!? 10 e5!? (10 Nde2 Bc6 11 Rd1 Be7 12 0-0 0-0 is rather comfortable for Black) 10...dxe5 11 Nb3 (perhaps more critical is 11 Ndb5 Rb8! 12 0-0-0, but after

12...Qb6 13 Bxf6 Bc6! 14 Rd8+ Rxd8 15 Bxd8 Qxb5! 16 Nxb5 Bxf3 17 gxf3 a6 Black regains his piece with an edge) 11...c4 12 Nd2 Rc8 is unclear as analysed by Lysenko.

b) 9...e5!? has perhaps been under-rated and also seems fine: 10 Nf5 Bxf5 11 Qxf5 Qd7 12 Qf3 Be7 13 0-0-0 0-0 14 Rd3 Ne8 15 Bxe7 Qxe7 16 Rhd1 Rd8 certainly sees Black holding the balance.

10 Nb3

Another move order is 10 0-0-0 Be7 11 e5 dxe5 12 Nb3, transposing.

10...Be7 11 e5 dxe5 12 0-0-0

Now 12...a5?! 13 Rhe1 a4 14 Nd2 h6 15 Nc4 saw Black come under some pressure in L.Yudasin-A.Shirov, Biel 1993; a game which did much to generate some interest in 7 Bb5. However, Black doesn't have to launch his a-pawn and instead 12...Rd8!? 13 Rhe1 c5 14 Qe2 (14 Rxe5 Bc6 15 Rxd8+ Bxd8 16 Qh3 Be7 is fine for Black) 14...h6 15 Bh4 0-0 16 Nd2 Bc6 17 Nc4 Qa6 supplied decent counterplay in L.Milov-Y.Teplitsky, Ajka 1992.

Theoretical Conclusion

As Botvinnik said, 'the development of the bishop to b5 in the Sicilian can work only in exceptional cases' as White must either concede the bishop on c6 or lose time retreating it. Indeed in the Richter-Rauzer 7 Bb5 gives Black a number of decent options, both after 7...Bd7 and with 7...Qb6!?.

White Plays 7 Qd2

1 e4 c5 2 Nf3 Nc6 3 d4 cxd4 4 Nxd4 Nf6 5 Nc3 Nc6 6 Bg5 e6 7 Qd2 (Diagram 5)

Diagram 5 (B)
White prepares to go long

Diagram 6 (W)
Black is solid, but also passive

7...Be7

Black completes the development of kingside with this natural move. It is still quite playable, although nowadays the more flexible 7...a6 is more popular as we will see in the next chapter. There are also two less popular options:

a) After 7...Qb6 8 Nb3 Be7 9 0-0-0 0-0 play transposes to a position which we'll consider in our next section via 7...Be7 8 0-0-0 0-0 9 Nb3 Qb6. More critical must be 8 0-0-0! Qxd4 9 Qxd4 Nxd4 10 Rxd4 which is not level.

 NOTE: Exchanging the queens does not bring Black equality since White has both more space and the better development.

The modern classic G.Kasparov-M.Mchedlishvili, Bled Olympiad 2002, continued 10...a6 (preventing Nb5, but weakening the b6-square) 11 f3 Bd7 12 Na4! Bc6 13 Nb6 Rd8 14 Nc4! Be7 15 Na5 Rc8 16 Rb4! with some advantage for White.

b) 7...h6 was a radical approach prepared by Botvinnik for his 1951 World Championship match: Black is prepared to lose a tempo in return for the bishop pair and a strong centre. However, after 8 Bxf6 gxf6 (8...Qxf6? might look more natural, but Black loses a pawn after 9 Ndb5 Qd8 10 0-0-0) 9 0-0-0 (the most energetic, although Botvinnik had some problems too after 9 Rd1: 9...a6 10 Be2 h5 – wisely preventing Bh5! – 11 0-0 Bd7 12 Nb3 Be7 13 Qe3 and it's hard for Black to gain sufficient counterplay) 9...a6 **(Diagram 6)** 10 f4 reaches a position which is not theoretically too important, but an understanding of such doubled f-pawn positions is important for all Classical Sicilian players. We will return to this unbalanced position in Game 27.

8 0-0-0 0-0 (Diagram 7)

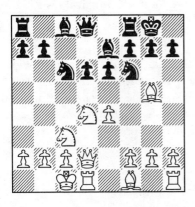

Diagram 7 (W)
White has a number of options

Diagram 8 (W)
A dangerous half-open b-file

Black continues to prioritize his kingside development. Instead 8...Qb6 9 Bxf6!

gxf6 (or 9...Bxf6 10 Nxc6 bxc6 11 Na4 Qb7 12 Qxd6 Be7 and here after 13 Qe5 0-0 14 Bc4 Black hasn't enough compensation according to Motylev) 10 Ndb5! 0-0 11 h4!? is awkward for Black.

TIP: White's h4 is not just a rather useful move in any kingside pawn-storm, but also enables him to swing his king's rook into play with Rh3.

Another option for Black is 8...Nxd4 9 Qxd4 a6 as Kramnik has employed and we will consider this approach in our next chapter via the move order 7...a6 8 0-0-0 Nxd4 9 Qxd4 Be7.

Following 8...0-0 White's two main options are 9 Nb3 and 9 f4, the subject of our next two sections respectively. He can also play in the spirit of the English Attack with 9 f3 and after 9...Bd7 (by no means essential: 9...d5 is a decent equalizer for those who like a simple life and 9...a6 is also possible) 10 h4 play has transposed to Game 32 (see the next chapter). Lesser options are:

a) 9 Be2?! Nxd4 10 Qxd4 Nxe4! wins a pawn in view of 11 Bxe7 Nxc3 12 bxc3 Qxe7 13 Qxd6 Qg5+ 14 Kb1 Qxg2.

b) 9 Kb1 is a better try, although after 9...Nxd4 10 Qxd4 Nxe4! 11 Nxe4 Bxg5 12 Nxg5 Qxg5 13 Qxd6 Bd7! Black hasn't any problems.

c) 9 Bxf6 Bxf6 10 Nxc6 bxc6 11 Qxd6 does win a pawn, but is rather risky. Indeed after 11...Qb6 **(Diagram 8)** 12 Qg3 Rb8 13 b3 Qa5!, White must defend with 14 Na4 Rb4 15 c4 since 14 Qxb8? Be5! 15 Qa8 Bxc3 16 Rd3 Be5 gives a winning attack.

d) 9 Ndb5!? is a better way of targeting d6 and the position after 9...Qa5 10 Bxf6 Bxf6 11 Nxd6 Rd8 12 f4 is complicated and in need of more practical tests.

Theoretical Conclusion

Developing the kingside with 7...Be7 8 0-0-0 0-0 remains quite playable, not least because grabbing the d-pawn does not promise White any advantage. Instead, as we will shortly see, he should prefer 9 Nb3 or 9 f4. On the other hand, Botvinnik's 7...h6 remains rather unfashionable. It might not be so bad, but is generally considered too passive for the taste of the modern-day player.

Illustrative Games

Game 27
□ **Ni Hua** ■ **A.Shabalov**
Qingdao 2002

1 e4 c5 2 Nf3 Nc6 3 d4 cxd4 4 Nxd4 Nf6 5 Nc3 d6 6 Bg5 e6 7 Qd2 h6 8 Bxf6 gxf6 9 0-0-0 a6 10 f4 Bd7

TIP: To gain some counterplay and to prevent any possibility of the awkward Be2-h5, Black should often advance his h-pawn in these doubled f-pawn positions.

That said, here 10...h5 **(Diagram 9)** does not solve all Black's problems. The classic game P.Keres-M.Botvinnik, Moscow 1954, continued 11 Kb1 (this will become necessary at some point; White wants to increase the pressure with f5 and without losing his queen to ...Bh6) 11...Bd7 12 Be2 Qb6 13 Nb3! (correctly keeping the knights on, whereas 13 Rhf1 Qxd4 14 Qxd4 Nxd4 15 Rxd4 Bc6 16 f5 Ke7 should be fine for Black) 13...0-0-0 14 Rhf1 Na5?! (14...Kb8 was probably a better try, although after 15 Rf3! h4 16 Qe1 Rg8 17 Qf1 White remains slightly for preference) 15 Rf3 Nxb3 16 axb3 Kb8 17 Na4 Qa7 18 f5 **(Diagram 10)** 18...Be7 19 fxe6 fxe6 20 Rxf6! Rh7 (20...Bxf6? fails to 21 Qxd6+ Kc8 22 Nb6+ and against 20...b5 Keres had prepared the dangerous 21 Rf7 Be8 22 Rg7! bxa4 23 Qb4+ Ka8 24 e5!) 21 Rg6 b5 22 Nc3 Qc5 23 Na2 Ka7 24 Nb4 and White enjoyed a significant advantage.

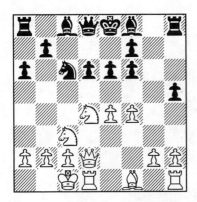

Diagram 9 (W)

Black seizes some useful space

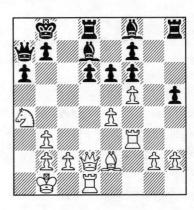

Diagram 10 (B)

Thematically increasing the pressure

11 Kb1 Qb6 12 Nf3

Another good option for White is 12 Nb3 0-0-0 13 Be2 Kb8 (13...h5 transposes back to Keres-Botvinnik) 14 Bh5! Rh7 15 Rhf1 Bc8 16 Qe2 Qc7 (or 16...Be7 17 Nd5! targeting the e7-bishop) 17 Nd4 Nxd4 18 Rxd4 Bg7 19 Rc4 Qe7 20 f5 which saw White achieve his strategic goals in Z.Almasi-B.Damljanovic, Cacak 1996.

12...0-0-0 13 Bc4 Kb8 14 Bb3 Bc8 15 Rhf1 h5 (Diagram 11) 16 g3!

Wisely halting the black h-pawn and thereby challenging Black to find some semblance of counterplay.

16...Qc5 17 Nh4 b5 18 f5 Bh6 19 Qe2 Be3!? 20 fxe6 fxe6 21 Ng6

Black was hoping for 21 Rxf6?! Bd4 22 Rff1 Bxc3 23 bxc3 Qxc3 24 Ng6 Rh6 25 Nf4

Ne5 which would have left him right back in the game.

21...Rhe8 22 e5! (Diagram 12) 22...f5!

Diagram 11 (W)
Can Black gain sufficient counterplay?

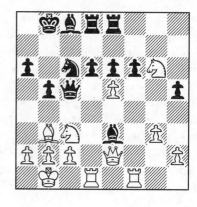

Diagram 12 (B)
Wrecking the black structure

Relatively best, whereas after 22...dxe5 23 Ne4 Rxd1+ 24 Rxd1 Qb6 25 Nxf6 Rd8 26 Qxh5 Black would have found his pawns dropping off, just as they also begin to after 22...fxe5 23 Ne4 Qb6 24 Nxd6.

23 exd6 Bd4 24 Qxh5 a5?!

A much better try was 24...Rxd6 when White only remains slightly better after 25 Ne5 Rf8 26 Nxc6+ Rxc6 27 Ne2.

25 a4! Bxc3 26 bxc3 bxa4 27 Bxa4 (Diagram 13)

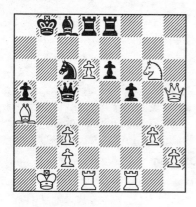

Diagram 13 (B)
Both kings become exposed

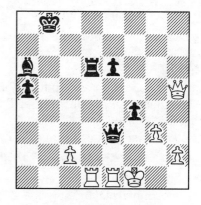

Diagram 14 (W)
White must be careful

27...Rd7

Now 27...Rxd6? fails to 28 Rxd6 Qxd6 29 Rd1 Qc7 30 Ne5 winning serious material.

28 Bxc6?!

Missing his chance: 28 Qf3! Rb7+ 29 Ka2 would have retained some advantage.

28...Qxc6 29 Ne5 Qb5+! 30 Kc1 Qxe5!

As ever Shabalov is quick to seize the initiative and rightly avoids 30...Rxd6? 31 Nc6+! Qxc6 32 Rxd6 Qxd6 33 Qxe8.

31 Qxe8 Qxc3 32 Rfe1 f4! 33 Qh5

Slightly risky. Instead 33 gxf4 would have left Black with nothing more than perpetual with 33...Qa1+ 34 Kd2 Qd4+ 35 Ke2 Qe4+ 36 Kf2 Qxf4+.

33...Qa3+ 34 Kd2 Rxd6+ 35 Ke2 Qe3+ 36 Kf1 Ba6+ (Diagram 14) 37 Rd3!

Accurate defence, whereas 37 Kg2? Rd2+ 38 Kh3 Rxh2+! would have turned this great scrap completely upset down.

37...Bxd3+ 38 cxd3 Qxd3+ 39 Kg2 fxg3 40 hxg3 Qd5+ 41 Qxd5 exd5 42 Ra1 Ra6 43 Rd1 a4 44 Rxd5 a3 45 Rd1 Kb7 46 Kf3 Ra4 47 Ke3 ½-½

The Old Main Line with 9 Nb3

1 e4 c5 2 Nf3 Nc6 3 d4 cxd4 4 Nxd4 Nf6 5 Nc3 d6 6 Bg5 e6 7 Qd2 Be7 8 0-0-0 0-0 9 Nb3 (Diagram 15)

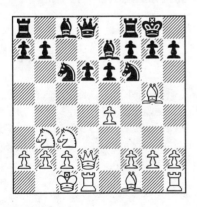

Diagram 15 (B)

Pressurizing the d6-pawn

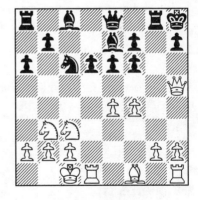

Diagram 16 (W)

Black's king is not so easy to attack

First played by Alekhine in 1936, White avoids the exchange of knights and takes aim at d6.

9...Qb6!

Taking counter aim at f2 is probably Black's best move, although he does have alternatives:

a) The liberating 9...d5 hasn't become popular because after 10 Bxf6 Bxf6 11 exd5 Bxc3 12 Qxc3 exd5 Black lacks any real compensation for the IQP.

b) Including first 9...a5 10 a4 makes 10...d5 a better try since after 11 Bxf6 Bxf6 12 exd5 Bxc3 13 Qxc3 exd5 Black's c6-knight can make good use of the b4-square. Unfortunately for Black, though, 11 Bb5! is much stronger; for example, 11...Nxe4 12 Nxe4 dxe4 13 Qxd8 Bxd8 14 Bxd8 Nxd8 15 Nc5 f5 16 Rd6 left White dominating in M.Tal-M.Sisniega, Taxco 1985.

c) 9...a6 looks a little suspect as it rather ignores White's designs against d6, but it was employed by a young Leko. E.Liss-P.Leko, Budapest 1993, saw 10 Bxf6 gxf6 (10...Bxf6 11 Qxd6 Bxc3 12 bxc3 Qf6 13 Qg3 e5 14 Bc4 is slightly better for White) 11 Qh6 (perhaps 11 h4!? should be preferred: 11...Kh8 12 g4 b5 13 g5 b4 14 Na4 Rg8 15 f4 Rb8 16 Kb1 Bf8 17 Be2 e5 18 f5! gave White serious pressure in N.Short-A.Karpov, 10th matchgame, Linares 1992, and even the superior 12...Rg8 13 g5 fxg5 14 hxg5 Rxg5 15 Bd3 Rg7 16 f4 leaves White with promising compensation) 11...Kh8 12 Qh5 Qe8 13 f4 Rg8 **(Diagram 16)** 14 g4 b5 15 Bd3 Rg7 16 h4 b4 17 Ne2 and now one reasonable option was 17...a5!? 18 g5 a4 19 Nbd4 Nxd4 20 Nxd4 Ra5 21 Bc4 Bd7 when the position remains extremely unbalanced and unclear.

10 f3

 NOTE: This is often a useful multipurpose move; overprotecting e4 and preparing an advance of the g-pawn.

Weaker is 10 f4?! due to 10...Rd8 11 Be2 h6 12 Bxf6 (Black meets 12 Bh4? with the standard trick 12...Nxe4!) 12...Bxf6 13 g4 a5 14 a4 Qb4 and Black's attack is the faster.

Sometimes White prefers to march the h-pawn and after 10 h4 Rd8 11 h5 Black must stop it and prepare counterplay with ...d5: for example, 11...h6 12 Be3 Qc7 13 f4 a6 14 Be2 b5 15 Bf3 d5 16 e5 Nd7 17 Qf2 Rb8 18 g4 (or 18 Bxd5 b4! 19 Bxc6 bxc3 20 Qf3 cxb2+ 21 Kxb2 a5 with an obvious initiative for a pawn) 18...Nb6! 19 Bc5 Bxc5 20 Nxc5 Na4! 21 N5xa4 bxa4 gave Black very real counterplay in J.Nunn-G.Sax, Skelleftea 1989.

10...Rd8 (Diagram 17)

Black immediately defends the pawn on d6 and prepares ...d5, but this is not strictly necessary despite its popularity. After the alternative 10...a6 it's rather risky for White to win a pawn: 11 Bxf6?! Bxf6 12 Qxd6 Rd8 13 Qc5 Rxd1+ 14 Nxd1 Qc7! gives Black promising compensation on the dark squares and with his bishop pair. It's better for White to attack on the kingside, although 11 g4 Qc7 12 Be3 b5

13 g5 Nd7 14 Kb1 b4 15 Ne2 (possibly better is 15 Na4!?, blocking Black's a-pawn) 15...Bb7 16 f4 a5 17 Ng3 (more careful is 17 e5 d5 18 Nbd4) 17...Rfc8 18 Bd3 a4 19 Nc1 Na5!? 20 Qxb4 a3 21 b3 d5! gave Black the initiative for his pawn in M.Tazbir-V.Shishkin, Krakow 2006.

11 Nb5!?

Suddenly the black queen finds itself rather short of space, whereas the alternatives are quite comfortable for the second player:

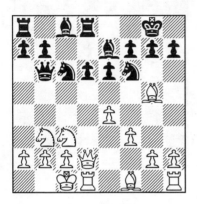

Diagram 17 (W)

Black prepares ...d5

Diagram 18 (W)

The struggle heats up

a) 11 Be3 Qc7 12 Qf2 d5 13 exd5 Nxd5 14 Nxd5 Rxd5 15 Rxd5 exd5 16 g4 Ne5 17 Kb1 (after 17 Bxa7?! Black gains a good game with 17...Nxf3! 18 h3 Ng5) 17...Nc4 18 Bd4 a5 19 Bd3 a4 20 Nc1 Bd7 21 h4 Bb5 saw the activity of Black's pieces compensate for the isolated d5-pawn in E.Ermenkov-V.Epishin, Burgas 1994.

b) 11 Kb1 is a crafty prophylactic move: 11...Qc7!? (wisely avoiding 11...d5?! due to Anand's 12 Bxf6 dxe4? – Black should prefer 12...Bxf6 13 exd5 Bxc3 14 Qxc3 exd5 15 Qc5 and try to defend this unpleasant endgame with an isolated pawn – 13 Bxe7 Rxd2 14 Nxd2 exf3 15 Nc4!) 12 Bf4 a6 13 g4 Ne5 14 g5 Nfd7 15 Qg2 b5 **(Diagram 18)** 16 Bc1 Bb7 17 f4 b4 18 Ne2 Nc4 19 Ng3 d5 was the course of M.Illescas Cordoba-V.Kramnik, 3rd matchgame, Alcobendas 1993, and here Kramnik suggests 20 f5!? Nd6 21 f6 Bf8 22 fxg7 Bxg7 23 Bd3 Ne5 with mutual chances.

11...Rd7 (Diagram 19)

A strange move but there is nothing else, especially since 11...Ne5 12 Be3 Qc6 13 Na5 Qd7 14 Bxa7 leaves White a clear pawn ahead.

12 Qe1

This old idea of Hübner's only became popular in this millennium: White's queen wisely escapes the vis-à-vis with the black rook down the d-file so that he can profitably meet 12...d5? with 13 e5. Previously 12 Be3 Qd8 13 N5d4 was preferred, but Black has now found how to free his game: 13...e5! **(Diagram 20)** 14 Nf5?! (better is 14 Nxc6 bxc6 15 Na5 Rc7!? with a complex game) 14...d5 15 Nxe7+ Qxe7 16 Bc5 Qe6 17 exd5 Rxd5 18 Qe1 b6 19 Bf2 (I.Chirila-V.Shishkin, Bucharest 2006) 19...Rxd1+ 20 Qxd1 Bb7 leaves Black with an easy game.

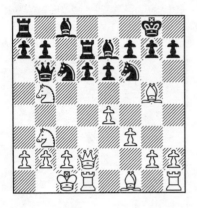

Diagram 19 (W)

Buying Black's queen a square

Diagram 20 (W)

A useful break-out

12...a6

White's knight must now retreat, but he can first include 13 Be3 Qd8 as we'll see in Game 28.

Theoretical Conclusion

The theory of this line continues to develop and remains in something of a state of flux. Nowadays Black usually eschews the slightly too solid 9...a6, which gives White good chances of an advantage, in favour of the fully satisfactory 9...Qb6, after which he combines queenside activity with preparing the ...d5-counter.

Illustrative Games

Game 28
☐ **H.Hamdouchi** ■ **B.Avrukh**
Athens 2005

1 e4 c5 2 Nf3 Nc6 3 d4 cxd4 4 Nxd4 Nf6 5 Nc3 d6 6 Bg5 e6 7 Qd2 Be7 8 0-0-0 0-0 9 Nb3 Qb6 10 f3 Rd8 11 Nb5 Rd7 12 Qe1 a6 13 Be3

A major alternative is 13 N5d4 when Black often plays 13...Rd8, but we also like

13...Nxd4!? 14 Nxd4 Qc7 15 h4 b5 16 g4 Bb7 which is far from clear. Play might continue 17 Bd2 Rc8 18 Bd3?!, but after 18...d5 19 e5 Ne4! (Dembo) Black seizes the advantage with a neat trick.

13...Qd8 14 N5d4 (Diagram 21)

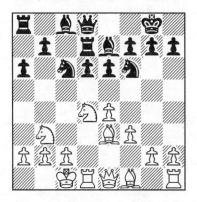
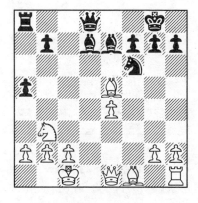

Diagram 21 (B)

Black will look to advance in the centre

Diagram 22 (W)

Black launches a strong attack

14...a5!?

TIP: Using the a-pawn to destabilize a white knight on b3 is an important theme in the Richter-Rauzer. Crucial to its success is whether Black can better exploit the weakened b4-square (after a4 from White) than White can the b5-square.

However, the text is by no means obligatory with a highly tempting alternative being 14...Nxd4 15 Bxd4 e5 16 Bc3 d5! offering a pawn for the initiative. Black is better after 17 exd5 Nxd5 18 Bxe5 Bg5+ since 19 Kb1?? fails to 19...Nc3+, and 17 Bxe5 dxe4 18 Rxd7 Bxd7 19 fxe4 a5! **(Diagram 22)** 20 Kb1 a4 21 Nc1 a3 22 b3 Ng4 23 Bc3 Qc7 retained excellent compensation for the pawn in R.Hübner-J.Piket, Lugano 1989.

15 a4

Prudent; the a-pawn needs halting. Instead 15 Bb5?! a4 16 Nd2 (16 Nxc6? bxc6 17 Bxc6 fails to 17...axb3! 18 Bxa8 bxa2 19 Kd2 Qa5+) 16...Rc7 17 Kb1 Bd7 18 Nxc6 bxc6 19 Bd3 Rb7 once again offers Black promising attacking prospects.

15...e5 16 Nf5 d5! 17 Nxe7+

After this Black's central counterplay compensates for the loss of the bishop pair, but it does too after 17 Qg3 Nh5 18 Qg4 g6 19 exd5 Nf6! 20 Nxe7+ Nxe7 21 Qg5 Nfxd5 22 Bf2 Qc7 23 Bb5 Rd8 (Avrukh).

17...Qxe7 18 Bc5 Qe8 19 exd5 Rxd5 20 Rxd5 Nxd5 (Diagram 23)

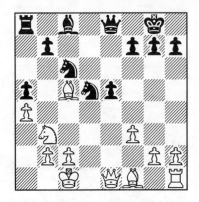

Diagram 23 (W)	Diagram 24 (W)
Black enjoys good central control	Should White play 30 Qd3?

> **NOTE: Black's extra central pawn and strongly-placed d5-knight promise him a good game, especially with White's own knight a little misplaced on b3.**

21 Bb5 Bd7 22 Qd2 Ncb4! 23 Bxb4

Wisely avoiding the offer of a piece: 23 c3?! Bxb5 24 cxb4 Bxa4 25 Qxd5 axb4 would have left White's queen rather overloaded and after 26 Kb1 Rd8 27 Qc4 Rc8 28 Qxb4 Bxb3 29 Qxb3 Rxc5 30 Qxb7 Qd8 Black enjoys some initiative in view of his somewhat safer king.

23...Bxb5 24 Ba3 Bc4 25 Nxa5 Qxa4 26 Nxc4 Qxc4 27 Rd1 Rc8 28 Kb1 Rd8 29 Ka1 Rd7 (Diagram 24) 30 Qa5

White might like to exchange the queens, but 30 Qd3?? had to be avoided on account of the nasty back-rank trick 30...Nb4!.

30...h5 31 b3 Qc6 32 c4 Ne3!

Allowing the position to open up which might favour the bishop, but Avrukh has realized that his ideal attacking team of queen and knight should always be able to force perpetual.

33 Rxd7 Qxd7 34 Qxe5 Nxg2 35 Bb2 f6 36 Qxh5 Ne1 37 Ka2 (Diagram 25) 37...Nd3?!

Overly ambitious play in the time scramble. Instead Black should have preferred 37...Qd2 when White has nothing better than perpetual after 38 Qe8+ Kh7 39 Qe4+ Kh8.

38 Bc3 b6 39 Qg4

Sensibly keeping the queens on, whereas after 39 Qd5+?! Qxd5 40 cxd5 Kf7 41 Ka3 b5 Black might be a pawn down, but his king is much the faster to centralize and his knight rather well placed.

39...Qd6 40 Qc8+ Kf7 41 Qb7+ Kg6 42 Qe4+ Kf7 43 h4 Nc5 (Diagram 26) 44 Qd5+?!

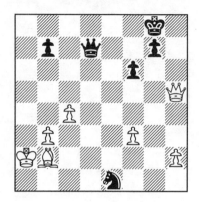

Diagram 25 (B)

Black should force a draw

Diagram 26 (W)

It's far from easy for White

Now Black wins back his pawn with a level ending and instead 44 Qd4 Qc6 45 Qg4 would have retained a few chances for White.

44...Qxd5 45 cxd5 Ke7 46 h5 Nd3 47 Ka3 Nf4 ½-½

The Old Main Line with 9 f4

1 e4 c5 2 Nf3 Nc6 3 d4 cxd4 4 Nxd4 Nf6 5 Nc3 d6 6 Bg5 e6 7 Qd2 Be7 8 0-0-0 0-0 9 f4 (Diagram 27)

With this standard and energetic advance White creates the threat of e4-e5. Indeed 9...a6?! is now rather misguided in view of 10 e5! dxe5 (or 10...Nd5 11 Nxc6 bxc6 12 Ne4 dxe5 13 Bxe7 Qxe7 14 fxe5 and the weakness of d6 gives White an edge) 11 Nxc6 bxc6 12 fxe5 Nd7 13 h4 Rb8 14 Qe3 when White was better and soon whipped up a strong attack in P.Keres-L.Szabo, Budapest 1955. Another strategy which we are not a fan of is to reach a French-type structure: 9...d5 10 e5 Nd7 11 Bxe7 Qxe7 12 Nf3 Nb6 13 Qe1 Bd7 14 Bd3 leaves Black quite passive and a little worse.

9...Nxd4

The modern preference, although a very important alternative is 9...h6!? **(Diagram 28)**:

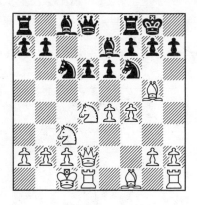

Diagram 27 (B)	**Diagram 28 (W)**
Sharp and critical	Black forces the pace

a) The attempt to win the d6-pawn again doesn't promise White any advantage: 10 Bxf6 Bxf6 11 Nxc6 (or 11 Ndb5 when the typical 11...e5!? gives Black easy play; for example, 12 Nd5 Bg4 13 Be2 Bxe2 14 Qxe2 exf4 15 Nxf6+ Qxf6 16 Nxd6 Rfd8 17 Nxb7 Nd4 leaves him rather active and most certainly not worse) 11...bxc6 12 Qxd6 Qb6 sees Black creating threats down the b-file and with his strong dark-squared bishop. Following 13 Qd3 (13 e5?! tries to blunt the f6-bishop, but after 13...Rd8 14 Qa3 Qe3+ 15 Kb1 Rxd1+ 16 Nxd1 Qxa3 17 bxa3 Be7 Black has a clear edge in the endgame) 13...Rb8 14 b3 Rd8 15 Qf3 Bd4 16 Bc4 Qb4 17 Rd3 Qa3+ 18 Kb1 Qc5 the careful 19 Kc1 led to a repetition of moves in A.Rodriguez-J.Van der Wiel, Biel 1985, but White could easily have gone astray: for instance, 19 Rhd1? loses to 19...Qxc4 20 Ne2 e5! 21 fxe5 c5 22 c3 Bg4!! 23 Qxg4 Rxb3+! with a crushing attack.

b) 10 h4!? **(Diagram 29)** is a critical offer of a piece: 10...Nxd4 11 Qxd4 hxg5 12 hxg5 Ng4 13 Be2 (best; 13 e5?! dxe5 14 Qe4 f5! 15 gxf6 Nxf6 leaves Black slightly better after 16 Rxd8 Nxe4 17 Rxf8+ Bxf8 18 Nxe4 exf4) 13...e5 14 Qg1 exf4 15 Bxg4 **(Diagram 30)** 15...Bxg5 (Black can also explore 15...Bxg4!? 16 Qh2 f5, hoping for 17 Qh7+ Kf7 18 exf5 Bxg5 19 Qg6+ Kg8 20 Qh7+ Kf7 with a repetition, but we suspect that White is a little better after Enders's 17 g6!? Bh4 18 Rd4 fxe4 19 Rxe4) 16 Bxc8 (another rather unclear situation arises after 16 Bf3 Re8 17 Nb5 Re6 18 e5!? Rxe5 19 Nxd6 Qc7) 16...Rxc8 17 Rd3 and now Black must choose between the common 17...Re8 and 17...Bh6!? 18 Kb1 Rc5 19 g3 Rg5 with a highly unclear situation in both cases.

c) 10 Bh4 e5! (probably best; 10...Qb6 was seen in P.Leko-V.Kramnik, Belgrade 1995, but has not found many followers because White got strong attack after 11 Nxc6 bxc6 12 e5! dxe5 13 fxe5 Ne4 14 Nxe4 Bxh4 15 Qf4 Be7 16 Bd3) 11 Nf5! **(Dia-**

gram 31)

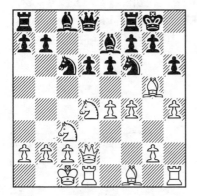

Diagram 29 (B)
Ambitious and dangerous

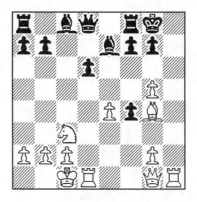

Diagram 30 (B)
A rather complex situation

11...Bxf5 12 exf5 (a highly unbalanced situation has been reached; Black has completed his development, but can easily come under pressure in the centre and on the light squares) 12...exf4 (Black does not get his usual counterplay with 12...Qa5; R.Hübner-J.Timman, Wijk aan Zee 1996, continued 13 Kb1 Rfe8 14 Bc4 Qb4 15 Bb3 Qxf4 16 Qxf4 exf4 17 Rhf1 and White was better) 13 Kb1 d5 14 Bxf6 (recapturing the pawn with 14 Qxf4 allows Black to advance his d-pawn and gain good play after 14...d4 15 Bxf6 Bxf6 16 Ne4 Be5 17 Qf3 Rc8) 14...Bxf6 15 Nxd5 Be5 **(Diagram 32)** reaches a theoretically quite important position and one which we will return to in Game 29.

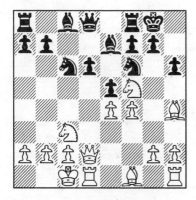

Diagram 31 (B)
The struggle quickly flares up

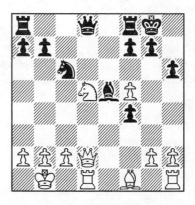

Diagram 32 (W)
Both sides have good trumps

WARNING: In this final variation Black must avoid the typical tactical shot 10...Nxe4?. It is often good, but here 11 Bxe7 Nxd2 12 Bxd8 Nxf1 13 Nxc6 bxc6 14 Be7 Re8 15 Rhxf1 Rxe7 16 Rxd6 leaves White clearly better due to his possession of the d-file and Black's queen-side weaknesses.

Returning to 9...Nxd4:

10 Qxd4 (Diagram 33)

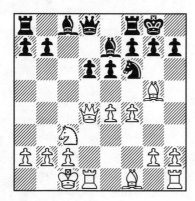

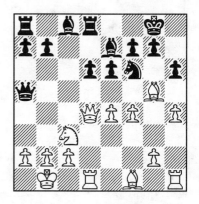

Diagram 33 (B)

White will look for the e5-advance

Diagram 34 (B)

Wisely declining the bishop

10...Qa5

The most principled response. Black's queen eyes White's bishop along the fifth rank, puts some pressure on a2 and prepares ...Rd8. Alternatively:

a) 10...a6 11 Be2 b5 12 Bf3 favours White since e5 is coming.

b) 10...h6 11 Bh4 a6 12 g4! (12 Be2 allows the equalizing 12...Nxe4!) 12...Nxg4 13 Bxe7 Qxe7 14 Qxd6 Qxd6 15 Rxd6 b5 16 Be2 Nf6 17 e5 gave White the advantage in the endgame in S.Dolmatov-I.Smirin, Manila Olympiad 1992.

11 Bc4

White finishes his development and prepares e4-e5. Instead the immediate 11 e5 only reaches an equal endgame after 11...dxe5 12 Qxe5 (weaker is 12 fxe5?! Rd8 13 Qf4 Rxd1+ 14 Kxd1 Nd5 15 Nxd5 Qxd5+ 16 Bd3 Bxg5 17 Qxg5 f5! with an edge for Black) 12...Qxe5 13 fxe5 Nd5 14 Bxe7 Nxe7 15 Bd3 b6 16 Be4 Rb8 17 Rhe1 Bb7 (I.Rausis-E.Miroshnichenko, Abu Dhabi 2006).

A more important alternative is the prophylactic 11 Kb1 h6 12 h4 (once again this ambitious idea; instead 12 Bh4 e5 13 Qd2 Nxe4! 14 Nxe4 Qxd2 15 Rxd2 Bxh4 16 g3 Be7 17 Nxd6 exf4 18 Nxc8 Raxc8 19 gxf4 is clearly fine for Black and here 13 fxe5 dxe5 14 Qf2 Ng4 15 Qe1 Bxh4 16 Qxh4 Be6 supplies good counterplay) and now:

a) 12...Rd8 **(Diagram 34)** 13 Bd3 (or 13 Be2 Bd7 14 Qe3 Rac8 15 Rd3 Bc6 16 Bxf6 Bxf6 17 Bf3 Be8 increasing the pressure against c3 with an unclear position) 13...Bd7 14 e5 dxe5 15 fxe5 Bc6 16 Qf4 (the best try, whereas 16 Qe3 runs into the equalizing 16...Ng4! 17 Qg3 hxg5 18 hxg5 Qxe5 19 Qxg4 Qxg5 20 Bh7+ Kf8 21 Bg6 Kg8) 16...Nh5 17 Qg4 Rxd3! (thematic and of course Black must avoid opening the h-file with 17...hxg5? 18 Qxh5 Rxd3 19 hxg5) 18 cxd3 (perhaps a better try for the advantage is 18 Rxd3!? hxg5 19 Qxh5 g6 20 Qe2 gxh4 21 Rd4) 18...hxg5 19 Qxh5 gxh4 20 Rxh4 Bxh4 21 Qxh4 Qd8! (calm and accurate defence from Black) 22 Qh3 Qg5 23 Rh1 Qh6 24 Qxh6 gxh6 25 Rxh6 Bxg2 26 Rh4 Bc6 27 Ne4 was agreed drawn here in P.Jaracz-E.Miroshnichenko, Bad Wiessee 2005.

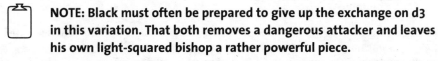

NOTE: Black must often be prepared to give up the exchange on d3 in this variation. That both removes a dangerous attacker and leaves his own light-squared bishop a rather powerful piece.

b) 12...e5!? 13 Qe3 exf4! 14 Bxf4 Be6 is a less forcing and decent alternative; for example, 15 Bd3 (or 15 Bxd6 Bxd6 16 Rxd6 Rac8 17 a3 Rxc3! 18 Qxc3 Qxc3 19 bxc3 Nxe4 with excellent play for the exchange in view of White's shattered structure) 15...Rac8 16 Nd5 Nxd5! 17 exd5 Bxd5 18 Qxe7 Qxa2+ 19 Kc1 Qa1+ 20 Kd2 Qxb2 21 Qxd6 Qc3+ 22 Kc1 Qa1+ forced a draw in I.Kurnosov-G.Guseinov, Kusadasi 2006.

Returning to the critical 11 Bc4 **(Diagram 35)**:

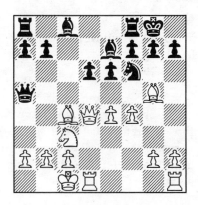

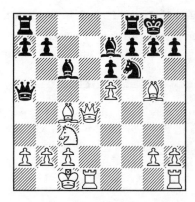

Diagram 35 (B)	**Diagram 36 (W)**
Black must know his theory here	Exploiting the pin along the fifth

11...Bd7

Notably Kotronias has recently employed the aggressive 11...b5!?, opening queenside files. After 12 Bxb5 Rb8 13 e5 a very unclear situation arises following 13...dxe5 14 fxe5 Rxb5 15 exf6 Rb4! 16 Qe3 Bxf6 17 Bxf6 gxf6. Stronger appears to be the solid 13 a4 when the analogous 13...a6 14 e5 dxe5 15 fxe5 Nd5 16 Bxe7 Nxe7 17 Qa7! gives White the advantage, but do expect further developments here!

12 e5

Another plan is to transfer the queen's rook to the kingside, but 12 Rd3 Rad8 13 Rg3 Kh8 14 e5 dxe5 15 fxe5 Bc6 16 Qe3 Ng8 17 Bd3 Qb6! saw Black maintaining the balance in J.Hodgson-V.Kramnik, Belgrade 1993.

12...dxe5 13 fxe5

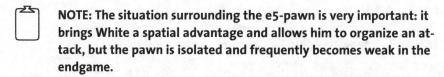

> NOTE: The situation surrounding the e5-pawn is very important: it brings White a spatial advantage and allows him to organize an attack, but the pawn is isolated and frequently becomes weak in the endgame.

After the alternative 13 Qxe5 Black obviously can't swap queens because of losing a piece. Instead he must follow the model game A.Karpov-G.Kamsky, Buenos Aires 1994: 13...Qb6 14 Qe2 (in the case of 14 f5 Black's defence becomes easier after 14...Ng4! 15 Qf4 Bxg5 16 Qxg5 Nf6) 14...Rad8 15 Ne4 Nd5 16 Bxd5 Bxg5 17 Nxg5 exd5 18 Rxd5 Bg4! 19 Qe4 g6 20 Rxd8 Rxd8 21 Qc4 Qf6 22 g3 Qe7 23 Qe4 Qd7 24 Qd3 Qe7 and neither side could make progress.

13...Bc6 (Diagram 36)

Black finishes the development of his key light-squared bishop, creates a retreat square on d7 for the f6-knight and prepares ...Rfd8.

14 Bd2 Nd7 15 Nd5 Qd8 16 Nxe7+ Qxe7 17 Rhe1

Following a number of forced moves we reach one of the most important positions of the Richter-Rauzer. See Game 30 for details.

Theoretical Conclusion

It currently seems that Black has some problems to solve after 9...Nxd4 10 Qxd4 Qa5 11 Bc4. Perhaps the sharp 9...h6!? should thus be preferred. Then 10 h4 appeals to aggressive players, but shouldn't promise any theoretical advantage and 10 Bh4 is somewhat more critical. Whichever line Black prefers one thing is clear: it is essential to be rather well prepared to deal with the dangerous 9 f4.

Illustrative Games

Game 29
□ **V.Tseshkovsky** ■ **J.Piket**
Wijk aan Zee 1989

1 e4 c5 2 Nf3 Nc6 3 d4 cxd4 4 Nxd4 Nf6 5 Nc3 d6 6 Bg5 e6 7 Qd2 Be7 8 0-0-0 0-0 9 f4 h6 10 Bh4 e5 11 Nf5 Bxf5 12 exf5 exf4 13 Kb1 d5 14 Bxf6 Bxf6 15 Nxd5 Be5 16 Bc4

Immediately activating the bishop is probably best. White can also try 16 c3 Rc8 17 f6!?, but after 17...Bxf6 18 Qxf4 Be5 19 Qg4 Qg5 20 Qxg5 hxg5 Black is fine.

 NOTE: Which side gains the upper hand in this variation is usually dependent on who can make better use of their key minor piece: White's dominant d5-knight being balanced by Black's powerful dark-squared bishop.

16...b5 (Diagram 37)

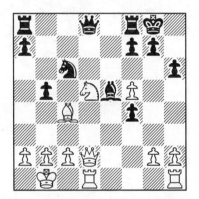

Diagram 37 (W)	**Diagram 38 (W)**
Black wants to attack	Two powerful knights

17 Bxb5

Opening lines for Black like this feels a little suspicious. Of course, allowing Black to advance his pawns after 17 Bb3! also looks quite dangerous for White, but we believe that this approach is actually quite problematic for Black and may even cast doubt on the viability of 9...h6: for example, 17...a5 18 a3 a4 (perhaps 18...b4!? 19 a4 Nd4 should be investigated, but after 20 Rhe1 Nxb3 21 cxb3 Re8 22 f6! gxf6 23 g3! White gains a strong attack) 19 Ba2 b4 20 Nxb4 Qf6 21 Nxc6 Qxc6 22 Bd5 Qb6 23 Qb4 Qc7 24 Bxa8 Rb8 25 Rd4!? Qa7 26 Qxa4 Qxd4 27 Qxd4 Bxd4 28 Rd1 Bxb2 29 Rd7 Bxa3+ 30 Bb7 left White a pawn up after some fascinating complications in B.Vuckovic-J.Todorovic, Vrnjacka Banja 2005.

17...Rb8 18 c4 Nd4 (Diagram 38)

Weaker players might be tempted by 18...a6? 19 Bxc6 Rxb2+, but after 20 Qxb2 Bxb2 21 Kxb2 Qd6 22 Rd3 White has a pretty much decisive material advantage.

WARNING: Try not to overestimate the power of the queen. Here extra White's rook, bishop and knight more than defend his slightly exposed king.

19 f6

White later tried 19 Rhe1, but after 19...f6! (both cementing the strong bishop and preventing f5-f6) 20 Ba4 Nxf5 21 Bb3 Nd4 22 Qd3 a5 Black had sufficient counter-play in A.Grischuk-A.Lugovoi, Moscow 1998.

19...gxf6

Black might want to make 19...Rxb5? work, but after 20 Ne7+ Kh8 21 cxb5 Bxf6 22 Rhe1 (Rajkovic) his compensation for the exchange is badly insufficient.

20 g3 f3 21 Ba4 Qd6 22 Rhe1 Qa3

Another option was 22...Qa6!? and after 23 Bb3 Rxb3 24 axb3 Nxb3 25 Ne7+ Kg7 26 Nf5+ Kg8 White would have had to force perpetual.

23 Re4 Qxa4 24 Rxd4 Rfe8 (Diagram 39)

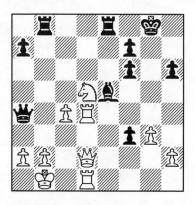
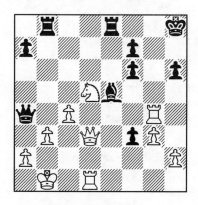

Diagram 39 (W)
White must counterattack, but how?

Diagram 40 (B)
It's Black to play and win!

25 Rg4+?

Tseshkovsky rather loses the plot around here and badly underestimates Black's attack. Instead 25 b3 Bxd4 26 Qxd4 Re2 would have been fine for him since 27 Nxf6+ Kf8 28 Nd7+ forces a draw.

25...Kh7 26 Qd3+?!

Black would have enjoyed some advantage after 26 b4 f5 27 Rh4 Bg7 28 Qc2 Qa3 29 Qb3 Qxb3+ 30 axb3 Re2, but at least this would have kept the game going.

26...Kh8

Missing the even stronger 26...f5! 27 Qxf5+ Kh8 when there is no defence down the b-file and White would have had to resign.

27 b3 (Diagram 40)

The attack is decisive too after 27 b4 Rxb4+! 28 Nxb4 Qxb4+ 29 Qb3 Qa5.

27...Rxb3+! 28 Qxb3 Rb8 29 Qxb8+ Bxb8 30 Nc3 Qb4+ 31 Kc2 Be5

> **NOTE:** Despite what we said earlier, the queen can be a very power-ful piece; it all depends on the position! Just observe here how she, ably supported by the active bishop, completely outclasses White's uncoordinated rooks.

32 Rgd4

Alternatively, 32 Rd8+ Kh7 33 Nd1 f2! 34 Nxf2 Qb2+ winning the knight and the game.

32...f2 33 R4d3 Qxc4 0-1

Brutal play from Piket.

Game 30
□ **V.Malakhov** ■ **R.Scherbakov**
Koszalin 1999

---

1 e4 c5 2 Nf3 Nc6 3 d4 cxd4 4 Nxd4 Nf6 5 Nc3 d6 6 Bg5 e6 7 Qd2 Be7 8 0-0-0 0-0 9 f4 Nxd4 10 Qxd4 Qa5 11 Bc4 Bd7 12 e5 dxe5 13 fxe5 Bc6 14 Bd2 Nd7 15 Nd5 Qd8 16 Nxe7+ Qxe7 17 Rhe1 (Diagram 41)

Diagram 41 (B)

A critical tabiya

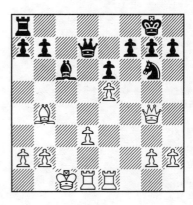

Diagram 42 (W)

There's some positional compensation

17...Rfd8

An important alternative is 17...Nb6, but after 18 Bf1 (worse is 18 Bd3?! due to the thematic 18...Rfd8 19 Qg4 Rxd3! 20 cxd3 Ba4; for example, 21 Bh6 f5 22 exf6 Qxf6 23 Be3 Rc8+ 24 Kb1 Bc2+ 25 Ka1 Bxd1 leaves Black better as pointed out by Wells) 18...Rfd8 19 Qg4 Qc5 20 Qb4! Qf2 21 Qf4 Qc5 22 Bb4 Rxd1+ 23 Rxd1 Qg1 24 c4 Nd7

25 Bd6 White enjoyed the initiative in Z.Efimenko-A.Muir, Hastings 2003/04.

18 Qg4 Nf8 19 Bd3 Rxd3!?

A typical idea, but one which is probably not quite sufficient here. Indeed leading Classical authority, Peter Wells, has tried instead 19...Rd5, but after 20 Be4 (Wells also feels that White is slightly better after 20 Bb4 Qd8 21 Bd6 Ng6 22 Kb1 Qh4 23 Qxh4 Nxh4 24 g3 Nf3 25 Re3! Nxh2 26 c4) 20...Rd7 21 Bb4 Rxd1+ 22 Rxd1 Qc7 23 Bd6 Qb6 24 Bxc6 Qxc6 (or 24...bxc6 25 b3 a5 26 Qd4 with an edge) 25 Qf3! Qxf3 26 gxf3 Ng6 27 Rd4 Rd8 28 c4 a6 29 c5 he had failed to equalize in M.Kobalia-P.Wells, Gibraltar 2006.

20 cxd3 Qd7 21 Bb4 Ng6 (Diagram 42) 22 Rd2

A little defensive and the much more active 22 Bd6! looks like the way to go. Following 22...f5 23 Qe2 Nh8!? 24 Rd2 Nf7 25 Rc2 Re8 (unfortunately for Black 25...Nxd6 26 exd6 Bd5?! fails to simply 27 Qe5) 26 Bc5 Qd5 27 b3 White was at least slightly better in V.Iordachescu-J.Campos Moreno, Linares 2000.

22...Bd5 23 Kb1 Bxa2+! 24 Kxa2 Qa4+ 25 Kb1 a5 26 Qc4

With the a-file set to open White must be careful: 26 Re4? axb4 27 Rxb4 Qa1+ 28 Kc2 would not have been the way to go since Black retains the initiative after 28...Nxe5 29 Qf4 Rc8+ 30 Kb3 Nc6 31 Ra4 Qe1.

26...axb4 27 Re4 (Diagram 43)

Diagram 43 (B)

Black has a perpetual

Diagram 44 (W)

Full compensation for the exchange

27...Ne7!?

Scherbakov wants to win. Instead he could have forced a draw with 27...Qa1+ 28 Kc2 Nxe5! 29 Rxe5 Qa4+ 30 Kb1 Qa1+.

28 Qxb4 Qa1+ 29 Kc2 Nd5 30 Qxb7 h6 31 Rd1 Qa5 32 Rc1 Ra7 33 Qc8+

The strength of the d5-knight would have been apparent even after an exchange of queens: 33 Qb8+ Kh7 34 Kd1 Qa6 35 Qb3 Rb7 36 Qa3 Qb6 37 d4 and now Black can go in for 37...Qxb2 38 Qxb2 Rxb2 since his knight is so well placed and fully the equal of White's extra rook.

33...Kh7 34 Kd1 Qb5 35 Qc2 Rb7 36 Ke2 Qxb2 37 Qxb2 Rxb2+ 38 Kf3 Rd2 (Diagram 44) 39 d4 g5

Just as in our last note, White finds himself an exchange ahead in the endgame but is unable to make any progress at all due to his inflexible structure and lack of a decent pawn break.

40 h4 Kg6 41 hxg5 hxg5 42 Rc4

Another try was 42 g4, but after 42...f5! 43 exf6 Nxf6 44 Rxe6 Rxd4 45 Rf1 Rf4+ 46 Ke2 Rxf1 47 Kxf1 Kf7 the final white pawn falls with a complete draw.

42...Rd3+ 43 Kf2 Kf5 44 Re1 g4 45 Kg1 g3 46 Rf1+ Ke4 47 Rcc1 ½-½

Chapter Eight

The Modern 7...a6

- Introduction
- Black Exchanges on d4
- Black Plays 8...Bd7
- Black Plays 8...h6

Introduction

1 e4 c5 2 Nf3 Nc6 3 d4 cxd4 4 Nxd4 Nf6 5 Nc3 Nc6 6 Bg5 e6 7 Qd2 a6 (Diagram 1)

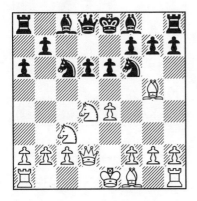 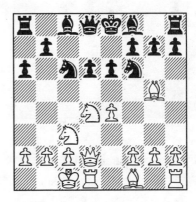

Diagram 1 (W)

Black takes control of b5

Diagram 2 (B)

A major divide

This tricky advance can nowadays be considered the main line of the Richter-Rauzer. Not only does this idea of Tartakower's eliminate any notion of Ndb5, but it also prepares an early ...b5.

8 0-0-0

By far White's main move, but in the last round of the 2006 Turin Olympiad Morozevich tried the questionable 8 Nxc6 bxc6 9 0-0-0 against Avrukh. We should note that this is not the same as the popular line 8 0-0-0 h6 9 Nxc6 bxc6 10 Bf4 which we will investigate below, and after 9...d5 10 e5 h6 11 Bh4 g5 12 Bg3 (Black seizes the initiative after 12 exf6?! Gxh4 13 Qd4 Rb8 14 Qxh4 Bd6) 12...Nd7 13 h4 g4 Avrukh had good counterplay.

Returning to 8 0-0-0 **(Diagram 2)** and here Black has a fairly wide choice:

a) To exchange knights and then develop with 9...Be7.

b) More popular is to continue Black's queenside development with 8...Bd7.

c) 8...h6 sees Black first opt to drive White's active bishop back from g5.

Black Exchanges on d4

1 e4 c5 2 Nf3 Nc6 3 d4 cxd4 4 Nxd4 Nf6 5 Nc3 Nc6 6 Bg5 e6 7 Qd2 a6 8 0-0-0 Nxd4 9 Qxd4 Be7 (Diagram 3)

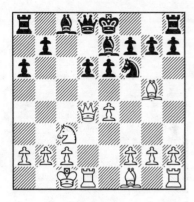

Diagram 3 (W)

Black frees his position

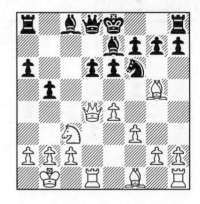

Diagram 4 (B)

White intends to pawn-storm

With the exchange of knights Black both opens the c-file and prepares a quick ...b5. Early queenside counterplay is most certainly the order of the day. However, the exchange has allowed White's queen to take up a strong central role and it is by no means uncommon in this variation for the situation in the centre to quickly become rather critical.

 NOTE: Black exchanges on d4 before playing ...Be7 because 8...Be7 9 Nb3! is a little awkward.

10 f4

White prepares to attack with either a rapid e5- or f5-advance. He can also build up more slowly and in the manner of the English Attack with 10 f3 and after 10...b5 11 Kb1 **(Diagram 4)** Black must decide what to do with his king:

a) 11...0-0 12 h4 Bb7 (as White has a strong central grip this doesn't seem sufficient and we prefer the more active 12...Qa5!? 13 g4 b4 14 Ne2 e5!; for example, 15 Qd2 Be6 16 Nc1 Rfc8!? 17 Bxf6 Bxf6 18 g5 Be7 19 Bh3 Rc7 leads to an unclear situation and one not unsatisfactory for Black) 13 Qd2 Qc7 14 Ne2! Rac8 15 Nd4 saw White making good use of his central control to gain an edge in V.Bologan-Ye Jiang-chuan, Beijing 2006. Note that here Black might like to counter in the centre with 15...d5?!, but after 16 e5! he must accept a grim version of the French since 16...Qxe5? fails to 17 Bf4 Qh5 18 g4.

b) Delaying castling with 11...Bb7 12 h4 Qc7!? 13 Qd2 Rc8 **(Diagram 5)** looks more to the point and after 14 Bd3 h6 15 Be3 (or 15 Bf4 b4 16 Ne2 e5 17 Be3 h5! with good counterplay according to Acs; Black's last is especially noteworthy, only holding up g4 once White has retreated his bishop and thereby prepared g4-g5) 15...b4 16 Na4 (this time 16 Ne2 d5! 17 e5 can be met by the powerful 17...Ne4! 18

fxe4 dxe4 19 Bb6 Qxb6 20 Bxe4 0-0, gaining the advantage) 16...d5! 17 Nb6 Rd8 18 e5 Ne4! 19 fxe4 dxe4 20 Nc4 exd3 21 cxd3 Qc6 22 Rhg1 Qb5 left Black with the bishop pair and an edge in G.Sax-P.Acs, Heviz 2003.

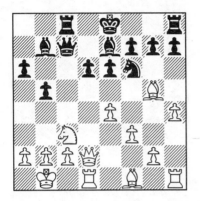

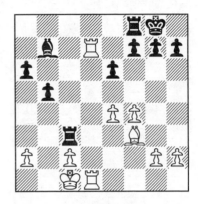

Diagram 5 (W)	**Diagram 6 (B)**
Pressure down the c-file	White has the better rooks

> **NOTE: As we've just seen, White's problem in the Richter-Rauzer whenever he opts for a kingside pawn-storm is that he must lose a tempo moving his g5-bishop out of the way of the g-pawn.**

Returning to 10 f4:

10...b5

Black wastes no time in advancing on the queenside and it is a little strange to us at least that this very interesting position wasn't really discussed in tournament practice until the mid-nineties.

11 Bxf6

This forces Black to recapture with his g-pawn, but also critical is 11 Be2!? Bb7 12 Bf3 Rc8 and only now 13 Bxf6 when Black must decide how best to recapture:

a) 13...Bxf6 14 Qxd6 Qxd6 15 Rxd6 Bxc3 16 bxc3 (after 16 Rb6!? Yermolinsky recommends 16...Bxb2+ 17 Kxb2 Rc7 18 e5 Bc8 19 Rd1 Ke7 when Black should equalize) 16...Rxc3 17 Rhd1 0-0 18 Rd7 **(Diagram 6)** gave White an edge in V.Malakhov-P.Blehm, Cappelle la Grande 2000, although Black should now have gained some counterplay with 18...Ba8 19 R1d4 f5!?.

> **NOTE: This type of endgame arises quite often in the Richter-Rauzer. At first glance Black seems to be fine due to his superior structure, but in reality White's possession of the d-file and slightly better development usually gives him the upper hand.**

b) 13...gxf6!? 14 f5 Qa5 15 fxe6 fxe6 16 Kb1 Rc4 17 Qe3 Qc7 18 Rhe1 Qc5 19 Qh6 was A.Motylev-R.Wojtaszek, Warsaw 2005, and now 19...Qg5!? 20 Qh3 Qe5 21 Bh5+ Kf8 would have remained rather unclear.

11...gxf6 (Diagram 7)

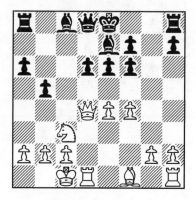

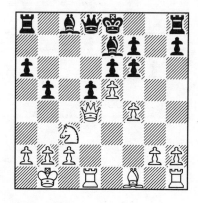

Diagram 7 (W)	Diagram 8 (B)
An essential recapture on f6	Kb1 is a typical prophylactic ploy

 WARNING: This isn't a dynamic choice, but rather an essential one. Instead 11...Bxf6? 12 e5! dxe5 13 Qc5 (another attractive and powerful continuation is 13 Qe4!? Bd7 14 Rxd7! Kxd7 15 Bxb5+!) 13...Bd7 14 Nxb5! is rather strong in view of 14...axb5 15 Rxd7!.

12 e5!?

The most direct and aggressive attempt to exploit White's lead in development. Also quite promising is the more positional 12 f5; for example, 12...Qc7 (more enterprising is 12...Qa5!? after which 13 Kb1 b4 14 Ne2 e5 15 Qd3 Bb7 16 Ng3 Rc8 17 Be2 Qc5 18 Rc1 Bf8! 19 c3 Bh6 gave Black decent counterplay in B.Jobava-K.Supatashvili, Tbilisi 2001, but White probably does better here with 16 Nc1!? and Nb3) 13 Be2 Qc5 14 fxe6 fxe6 (or 14...Bxe6 15 Nd5 and it is obvious that White is better) 15 Qxc5 dxc5 16 Bh5+ Kf8 17 e5! f5 18 g4! gave White a strong initiative despite the exchange of queens in A.Grischuk-A.Grosar, Batumi 1999.

12...d5

Black must keep the position closed. Otherwise he runs into trouble down either the d-file or the f-file, such as after 12...dxe5? 13 Qe4! Bd7 14 Rxd7! Kxd7 15 Bxb5+!.

13 Kb1 (Diagram 8)

The position is quite unclear, although it is clear that White has the safer king. We will return to it in Game 31.

Theoretical Conclusion

The exchange of knights is not so common these days, probably because many black players dislike the lack of a safe home for their king after 10 f4. Instead the English Attack approach is less of a challenge, especially if Black delays castling.

Illustrative Games

Game 31
☐ **V.Anand** ■ **V.Kramnik**
Wijk aan Zee 2000

1 e4 c5 2 Nf3 Nc6 3 d4 cxd4 4 Nxd4 Nf6 5 Nc3 d6 6 Bg5 e6 7 Qd2 a6 8 0-0-0 Nxd4 9 Qxd4 Be7 10 f4 b5 11 Bxf6 gxf6 12 e5 d5 13 Kb1 Bb7

Another option is to keep the light-squared bishop in touch with e6, as Black did in A.Volokitin-D.Shengelia, Batumi 2003: 13...Bd7!? 14 f5 fxe5 (but not 14...0-0? due to 15 fxe6 fxe6 16 Nxd5!) 15 Qxe5 Bf6 **(Diagram 9)** 16 Qe3 0-0 17 Qh3 b4 with good counterplay, not least due to the unopposed dark-squared bishop.

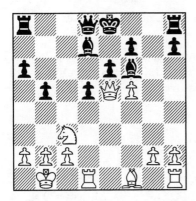

Diagram 9 (W)

A useful dark-squared bishop

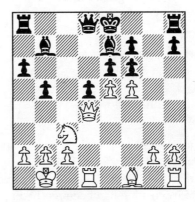

Diagram 10 (B)

Blowing open the centre

14 f5! (Diagram 10)

The sharpest and most challenging continuation. A more positional option is 14 Ne2 Rc8 15 Qe3, but after 15...fxe5 16 fxe5 Bc5 17 Qg3 Qc7 18 c3 b4 Black has sufficient counterplay.

14...fxe5 15 Qxe5 Bf6 16 Qg3 Qe7!

Wisely keeping e6 covered and preparing to go long. Instead 16...Qb8 17 Qh3 b4

149

18 Na4 Bc6 19 Nc5 Qb6 20 Nd3 would have only served to leave White in control of the position.

17 fxe6 fxe6 18 Be2 h5

A useful positional move, but Black can also prefer 18...0-0-0!? and if 19 Bg4 then 19...h5 **(Diagram 11)**.

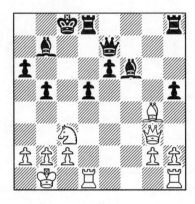

Diagram 11 (W)	Diagram 12 (W)
Both sides have their trumps	It's not so easy to attack e6

This appears risky since White has some pressure against e6 following 20 Bh3, as was played in G.Kasparov-V.Ivanchuk, Frankfurt (rapid) 1998, but after 20...Rhg8! 21 Qe3 Kb8 22 Qxe6 Qxe6 23 Bxe6 Rg5! 24 Rhf1 Bxc3 25 bxc3 Rxg2 (Karolyi) the game simplifies down to a draw.

19 Bf3

A sharper option is 19 a4!? and after 19...h4 20 Qg6+ Qf7 21 Qd3 (or 21 Qxf7+ Kxf7 22 axb5 Bxc3 23 bxc3 axb5 24 Bxb5 Rhb8 25 Kc1 e5 with good compensation, as analysed by Gelashvili) 21...bxa4 22 Bg4 Bc8 23 Rhe1 0-0 24 Nxa4 Rb8 25 b3 a rather complex position had been reached in P.Smirnov-D.Shengelia, Moscow 2004.

19...0-0-0 (Diagram 12) 20 h4?!

Trying to fix h5 as a weakness, but now Black gets to dangerously advance his central pawns. Thus White should have tried to keep them in check with 20 Qh3 Kb8 21 Rhe1, not that this would have brought him any advantage after 21...Bc8; for example, 22 Nxd5!? Rxd5 23 Rxd5 exd5 24 Rxe7 Bxh3 25 Rf7 Bxg2 26 Rxf6 Bxf3 27 Rxf3 fizzles out to a level rook ending.

> **WARNING: Always beware pursuing small positional gains. Sometimes one can, but do first make sure that doing so doesn't allow the opponent to strike back on another part of the board.**

20...b4! 21 Ne2

Wisely avoiding 21 Na4? Bc6 22 Nb6+? Kb7 23 Qf2 Qc7 when the knight would have been trapped.

21...e5 22 Nc1 Kb8 23 Nb3 Qc7 (Diagram 13)

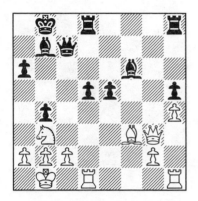

Diagram 13 (W)

The f6-bishop is loose

Diagram 14 (B)

White regains the exchange

Kramnik wants to prevent Na5, but perhaps there was no need to and after 23...Ka8!? 24 Na5 e4 25 Nxb7 Kxb7 26 Be2 Rhg8 Black would have been slightly better due to his superior activity and strong centre.

24 Bxh5! Rxh5

Now the game begins to fizzle out. If Black wanted to keep things going he might have given up his kingside with 24...a5!? and after 25 Bg6 a4 26 Nd2 a3 27 bxa3 bxa3 28 h5 Rd6 29 Qxa3 Ra6 Black's attacking chances fully compensate for the pawns.

25 Qg6 Rxh4 26 Qxf6 Rf4 27 Qg6 d4 28 Rh7 Be4

This just leads to further exchanges, but after 28...Rg4 29 Qh6 Qd6 White would have had no problems making a draw with 30 Qxd6+ Rxd6 31 Nc5 Bc8 32 Re7.

29 Qxe4!

Neat.

29...Rxe4 30 Rxc7 Kxc7 31 Nc5 (Diagram 14) 31...Re3 32 Ne6+ Kd7 33 Nxd8 Kxd8 34 Kc1 Ke7 35 Rd3

Forcing the draw, whereas 35 Kd2? Rg3 36 Rg1 Ke6 would have left White rather passive and suffering.

35...Re2 36 Rd2 Re1+ 37 Rd1 Re2 38 Rd2 Re4 39 Rd3 Ke6 40 c3 ½-½

Black Plays 8...Bd7

1 e4 c5 2 Nf3 Nc6 3 d4 cxd4 4 Nxd4 Nf6 5 Nc3 Nc6 6 Bg5 e6 7 Qd2 a6 8 0-0-0 Bd7 (Diagram 15)

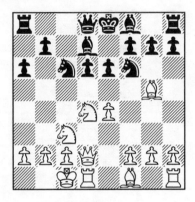

Diagram 15 (W)	**Diagram 16 (B)**
Preparing queenside counterplay	Can Black capture on e4?

Now that the c6-knight is defended Black is ready to advance with ...b5.

9 f4

White's usual response, but he does have alternatives:

a) 9 Nxc6 Bxc6 10 Qe1 hopes to generate some pressure down the d-file, but Black can easily sidestep it with 10...Qa5 and after 11 f4 Be7 12 Bh4 Qc7! (wisely covering the e5-square; an immediate 12...0-0? would have run into the powerful 13 e5) 13 Bd3 b5 14 Kb1 0-0 15 e5 dxe5 16 fxe5 Nd5 Black was fine in V.Belikov-V.Baklan, Sochi 2006.

 WARNING: Whenever White plays f4 in the Richter-Rauzer, Black must always be alert to the e5-advance and its ramifications. Sometimes Black is happy to encourage e4-e5 followed by an opening of the centre, but it's not unknown for the advance to leave him in serious difficulties should he have handled the opening in a careless manner.

b) 9 Be2 h6 10 Bh4 **(Diagram 16)** 10...Rc8! (and not the immediate 10...Nxe4? because after 11 Bxd8 Nxd2 12 Bb6 Nxd4 13 Bxd4 the d2-knight is trapped; 10...Rc8 prepares a retreat for it on c4) 11 f4 Nxe4!? 12 Nxe4 Qxh4 13 Nf3 Qe7 14 Nxd6+ Qxd6 15 Qxd6 Bxd6 16 Rxd6 Ke7 17 Rhd1 Be8 was about equal in A.Delchev-Z.Kozul, Pula 1999.

c) A more popular alternative is 9 f3, both strengthening e4 and preparing to advance the g-pawn. We'll see this typical strategy in action in Game 32.

9...b5

Consistent, but Black has two important alternatives:

a) 9...Be7 became popular after the famous Fischer-Spassky match: 10 Nf3 (the main line, but in the 20th game the American preferred 10 Be2; against this Black should seriously consider a strong piece sacrifice: 10...0-0 11 Nf3 Qa5! after which both 12 e5 dxe5 13 Bxf6 Bxf6 14 Qxd7 exf4 15 Qd2 Nb4 and 13 fxe5 Nxe5 14 Nxe5 Qxe5 15 Bxf6 Bxf6 16 Qxd7 Rad8 give Black excellent play) 10...b5 **(Diagram 17)** reaches another theoretically important divide:

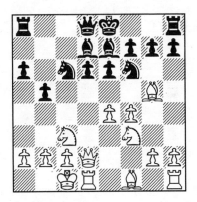

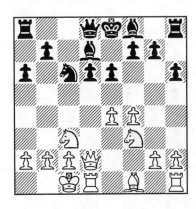

Diagram 17 (W)

Nf3 prepares both e4-e5 and Bxf6

Diagram 18 (W)

Black has the long-term trumps

a1) 11 e5 b4 12 exf6 bxc3 13 Qxc3 gxf6 14 Bh4 (and not 14 Rxd6? Bxd6 15 Bxf6 due to 15...Bb4) 14...d5 is a forcing line leading to a complex and roughly balanced situation; for example, 15 Kb1 Rc8 16 Nd4 Qb6 17 Nxc6 Qxc6 18 Qd2 Rb8 19 c4! dxc4 20 Bxc4 Bc8 21 Rc1 Bb7 is about equal, as analysed by Wells.

a2) 11 Bxf6 gxf6 12 Bd3 (12 Kb1!? Qb6 13 f5 0-0-0 14 g3 Kb8 15 fxe6 fxe6 16 Bh3 Bc8 17 Qe1 Rhe8 18 Ne2! gave White a small edge in S.Dolmatov-M.Bluvshtein, Moscow 2004) 12...Qa5 13 Kb1 b4 14 Ne2 Qc5 15 f5 a5 16 Nf4 a4 17 Rc1! Rb8 18 c3 b3 (after 18...a3 White seizes the initiative with 19 b3 Ne5 20 Nxe5 fxe5 21 Nh5) 19 a3 Ne5 was R.Fischer-B.Spassky, World Championship (Game 18), Reykjavik 1972, and now 20 Nd4!? Nxd3 21 fxe6 fxe6 22 Qxd3, with the point 22...e5? 23 Nfe6 Qc8 24 Ng7+ Kf7 25 Ndf5, would have given White the edge according to Keres.

> **TIP: Whenever White doubles Black's pawns on f6 he should look to attack Black's centre with f4-f5, pressurizing e6 and facilitating Ne2-f4.**

b) The uncompromising 9...h6 leads to a further split:

b1) 10 Bxf6 Qxf6 11 Nf3 leaves White ahead in development and threatening 12 e5, but after 11...Qd8! **(Diagram 18)** Black is very solid and has the useful long-term advantage of the bishop pair. Thus in A.Morozevich-A.Timofeev, Sochi 2006, White tried 12 Kb1 Be7 13 e5!? and now Black should probably keep the position closed with 13...d5!? 14 f5 Qc7 15 Qe3 0-0-0.

b2) More challenging is 10 Bh4!, since both 10...g5!? (a typical Sicilian freeing break) 11 fxg5 Ng4 12 Be2! (see Game 33) and 10...Nxe4 11 Qe1! (a powerful sacrifice, whereas 11 Nxe4 Qxh4 12 Nf3 Qe7 13 Nxd6+ Qxd6 14 Qxd6 Bxd6 15 Rxd6 Ke7 lets Black equalize) 11...Nf6 12 Nf5 **(Diagram 19)** currently seem to favour White; for example, after the latter 12...Qa5 (or 12...Qc7 13 Bxf6 gxf6 14 Nd5 Qd8 15 Qe3 which is very unpleasant for Black) 13 Nxd6+ Bxd6 14 Rxd6 Qc7 15 Rd2 0-0-0 16 Bxf6 gxf6 17 Qh4! f5 18 Be2 Be8 19 Rhd1 Rxd2 20 Rxd2 Qe7 21 Qf2 retained the advantage in M.Roiz-D.Tyomkin, Israel 2005.

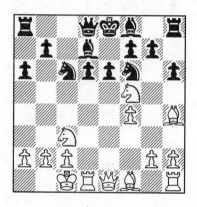

Diagram 19 (B)

White has heavy pressure

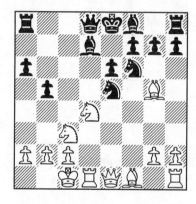

Diagram 20 (B)

White hasn't quite enough

Returning to 9...b5:

10 Bxf6

Once again White decides to damage Black's structure. He might try and blow open the centre with Vitolinsh's 10 e5?!, but this is probably too optimistic: for example, 10...dxe5 11 fxe5 Nxe5 12 Qe1 **(Diagram 20)** 12...h6!? 13 Bh4 (13 Qxe5 hxg5 14 Qxg5 regains the pawn, but after 14...b4 15 Nce2 Rh5 16 Qe3 Qa5 Black's pieces are clearly the more active) 13...Ng6 14 Bxf6 Qxf6 15 Bd3 Bc5 16 Nd5!? Qg5+ 17 Kb1 0-0 18 Nc7 was a rare recent example, T.Radjabov-Z.Kozul, Warsaw 2005, and here Radjabov recommends 18...Rac8! when Black is slightly for preference in the complex situation arising after 19 Ncxe6!? fxe6 20 Nxe6 Qf6! 21 Nxf8 Nxf8.

10...gxf6

WARNING: 10...Qxf6 leaves the d7-bishop unprotected and 11 e5! dxe5 12 Ndb5 Qd8 13 Nd6+ Bxd6 14 Qxd6 gives White a clear advantage.

11 Kb1 (Diagram 21)

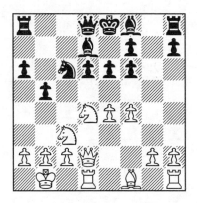

Diagram 21 (B)	Diagram 22 (W)
Tucking the king away	A fashionable choice

A useful prophylactic move, preventing any problems with ...Bh6(+). Indeed after the immediate 11 f5!? Black's dark-squared bishop comes to the fore with 11...Nxd4 12 Qxd4 Bh6+ 13 Kb1 Bf4, although after 14 fxe6 fxe6 15 Ne2 Be5 16 Qf2!? Bc6 17 Nf4 Qe7 18 Bd3 Rg8 19 g3 White still retained a small pull in M.Al-Modiahki-T.Bakre, Gibraltar 2006. Another potentially under-rated option is 11 Nxc6 Bxc6 12 Qe1!?; for example, 12...b4 (and not 12...Qb6? 13 Nd5!) 13 Nd5 a5 14 Bd3 Bg7 15 f5 Bxd5 16 exd5 e5 17 Bb5+ Ke7 18 Bc6 Ra6 19 Rd4 left one of the leading 8...Bd7 experts somewhat worse in M.Palac-Z.Kozul, Vinkovci 1989.

11...Qb6

The usual choice of leading Classical exponent, Zdenko Kozul, although even he has recently been experimenting with 11...b4!? 12 Nce2 Qb6 **(Diagram 22)**, preventing any possibility of a Nd5 sacrifice. S.Erenburg-Z.Kozul, Kusadasi 2006, continued 13 Nxc6 (13 f5 e5 14 Nxc6 Bxc6 transposes, although here Black can also consider Atalik's 13...Nxd4!? 14 Nxd4 e5) 13...Bxc6 14 f5 e5 15 Ng3 Qc5 16 Bd3 (Black also gains decent counterplay after 16 Nh5 Ke7 17 Bd3 Rg8 18 Rhg1 a5 19 g4 a4 20 h4 a3! 21 g5 fxg5 22 hxg5 axb2) 16...Ke7! 17 Bc4!? h5 (but not 17...Qxc4? due to 18 Qxd6+ Ke8 19 Qxf6 Rg8 20 Qxe5+ Be7 21 f6) 18 Bd5 Rc8 19 Bxc6 Rxc6 20 Rhe1 Bh6 21 Qd3 h4 22 Nf1 Rhc8 with thematic counterplay.

TIP: After the fashionable 11...b4 Black's king must usually stay in the centre, but it is actually fairly safe on e7 from where it both defends f6 and connects the rooks.

12 Nxc6

White can also maintain a knight on d4 with 12 Nce2 and after 12...h5 13 g3 Rc8 14 Bg2 we quite like Hillarp Persson's 14...b4!?; for example, 15 Rhf1 a5 16 Nxc6 Bxc6 17 Nd4 Bd7 18 e5!? (J.Timman-T.Hillarp Persson, Malmö 2006) 18...fxe5! 19 fxe5 dxe5 20 Nf3 Ba4!? 21 b3 Bh6 22 Qe2 Bb5 23 Qxe5 0-0 remains sharp and unclear.

12...Bxc6 13 Qe1 (Diagram 23)

Diagram 23 (B)

White prepares Nd5

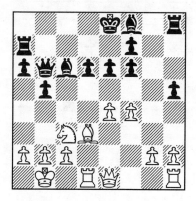

Diagram 24 (W)

e6 and f6 will be pressurized

An important alternative is Robert Byrne's 13 f5!? when 13...b4 14 Ne2 e5! transposes back to Erenburg-Kozul (see the note to Black's 11th move). Black can also consider 13...h5!? and 14 fxe6 fxe6 15 Qf4 (or 15 Bd3 b4 16 Ne2 Bh6 17 Qe1 Ke7 when Black's king again feels quite comfortable in the centre)15...Qc5!? 16 Qxf6 Rh6 17 Qd4 Qxd4 18 Rxd4 Ke7 19 e5!? dxe5 20 Rh4 Bg7 again gave the man himself quite a decent position in D.Svetushkin-Z.Kozul, Kusadasi 2006

13...Ra7!?

A popular continuation, ruling out 14 Nd5? because of 14...exd5 15 exd5 Re7. Instead 13...0-0-0 14 Bd3 b4 15 Ne2! d5 16 e5 f5 17 Nd4 gives White a French-like edge, but Acs's 13...Be7 14 f5 Qc5 15 Bd3 b4 16 Ne2 a5 is a possible alternative.

14 Bd3 h5 (Diagram 24)

Black prevents White's queen from invading his position, but this might not be enough to fully equalize. Indeed in D.Navara-Z.Kozul, Turin Olympiad 2006, 15 Qh4 Bg7 16 Rhe1 Kf8 17 f5 b4 18 Ne2 e5 19 Ng3 Qf2 20 Rf1 saw White gain the upper hand.

Theoretical Conclusion

Currently 8...Bd7 is quite a popular way of countering the Richter-Rauzer. After the critical 9 f4 both 9...Be7 and 9...h6, while far from exhausted, appear to give White good chances of gaining an edge. Thus Black nowadays generally prefers 9...b5 after which a rather complex situation occurs: Black must handle the early middlegame quite carefully, but if he emerges unscathed he has a good chance of gaining the initiative. Above all one should keep an eye on Kozul's games in this variation!

Illustrative Games

Game 32
□ **D.Neelotpal** ■ **A.Timofeev**
Abu Dhabi 2004

1 e4 c5 2 Nf3 Nc6 3 d4 cxd4 4 Nxd4 Nf6 5 Nc3 d6 6 Bg5 e6 7 Qd2 a6 8 0-0-0 Bd7 9 f3 Be7

This can also be delayed and 9...Rc8!? is a reasonable alternative; for example, 10 Nxc6 Bxc6 11 Kb1 Be7 12 Bd3 Qc7 13 Ne2 0-0 14 g4 d5! was about equal in O.Korneev-Z.Kozul, Nova Gorica 2006.

10 h4 h6 11 Be3 h5!? (Diagram 25)

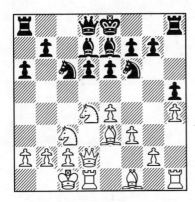

Diagram 25 (W)
Prophylaxis against g2-g4

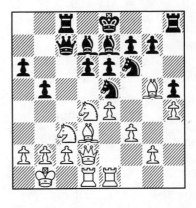

Diagram 26 (W)
Black builds on the queenside

Black borrows an idea from certain English Attack lines of the Najdorf to hold up White's ideal g4-advance.

12 Kb1

White might also return his bishop with 12 Bg5!? and after 12...Ne5 13 f4 Neg4 14 Qe1 Qc7 15 Rh3 b5 16 a3 0-0 both sides had their chances in R.Kasimdzhanov-K.Sasikiran, Vlissingen 2004.

12...Qc7 13 Bd3 Ne5 14 Bg5 b5 15 Rhe1 Rc8 (Diagram 26)

Black can be fairly happy with the outcome of the opening. He is well massed on the queenside and for the time being White lacks active counterplay, although that will come with his f- and g-pawns.

16 a3 Qb6 17 Bf1 0-0 18 f4 Nc4 19 Bxc4 Rxc4

It was also tempting to open the b-file and after 19...bxc4!? 20 Ka1 Rb8 21 Rb1 Bd8 22 f5 Ng4 the situation remains rather unclear.

20 g4!? a5!?

Timofeev has no desire to open kingside lines, even at the gain of a pawn, and so sticks to his guns on the queenside.

21 e5 b4 (Diagram 27)

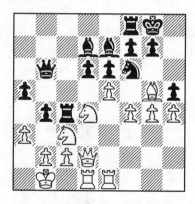

Diagram 27 (W)

The struggle sharpens

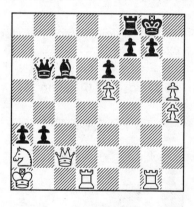

Diagram 28 (W)

Black enjoys a strong attack

22 Na2?!

A little risky. More challenging would have been 22 axb4 axb4 23 Na4!? when, for example, 23...Bxa4 24 exf6 gxf6 25 b3 Rxd4 26 Qxd4 Qxd4 27 Rxd4 Bc6 28 Bh6 Rb8 leads to a rather unclear ending.

22...bxa3 23 b3 dxe5 24 fxe5 Nd5 25 Bxe7 Nxe7 26 gxh5 a4 27 Ka1 Nc6 28 Nxc6 Bxc6 29 Rg1 Rxc2!?

Timofeev must have been tempted by 29...Be4 30 Nc3 Bf5, but rejected it because White can save the day with the neat 31 Qg5 g6 32 hxg6 fxg6 33 Rd7 axb3 34

Qxg6+! Bxg6 35 Rxg6+ Kh8 36 Rh6+ when it's perpetual.

30 Qxc2 axb3 (Diagram 28) 31 Qe2?

A much better defence was 31 Qd3 bxa2 32 Qd4 and after 32...Qb7 33 Kxa2 Bd5+ 34 Ka1 Rc8 Black retains good compensation for the exchange, but no more than that.

31...bxa2 32 h6 Rb8!

Now there's no defence.

33 Rxg7+ Kh8 34 Qxa2 Qb2+ 35 Qxb2 axb2+ 36 Ka2 Bd5+ 37 Ka3 b1Q 38 Rxb1 Rxb1 39 Rxf7 Re1 0-1

Game 33
□ **P.Acs** ■ **J.Van der Wiel**
Wijk aan Zee 2003

---

1 e4 c5 2 Nf3 Nc6 3 d4 cxd4 4 Nxd4 Nf6 5 Nc3 d6 6 Bg5 e6 7 Qd2 a6 8 0-0-0 Bd7 9 f4 h6 10 Bh4 g5 11 fxg5 Ng4 12 Be2 Nge5 (Diagram 29)

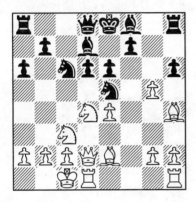
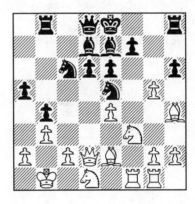

Diagram 29 (W)	Diagram 30 (B)
Black relies on his control of e5	Holding up Black's attack

13 Nf3

Another promising option is 13 Nxc6!? Bxc6 14 g3 and after 14...Ng6 15 Kb1 Qa5 16 Rhf1 hxg5 17 Bxg5 Rxh2 18 Bf6 White had an edge in Z.Almasi-K.Sasikiran, Paks 2005.

13...Be7 14 Rhg1 b5

Trying to gain counterplay. Black might prefer to try and regain his pawn, but after 14...Rg8?! 15 Bg3! hxg5 16 Nxe5 Nxe5 17 Bxe5 dxe5 18 Bh5! he finds himself under serious pressure.

TIP: When you're a pawn up for some compensation, always look for a way to return the pawn to gain either the initiative or a positional advantage.

15 Rdf1 b4 16 Nd1 Rb8 17 Kb1 a5 18 b3! (Diagram 30)

It's always a little risky to advance pawns in front of one's own king, but this advance is rather strong and pretty much breaks up Black's attack

18...hxg5

Another Dutch GM preferred 18...a4, but after 19 Nb2 axb3 20 cxb3 Qa5!? 21 g6! fxg6 22 Bxe7 Kxe7 23 Rd1 Qc7 24 Nc4 Black came under a heavy attack in S.Karjakin-F.Nijboer, Wijk aan Zee 2003. Perhaps if Black wants to resurrect this variation he should examine 18...Ng6!?, although after 19 g3 Nce5 20 gxh6 Nxf3 21 Rxf3 Ne5 22 Rf4 White seems to retain a small advantage.

19 Bxg5 Nxf3

It's far from easy for Black to regain his pawn here, not least because 19...Bxg5 20 Nxg5 Rxh2? fails to 21 Qf4.

20 gxf3 Bxg5

This time 20...Rxh2? had to be avoided on account of 21 Bh6!, cutting the rook off from defending Black's back-rank.

21 Rxg5 Qf6 22 Bb5! (Diagram 31)

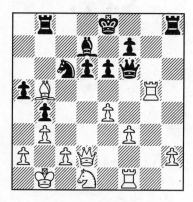

Diagram 31 (B)
White fights for the initiative

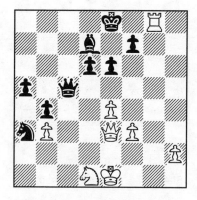

Diagram 32 (B)
A decisive counterattack

22...Qd4 23 Qg2 Na7 24 Rg8+ Rxg8 25 Qxg8+ Ke7 26 Qg5+ Ke8 27 Bc4 Rb5

Perhaps a better try was 27...Rc8!?, although after 28 Qxa5 Nc6 29 Qg5 Ne5 30 Nb2 there's no doubting White's advantage.

28 Bxb5 Nxb5 29 Qe3 Na3+ 30 Kc1 Qa1+ 31 Kd2 Qxa2

White would also have gained a decisive counterattack in the event of 31...Nb1+ 32 Ke1 Nc3 33 Qd4 Bb5 34 Rg1 Be2 35 Qa7.

32 Rg1 Qxc2+ 33 Ke1 Qc5 34 Rg8+ (Diagram 32) 34...Ke7 35 Qh6! e5 36 Qf8+ Ke6?

A blunder in time trouble. As indicated by Acs Black had to try 36...Kf6, although in that case he was ready to finish with the accurate 37 Qg7+ Ke7 38 Qg5+! Ke6 39 Rh8 Bc6 40 Qg7 Bb5 41 Rc8!.

37 Rg7 1-0

Black Plays 8...h6

1 e4 c5 2 Nf3 Nc6 3 d4 cxd4 4 Nxd4 Nf6 5 Nc3 d6 6 Bg5 e6 7 Qd2 a6 8 0-0-0 h6 (Diagram 33)

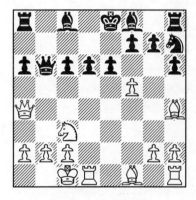

Diagram 33 (W)	**Diagram 34 (B)**
Forcing the bishop backwards	Has White really enough?

By immediately forcing the bishop to move Black ensures that he avoids any doubling of his f-pawns. He also makes certain that the pin is broken since 9 Bh4 promises White equality at best. The reason being the standard blow 9...Nxe4! and after 10 Qf4! (not the primitive 10 Nxe4? Qxh4 11 Nxc6 because of 11...Qxe4 when Black is simply a pawn up), Black has a reasonable choice:

a) 10...g5!? 11 Qxe4 gxh4 12 Nxc6 bxc6 13 Qxc6+ Bd7 14 Qe4 is quite unclear: Black's strong pawn centre and bishop pair being counterbalanced by the fact that his king must stay in the centre.

b) 10...Ng5 is the old recipe and still good; e.g., 11 Nxc6 bxc6 12 Qa4 Qb6 13 f4 Nh7 14 f5!? **(Diagram 34)** 14...Rb8! still leaves White having to prove his compensation and Black was fine after 15 Bd3 Be7 16 fxe6 Bxe6 17 Bxh7 Rxh7 18 Bxe7 Kxe7 19 b3 Rhh8 20 Rhe1 Rhd8 in D.Bunzmann-A.Raetsky, Schwaebisch Gmuend 2001.

9 Be3

Traditionally White's main response to 8...h6, but those tempted to take up this line as Black nowadays need to be very well prepared too for White's alternatives:

a) 9 Bf4 Bd7 (and not 9...Nxd4? 10 Qxd4 e5 on account of 11 Bxe5) 10 Nxc6 Bxc6 11 f3 (White is correct to defend f3: 11 Bxd6?! Bxd6 12 Qxd6 Qxd6 13 Rxd6 Bxe4 14 Rd4 Bc6 15 f3 Ke7 16 Be2 g5! 17 b4 h5 only helped Black to gain the upper hand in F.Berend-V.Jansa, Bennevoie 1999, and the once popular 11 Qe1 is now seen much less often, partly because Black has a reasonable choice between Chernyshov's 11...Qa5!? 12 f3 0-0-0 13 Bc4 g5 and Shirov's 11...Be7 12 e5 Nh5 13 Be3 Qc7) leads to some quite complex positions **(Diagram 35)**:

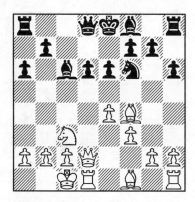

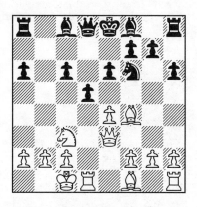

Diagram 35 (B)	Diagram 36 (B)
11...d5 is not the only option!	Black faces problems developing

a1) The usual response is 11...d5 12 Qe1 Bb4 13 a3 Ba5 after which 14 Bd2 (we must also note the instructive queen sacrifice 14 exd5 Nxd5 15 b4 Nxf4! 16 Rxd8+ Bxd8 17 h4 0-0, gaining excellent counterplay due to Black's strong dark-squared bishop and White's weakened queenside) 14...d4 15 e5! (White respond energetically, whereas 15 Ne2 Bc7 16 Nf4 a5 17 e5 Nd7 18 Nd3 b5 19 Qg3 g6 20 h4 b4 21 a4 b3! gives Black good attacking chances, as pointed out by Atalik) 15...Qc7 16 Ne2 Bxd2+ 17 Qxd2 Qxe5 18 Nxd4 0-0! 19 Nxc6 bxc6 was finely balanced in V.Kotronias-S.Atalik, Kardifia 1994; two great Classical authorities in opposition here.

a2) Chernyshov's 11...Qa5!? is an intriguing alternative based on the point that 12 Bxd6 0-0-0 13 Qf4 can be met by 13...Nd5!; for example, 14 exd5 Bxd6 15 Qxf7 exd5 16 Qxg7 Kb8 17 Kb1 d4! 18 Ne4 Bd5 19 Nxd6 Qxa2+ 20 Kc1 Qa1+ 21 Kd2 Qxb2 gave Black the initiative in K.Pilgaard-K.Chernyshov, Budapest 2002.

b) The Twenty-First Century has seen White more and more often adopting a new and quite formidable weapon, namely 9 Nxc6!? bxc6 10 Bf4 d5 11 Qe3 **(Diagram**

36). It looks suspicious to strengthen Black's centre thus, but in practice White has scored very well largely due to his lead in development as we will see further in Game 34.

 WARNING: We hope that both grandmasters and our readers will be able to find a satisfactory path for Black through the complexities created by 9 Nxc6, but for now the line seems to promise White some advantage.

Returning to the older 9 Be3:

9...Bd7

Black wants to play on the queenside. Instead he should avoid 9...Ng4?! which only causes him problems after 10 Nxc6 bxc6 11 Bc5. A more popular alternative is 9...Be7 10 f4 Nxd4 11 Bxd4 b5 which we will see Kramnik successfully employing in Game 35.

10 f4

Yet again the English Attack-style 10 f3 is a decent alternative and after 10...b5 White has a choice:

a) 11 g4 wastes no time on the kingside, but after the 11...Ne5 12 Bd3 (12 h4 b4 13 Nb1 d5 14 Bf4 Nc4 15 Qe1 Rc8 16 b3 Qa5! gives Black promising counterplay, as pointed out by Wells) 12...b4 13 Nce2 d5 **(Diagram 37)** 14 exd5 Nxd5 15 Nf4 of E.L'Ami-H.Rau, German League 2003, Black can maintain an unclear situation with 15...Nxe3!? 16 Qxe3 Bd6 17 Qe4 Ra7.

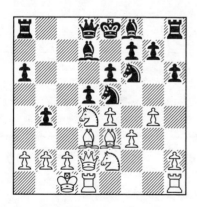

Diagram 37 (W)

Thematically striking back in the centre

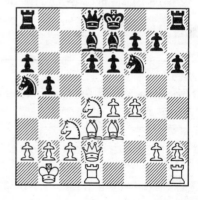

Diagram 38 (W)

Black begins his queenside offensive

b) 11 Nxc6 Bxc6 12 Kb1 is a more prophylactic approach, after which 12...Qc7 13 Bd3 Be7 14 Qf2 Nd7 15 Rhe1 Rc8! (and not 15...Bf6?! due to 16 Nd5!) 16 Qg3 b4 17

Ne2 Bf6 18 Bd4 0-0 19 Bxf6 Nxf6 20 Nd4 Bb7 gave Black sufficient counterplay in P.Leko-A.Groszpeter, Hungary 1995.

10...Qc7

Also quite reasonable is 10...Be7 after which Black might be able to develop his queen straight to a5; for example, 11 h3 b5 12 Bd3 Nxd4 13 Bxd4 b4 14 Ne2 e5! 15 Be3 Qa5 gave Black decent counterplay in L.Yudasin-P.Svidler, Pula 1997.

11 Kb1 b5 12 Bd3 Na5 (Diagram 38)

Both sides have developed quite logically and White must now decide how ambitious he wishes to be:

a) 13 e5!? dxe5 14 fxe5 Qxe5 15 Nf5!? exf5 16 Rhe1 was the sharp course of V.Tseshkovsky-V.Nevednichy, Cetinje 1993, and now Black should have returned the piece to gain equality with 16...Be7! 17 Bb6 Qd6 18 Bxa5 0-0 19 a3 Be6 20 Bb4 Qc7 21 Bxe7 Qxe7.

b) 13 Qe1 b4! (and not the immediate 13...Nc4?! due to 14 Bxc4 Qxc4 15 e5! – remember to never underestimate this advance) 14 Nce2 Nc4 15 Bc1 Rb8 16 h3 g6! 17 Ng3 Bg7 was quite acceptable for Black in G.Shahade-V.Baklan, Groningen 1998.

Theoretical Conclusion

The fact that Black avoids any doubling of his pawns with 8...h6 once helped to make this a popular option. Perhaps it will be again, and Black certainly has decent counterplay after both 9 Be3 and 9 Bf4, but for the time being the modern 9 Nxc6!? Bxc6 10 Bf4 is causing a headache.

Illustrative Games

Game 34
□ **R.Ponomariov** ■ **Bu Xiangzhi**
Lausanne 2001

1 e4 c5 2 Nf3 Nc6 3 d4 cxd4 4 Nxd4 Nf6 5 Nc3 d6 6 Bg5 e6 7 Qd2 a6 8 0-0-0 h6 9 Nxc6 bxc6 10 Bf4 d5 11 Qe3 Qa5

Neither do the alternatives solve Black's difficulties:

a) 11...Bb4 12 a3 Ba5 (or 12...Bxc3 13 Qxc3 Nxe4 14 Qxg7 Qf6 15 Qxf6 Nxf6 16 c4 with a pleasant edge due to the bishop pair, as pointed out by Goloshchapov) 13 Be2 0-0 14 e5 Nd7 15 Qg3 Bc7 16 Bd3 Qe7 17 Rhe1 **(Diagram 39)** 17...Kh8 18 Qh3! gives White good attacking chances, especially after 18...f6? 19 Bxh6! gxh6 20 Qxh6+ Kg8 21 Re3 Bxe5 22 f4 (Wells).

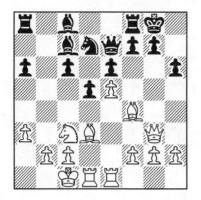

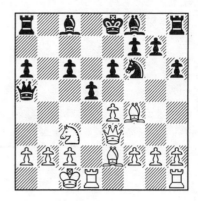

Diagram 39 (B)

Black is a little cramped

Diagram 40 (B)

A strong pawn sacrifice

b) 11...Be7 12 Be2 0-0 (or 12...Nd7 13 h4! e5 14 Bxe5! Nxe5 15 exd5 Bf6 16 f4 – Nataf – regaining the piece with advantage) 13 h4 Nd7 14 Qg3 Kh8 15 Bc7 Qe8 16 Rhe1 Bb7 17 Bf3 Rc8 18 Bd6 Bxd6 19 Qxd6 Qd8 20 Na4 left White in control in Zhang Pengxiang-Wang Rui, Yongchuan 2003.

12 Be2! (Diagram 40) 12...Bb4

Black has also tried 12...dxe4!?, but after 13 Qg3! (even stronger than the tempting exchange sacrifice 13 Nxe4 Nd5 14 Rxd5 cxd5 15 Nd6+ Bxd6 16 Bxd6 Qd8 17 Ba3) 13...Nd5 14 Nxd5! cxd5 15 Kb1 Bd7 16 Be5 Rg8 17 f4!? Bb5 18 Bh5 g6 19 f5!? (Wells) White has a strong initiative.

13 Be5 dxe4

The strength of White's set-up can also be seen in the variation 13...Bxc3 14 Bxc3 Qxa2 15 Bd3!? dxe4 16 Qg3! exd3 17 Qxg7 Rg8 18 Qxf6 d2+ 19 Kxd2 Qd5+ 20 Kc1 Qg5+ 21 Qxg5 hxg5 22 Bf6 Bb7 23 h4! which left him with some advantage in Y.Balashov - M.Makarov, Smolensk 2000.

14 Qg3!?

The most ambitious, although it's also possible to settle for an edge with the 14 Bxf6 gxf6 15 Qxe4 Ke7 16 Rd3 Ra7 17 a3 Bxc3 18 Rxc3 of J.Degraeve-K.Lerner, Koszalin 1999.

14...Bxc3 15 Bc7 Bxb2+

 WARNING: The text was essential with 15...Qb4? impossible due to the decisive 16 Rd8+ Ke7 17 Bd6+! Kxd8 18 Bxb4 Bxb4 19 Qxg7.

16 Kxb2 Qb4+ 17 Ka1 (Diagram 41)

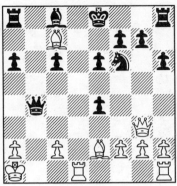

Diagram 41 (B)

Strong dark-square pressure

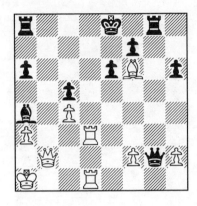

Diagram 42 (B)

The attack is overwhelming

17...Nd5 18 Qxg7 Qf8

Black would also have found himself rather tied in knots after 18...Rf8 19 Be5 Bd7 20 c4 Ne7 21 Bd6 Qa5 22 Qf6.

19 Qd4 Bd7 20 Bg3 Rg8 21 c4! c5 22 Qb2 Nb4 23 a3 Nd3 24 Bxd3 exd3 25 Rxd3

Rather useful too would have been 25 Qb7 Qg7+ 26 Ka2 Rd8 27 Rxd3.

25...Qg7 26 Be5 Qxg2 27 Rhd1

Now Black is destroyed on the dark squares. Not that this is a surprising outcome considering White's far superior coordination and safer king.

27...Ba4 28 Bf6 (Diagram 42) 28...Kf8 29 Rd8+ Be8 30 Qb6! Rg6 31 Bb2 Rxd8

White also wins after 31...f5 32 Qxc5+ Kg8 33 Rxa8 Qxa8 34 Qe7.

32 Qxc5+ Rd6 33 Qxd6+ Kg8 34 Qe5 f5 35 Qh8+ Kf7 36 Be5 Ba4 37 Rb1 1-0

Game 35
□ **V.Ivanchuk** ■ **V.Kramnik**
Dos Hermanas 1996

---

1 e4 c5 2 Nf3 Nc6 3 d4 cxd4 4 Nxd4 Nf6 5 Nc3 d6 6 Bg5 e6 7 Qd2 a6 8 0-0-0 h6 9 Be3 Be7 10 f4 Nxd4 11 Bxd4 b5 (Diagram 43) 12 Qe3

Nowadays White is more likely to prefer to develop his light-squared bishop:

a) 12 Be2!? b4 13 Na4 Nxe4 14 Qe3 Nf6 15 Bf3 is a dangerous pawn sacrifice and after 15...d5 16 Bxf6 gxf6 17 f5 Qc7 18 fxe6 fxe6 19 Bh5+ Kf8 20 Nb6!? (A.Shabalov-G.Serper, USA 1996) White retains reasonable compensation even in the event of 20...Rb8 with simply 21 Nxc8 Rxc8 22 Rd2 (Serper).

b) 12 Bd3 b4 (12...Bb7 13 Kb1 0-0 14 e5! dxe5 15 fxe5 Nd7 16 Ne4 gave White the upper hand in G.Kasparov-V.Kramnik, Novgorod 1997) 13 Ne2 Qa5 14 Kb1 e5 15 Be3 0-0 16 Ng3 Rd8 17 f5 d5 **(Diagram 44)** gave Black decent counterplay in S.Dvoirys-P.Svidler, Elista 1997.

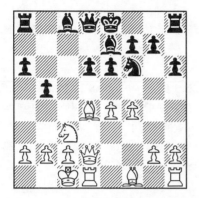

Diagram 43 (W)

Black begins his counterplay

Diagram 44 (W)

The ideal Sicilian break

12...Qc7 13 e5 dxe5 14 Bxe5?!

This is rebuffed by a strong exchange sacrifice. White should prefer 14 fxe5 Nd7 15 Ne4, although after 15...Bb7 (but not 15...0-0? due to 16 Nf6+! gxf6 17 exf6 Nxf6 18 Qxh6 Rd8 19 Be2! with some advantage) 16 Nd6+ Qxd6! 17 exd6 Bg5 18 Qxg5 hxg5 19 Bxg7 Rh7!? 20 Bc3 f5 21 h3 Nc5! Black had good activity for his pawn in G.Timoshenko-D.Tyomkin, Budapest 1999.

14...Ng4! (Diagram 45)

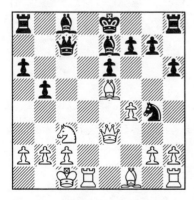

Diagram 45 (W)

A powerful exchange sacrifice

Diagram 46 (W)

A raking light-squared bishop

15 Qf3 Nxe5 16 Qxa8

White didn't have to accept the material, but he would have been struggling too in the event of 16 fxe5 Bb7 17 Qg3 b4 18 Na4 Rc8 19 Bd3 0-0.

16...Nd7 17 g3

Subsequent to this game White has usually steered clear of the line. Perhaps he might try 17 Qf3!?, although after 17...Bb7 18 Qg3 b4 19 Na4 Bc6 20 b3 Bd6 21 Rd4 0-0 we still rather like Black's compensation.

17...Nb6 18 Qf3

A more unbalancing alternative was 18 Nxb5, but then 18...Nxa8 19 Nxc7+ Nxc7 20 Bg2 Bc5 21 Rd3 Ke7 leaves Black's minor pieces superior to White's extra rook.

18...Bb7 (Diagram 46) 19 Ne4 f5!? 20 Qh5+ Kf8 21 Nf2 Bf6!

Beginning to take aim at the white king, whereas the materialistic 21...Bxh1?! 22 Nxh1 Bf6 would have been less clear after 23 Nf2 Na4 24 Nd3.

22 Bd3?!

A slip. White would also have come under a heavy attack after 22 Rg1 Na4 23 Nd3 Be4 (for example, 24 Qe2?! Nxb2! 25 Nxb2 Qc3 26 Nd3 Qa1+ 27 Kd2 Bc3+ 28 Ke3 Bd4+ 29 Kd2 Qc3+ 30 Kc1 Qa3+ 31 Kd2 Qa5+ 32 Kc1 Qxa2 is terminal), but he might have tried 22 Qe2 when Black is only a little better following 22...Bxh1 23 Nxh1 Kf7.

22...Na4 23 Rhe1 Bxb2+ 24 Kb1

It wasn't possible to run away with 24 Kd2? Qa5+ 25 Ke2 on account of 25...Bg2!.

24...Bd5!? (Diagram 47)

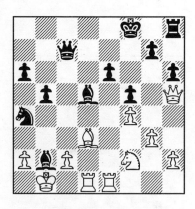

Diagram 47 (W)

A hapless white king

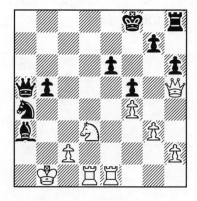

Diagram 48 (W)

The end is nigh

25 Bxb5

Kramnik's devious last prepared to meet 25 Bxf5? with 25...Bxa2+! 26 Kxa2 Qc4+ 27 Kb1 Nc3+ 28 Kxb2 Qb4+ 29 Kc1 Na2 mate.

25...Bxa2+! 26 Kxa2 axb5 27 Kb1 Qa5?!

A slip as time trouble begins to rear its ugly head. Kramnik later pointed out the correct path: 27...Qe7! 28 Rd3 Qb4! 29 Rd8+ Ke7 30 Re8+ Rxe8 31 Rxe6+ Kxe6 32 Qxe8+ Kf6 and wins.

28 Nd3?

Ivanchuk immediately returns the favour. Instead he could have fought on with 28 c3! Nxc3+ 29 Kxb2 Na4+ 30 Ka2! and after 30...Qb4! 31 Rd8+ Ke7 32 Re8+ Rxe8 33 Rxe6+ Kxe6 34 Qxe8+ Qe7 35 Qg6+ Qf6 36 Qxf6+ Kxf6 Black's advantage is by no means that large in the knight ending.

28...Ba3! (Diagram 48) 29 Ka2 Nc3+ 30 Kb3 Nd5 31 Ka2

Now it's mate, but it would have been too in the case of 31 Rxe6 Qa4+ 32 Ka2 Nc3+ 33 Ka1 Bc1.

31...Bb4+ 32 Kb1 Bc3 0-1

Index of Variations

Rare 6th Moves

1 e4 c5 2 Nf3 Nc6 3 d4 cxd4 4 Nxd4 Nf6 5 Nc3 d6 (Diagram)

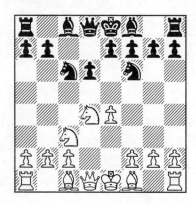

6 f3

6 Be3 Ng4 – *9*; 6 g3 e5 – *16*; 6 f4 – *20*; 6 h3 – *20*

6...e5 7 Nb3 Be7 – *10*

The Boleslavsky: 6 Be2 e5

1 e4 c5 2 Nf3 Nc6 3 d4 cxd4 4 Nxd4 Nf6 5 Nc3 d6 6 Be2 e5 (Diagram)
7 Nf3

7 Nb3 Be7 8 0-0 0-0

9 Be3 – *25*; 9 f4 – *26*; 9 Kh1 – *26*

7...h6 8 0-0 Be7 9 Re1 0-0 10 h3 Be6 11 Bf1 Nb8 – *32*

11...Qd7 – 32

The Sharp 6 Bc4

1 e4 c5 2 Nf3 Nc6 3 d4 cxd4 4 Nxd4 Nf6 5 Nc3 d6 6 Bc4 (Diagram)

6...Qb6

    6...e5 – 39; 6...Na5 – 39

7 Nb3

    7 Ndb5

        7 Be3 – 45; 7 Nxc6 – 46; 7 Nde2 – 47

    7...a6 8 Be3 Qa5 9 Nd4

        9...e6 – 53; 9...Ne5 – 54

7...e6 8 0-0 – 60

    8 Bf4 – 60

The Sozin Attack

1 e4 c5 2 Nf3 Nc6 3 d4 cxd4 4 Nxd4 Nf6 5 Nc3 d6 6 Bc4 e6 (Diagram)

7 Be3

>   7 0-0 Be7 8 Bb3 0-0
>
>>   9 Be3 – *80*; 9 Kh1 – *82*

7...a6 8 Bb3 Qc7 9 f4 Be7 10 Qf3 0-0 11 0-0-0 – *72*

>   11 0-0 – *72*

The Velimirovic Attack

1 e4 c5 2 Nf3 Nc6 3 d4 cxd4 4 Nxd4 Nf6 5 Nc3 d6 6 Bc4 e6 7 Be3 (Diagram)

7...a6

7...Be7 8 Qe2 0-0 9 0-0-0 a6 (9...Qa5 – *90*) 10 Bb3 Qc7
      1 g4 – *91*; 11 Rhg1 – *91*
8 Qe2 Qc7 9 0-0-0 Be7 10 Bb3 Na5 11 g4 b5 12 g5 Nxb3+ 13 axb3 Nd7 14 Nf5 – *103*
    14 h4 – *103*

6 Bg5: The Richter-Rauzer

1 e4 c5 2 Nf3 Nc6 3 d4 cxd4 4 Nxd4 Nf6 5 Nc3 d6 6 Bg5 (Diagram)

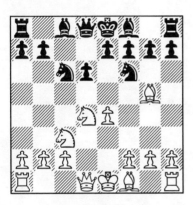

6...Bd7
    6...g6 – *109*; 6...Qb6 – *109*
7 Bxf6 – *111*
    7 Qd2 – *111*

The Traditional 6...e6 7 Qd2 Be7

1 e4 c5 2 Nf3 Nc6 3 d4 cxd4 4 Nxd4 Nf6 5 Nc3 d6 6 Bg5 e6 (Diagram)

7 Qd2
    7 Bb5 – *120*
7...Be7
    7...h6 – *123*
8 0-0-0 0-0 9 f4
    9 Nb3 – *127*
9...Nxd4 – *133*
    9...h6 – *133*

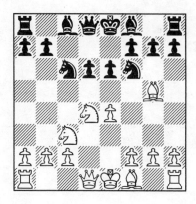

The Modern 7...a6

1 e4 c5 2 Nf3 Nc6 3 d4 cxd4 4 Nxd4 Nf6 5 Nc3 d6 6 Bg5 e6 7 Qd2 a6 (Diagram)

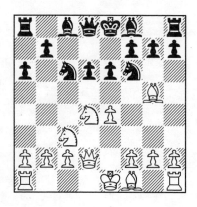

8 0-0-0 Bd7

    8...Nxd4 9 Qxd4 Be7 – *145*

    8...h6

        9 Nxc6 – *162*; 9 Be3 – *162*

9 f4 – *152*

    9 f3 – *153*

Index of Complete Games

Abergel.T-Bolding.K, Val d'Isere 2004 .... *40*

Acs.P-Van der Wiel.J, Wijk aan Zee 2003 .... *159*

Anand.V-Kramnik.V, Wijk aan Zee 2000 .... *149*

Burijovich.L-Atalik.S, Mar del Plata 2003 .... *27*

Caldeira.A-Milos.G, Sao Paulo 2002 .... *29*

Carlsson.P-Kogan.A, Bajada de la Virgen 2005 .... *114*

Cela.A-Kotronias.V, Ano Liosia 1997 .... *62*

De Firmian.N-Smirin.I, Antwerp 1994 .... *58*

Fernando.D-De Firmian.N, Lisbon 2000 .... *106*

Fischer.R-Geller.E, Skopje 1967 .... *93*

Gross.D-Chernyshov.K, Prague 2001 .... *42*

Hamdouchi.H-Avrukh.B, Athens 2005 .... *130*

Hector.J-Stefansson.H, Aarhus 2003 .... *48*

Howell.J-Wahls.M, Gausdal 1986 .... *98*

Illescas.M-Polgar.J, Dos Hermanas 1997 .... *85*

Ivanchuk.V-Kramnik.V, Dos Hermanas 1996 .... *166*

Kaidanov.G-Serper.G, Asheville 1997 .... *82*

Kholmov.R-Kovalevskaya.E, Pardubice 1997 .... *18*

Kononenko.D-Kovalev.A, Alushta 2003 .... *33*

Malakhov.V-Scherbakov.R, Koszalin 1999..*141*

Movsziszian.K-Spraggett.K, Tarragona 2006.......................................*96*

Neelotpal.D-Timofeev.A, Abu Dhabi 2004...*157*

Negi.P-Mamedov.N, Dubai 2004...*65*

Ni Hua-Shabalov.A, Qingdao 2002..*124*

Ponomariov.R-Bu Xiangzhi, Lausanne 2001..*164*

Rechlis.G-Piket.J, Gausdal 1986...*104*

Reinderman.D-Kasparov.G, Wijk aan Zee 1999.....................................*72*

Rodriguez.A-Hernandez.G, Ayamonte 2004..*11*

Rublevsky.S-Lugovoi.A, Sochi 2004..*76*

Solodovnichenko.Y-Miroshnichenko.E, Alushta 2001.......................*116*

Topalov.V-Gavrikov.V, Geneva (rapid) 1996...*50*

Topalov.V-Kramnik.V, Belgrade 1995...*54*

Tseshkovsky.V-Piket.J, Wijk aan Zee 1989...*138*

Tseshkovsky.V-Scherbakov.R, Ekaterinburg 2002 ....*13*

Yagupov.I-Aseev.K, St Petersburg 1999..*35*